THANGLIENA

John Whitehead

Thangliena

THE LIFE OF
T.H. LEWIN

Paul Strachan
KISCADALE

**This book is
for Ella, with love**

Designed and Published in 1992 by
Paul Strachan
Kiscadale Publications
[Paul Strachan - Kiscadale Ltd.]
Gartmore, Stirlingshire
FK8 3RJ

Printed in Hong Kong by Colorcraft

ISBN 1 870838 06 8

CONTENTS

PART III (1874-1916)
Limits and Renewals

ILLUSTRATIONS

In Memory of
Lt. Colonel Tom Herbert Lewin, B.S.C.
Once superintendent of these hill tracts
born 1839, died 1916

HE came to this people in 1865, & worked among them & for them for nine years, when loss of health compelled him to return to England.

THE people trusted him & loved him for his sympathy and sense of justice, for his untiring interest in their welfare & for his intrepid & dauntless courage.

HE travelled in their unknown land, visiting their chiefs, their villages & their homes, alone & unafraid.

HE was the first to interpret & write down their language, preparing the way for schools & progress.

HE studied & improved their agriculture & their laws & helped them in all their difficulties.

THE people knew him as THANGLIENA, tom lewin, & honoured him as a chief.

THEY called him the LUSHAIS FIRST WHITE FRIEND.

THEY built a house for him voluntary in token of his devotion.

THEIR children now have voluntarily brought stones here, near where his house once stood & have helped the one who knew him best of all & who knew how his heart was ever with this people to build up the stones to the memory of
THANGLIENA.

Inscription engraved on the memorial stone, or lungdawh, erected at Demagri in the Lushai Hills, 1921.
The place is now called Tlabung in Mizoram State, India.

ACKNOWLEDGEMENTS

My greatest debt is to Mrs Everest Ursula Currie, Colonel
Lewin's eldest grandchild, who not only entrusted to me
all his private papers which have been in her care since
the death of her mother Mrs Everest Macdonald, but also
spent many hours talking to me about her family and
sharing with me her childhood memories of her grandparents at Parkhurst. For reading and commenting on
an early draft of the text, for permitting me to include her
delightful memoir as an appendix, and for her kindness
and encouragement during my research for this
biography, I am deeply grateful to her. I am, of course,
responsible for any errors of fact or interpretation that
remain.

I am also much indebted to Ms Sarah Lewin of the
Hampshire Record Office, Winchester, whose comprehensive index to the T.H. Lewin archive on permanent
loan to the University of London Library greatly facilitated
my task. My thanks, too, to Ms H.M. Young of that library
and to her staff for their assistance and courtesy during
the days I spent examining the archive.

I am grateful to the following for generously
responding to my requests for information about their
families: Lady Bednall (formerly Eileen Lewin); Lady
Crofton (formerly Mary Friend); Lady Eliott of Stobs
(formerly Frances McClean); Richard Lewin of

Littlehampton; Mrs Betsy Macdonald; Mrs Spillane (formerly Betty Hicks) and her son Robert Stuart concerning the Terriss family.

I am also grateful to Mr R.L. Thanzawna, formerly deputy commissioner of Lunglei District, Mizoram, and to Dr C. Lal Hminga of Serkawr, Mizoram, for information about the Lushai Hills. My thanks, too, to Ms Za Tuah Nguri of Satawm, Chin State, Burma, for translating for me a recent article on Colonel Lewin written in the Lushai language.

For their expert opinions on Lewin's contributions to the study of the Lushai and Tibetan languages I am indebted to Dr F.K. Lehman, Professor of Anthropology & Linguistics at the University of Illinois, and to Dr Michael Aris of the Department of Sanskrit & Indian Studies at Harvard University.

For preparing the photographs and drawing the map of northern India I am grateful to Tom Foxall of Forty-five Design, Much Wenlock.

Acknowledgements are due to the following for help of one kind or another: the late Ian Bowman, ICS; John Boyes-Watson; Alan Dawes; J.S. Dearden, curator of the Ruskin Galleries; Mr and Mrs J.C. Dempster of Parkhurst; Alisdair Fraser, FRCS; P.N. Furbank; Mrs Sally Hofmann; Dr Wolfgang Mey; M.J. Proffitt of OWLS; George Rowell of the Society for Theatre Research; John and Thanni Willis.

The following librarians have greatly assisted my research: Lionel Carter, Secretary-Librarian, Centre of South Asian Studies, University of Cambridge; B.C. Bloomfield, formerly Director of the India Office Library

& Records, and Ms Jill Geber of that library; Ms Mary Murphy, Archivist, Institution of Civil Engineers; the Librarian, Ludlow Public Library; John Andrews, Chief Librarian, Ministry of Defence Central Library; Dr Linda Washington, Department of Printed Books, National Army Museum; Ms Liza Verity, Enquiry Section, National Maritime Museum; National Portrait Gallery; Stephen Rabson, P&O Librarian; Rolf Linde of the Riksarkivet, Stockholm; Kevin Brown, Archivist, St Mary's Hospital and Medical School, Praed Street; Ms Anna Allott, School of Oriental & African Studies.

Finally, I must thank my wife Ella not only for converting several drafts of the biography into immaculate typescript, but also for much help and support in other ways at every stage of my long quest for Thangliena, whose work among the Lushais I first heard about when I was serving with the Chin Hills Battalion in Burma many years ago.

John Whitehead
June 1992

LEWIN GENEALOGY

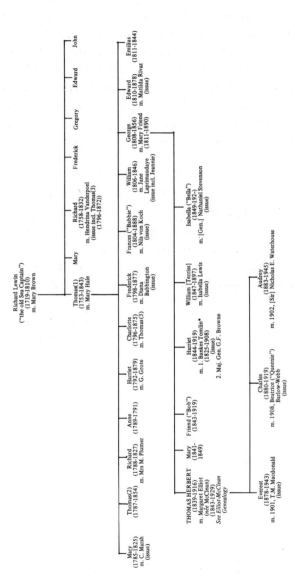

Richard Lewin ("the old Sea Captain") (1719-1810) m. Mary Brown

- Thomas(1) (1753-1843) m. Mary Hale
- Mary
- Richard (1758-1832) m. Hendrina Vanderpoel (issue incl. Thomas(3) (1796-1872))
- Frederick
- Gregory
- Edward
- John

Children of Thomas(1):
- Mary (1785-1825) m. C. Marsh (issue)
- Thomas(2) (1787-1854)
- Richard (1788-1827) m. Mrs M. Plumer
- Anne (1789-1791)
- Harriet (1792-1879) m. G. Grote
- Charlotte (1796-1875) m. Thomas(3)
- Frederick (1798-1877) m. Diana Babbington (issue)

Children of Richard (1758-1832):
- Frances ("Babbie") (1804-1888) m. Nils von Koch (issue)
- William (1806-1846) m. Jane Laprimaudaye (issue incl. Jeannie)
- George (1808-1856) m. Mary Friend (1811-1890)
- Edward (1810-1878) m. Matilda Rivaz (issue)
- Emilius (1811-1844)

Children of Thomas(2):
- THOMAS HERBERT (1839-1916) m. Margaret Elliot (née McClean) (1843-1929) *See Elliot-McClean Genealogy*
- Mary (1841-1849)
- Friend ("Bob") (1843-1919)

Children of Frederick (1798-1877):
- Harriet (1844-1919) m. 1. Bankes Tomlin* (1825-1908) (issue) 2. Maj. Gen. G.F. Browne
- William [Terriss] (1847-1897) m. Isabella Lewis (issue)

Children of George (1808-1856):
- Isabella ("Bella") (1849-192–) m. [Gen.] Nathaniel Stevenson (issue)

Children of Thomas Herbert:
- Everest (1878-1943) m. 1901, T.M. Macdonald (issue)
- Charles (1880-1919) m. 1908, Beatrice ("Queenie") Barlow-Webb (issue)
- Audrey (1883-1945) m. 1902, [Sir] Nicholas E. Waterhouse

*Son of Robert Sackett Tomlin of Dane Court, St. Peter's-in-Thanet and Elizabeth Anne (née Bankes), the younger sister of Mary Friend's mother Isabella who married James Friend (1781-1819)

JRW

ELLIOT-McCLEAN GENEALOGY

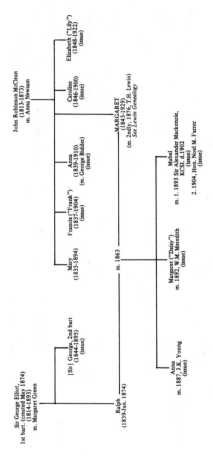

Sir George Elliot,
1st bart. (created May 1874)
(1814-1893)
m. Margaret Green

John Robinson McClean
(1813-1873)
m. Anna Newsam

[Sir] George, 2nd bart.
(1844-1895)
(issue)

Ralph
(1839-Jan. 1874)

m. 1863

Mary
(1835-1894)

Francis ("Frank")
(1837-1904)
(issue)

Anna
(1839-1910)
(m. George Bidder)
(issue)

MARGARET
(1843-1929)
(m. 2ndly. 1876, T.H. Lewin)
See Lewin Genealogy

Caroline
(1846-1900)
(issue)

Elizabeth ("Lily")
(1848-1922)
(issue)

Anna
m. 1887, J.K. Young
(issue)

Margaret ("Daisy")
m. 1892, W.M. Meredith
(issue)

Mabel
m. 1. 1893 Sir Alexander Mackenzie,
KCSI. d.1902
(issue)
2. 1904, Hon. Noel M. Farrer
(issue)

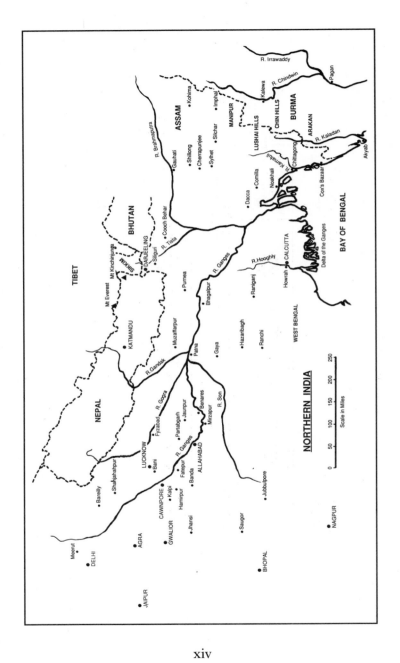

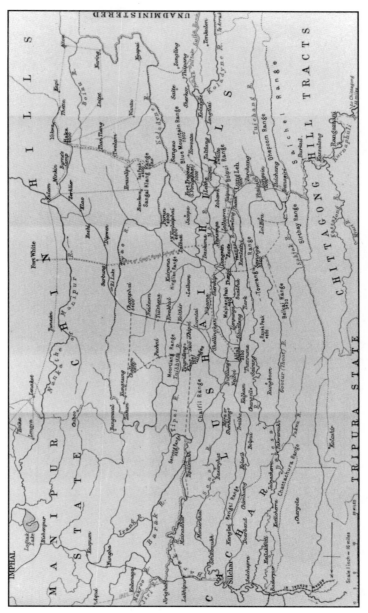

THE LUSHAI HILLS

Part I (1839-1865)

The Day's Work

Chapter One
Thomas Lewin
of The Hollies

On the morning of Wednesday, 5 February 1794, James Boswell of Auchinleck esqr., author of a successful biography of Dr Samuel Johnson and having little more than a year to live, awoke in his London house in Great Portland Street with a violent headache, necessitating recourse to the drop of brandy he had often found a sure remedy for a hangover. The previous night had been one to tax the strongest constitution. At three in the afternoon his friend John Penn — once lieutenant-governor of Pennsylvania, the colony in America founded by his grandfather — had called for Boswell in his coach, in which they had been driven to a tavern in Bishopsgate Street Within known as The London, where with nine others they sat down to dine as the guests of the landlord Mr Bleaden. The fare he set before them consisted of a course of two soups, two dishes of fish, stewed beef, boiled lamb and spinach, roast mutton, fricandeau of veal, *petit pâté*, beefsteaks, game, omelette, pasty and an elegant dessert. To accompany the meal the company drank madeira, sherry, port, old hock, burgundy, champagne and Scotch pints (said to be three times as large as English ones) of claret. The bottle, as Boswell noted afterwards in his journal, had circulated so frequently as to produce in him total oblivion until he woke up next morning in his own bed, to which friendly hands had carried him. Not surprisingly, when he tried to recollect the names of his fellow guests he was a trifle hazy about one of them, a ship's captain in the East India naval service: "Mr Lewin, I think".

Then in his mid-seventies, Richard Lewin was the son of a Kentish yeoman farmer who cultivated his own acres at Foots Cray. He went to sea at the age of thirteen in the service of the East India Company and, while his three brothers dwindled into obscurity, rose to be commander of one of the Company's ships of the first class. This was a lucrative command because the master of an East Indiaman, besides receiving a substantial salary, was allowed to allocate part of the cargo space for the storage of his own trade goods and to pocket the passage money paid by private passengers for the berths provided for them between-decks; perquisites that might bring him in several thousand pounds for a single voyage. The fortune Lewin thus amassed he laid out in the purchase of two ships, the *Exeter* and the *Vansittart*, and an estate of four hundred acres at Bexley in Kent, where he settled on retiring from the sea. He refused to live in the big house called Marrowbone Hall, because he found its spaciousness uncongenial after the cramped quarters he was used to, preferring instead a cottage by the forge in the village of Halfway Street nearby. He had made a good marriage with Mary Brown, daughter of a gentleman who owned an estate that extended along the ridge between

Hampstead and Highgate, now called Kenwood, who bore him seven children. Known as the old Sea Captain, he is described as having been a little man, his bald pate hidden under a wig, wearing knee-breeches and a scarlet waistcoat. It is recorded that "he suffered a good deal from heat in the head, and used to make his grand-daughters pump [water] on his head at the trough in the yard" of his cottage, perhaps after such convivial nights as the one he had enjoyed with Boswell, Penn and the others at The London tavern.

The Lewin connection with India was to last for five generations spanning more than two hundred years. When Richard Lewin first saw it from the deck of an East Indiaman the country, still in a state of anarchy following the death of the Mogul emperor Aurangzeb, was ripe for exploitation by European interests competing for trade in the East. The Portuguese had early on been left with a mere toe-hold at Goa, but the factories of the East India Company at Madras, Bombay and Calcutta were already assuming the character of presidency towns, while the French were developing factories of their own at Pondicherry a hundred miles south of Madras and at Chandernagore twenty miles north of Calcutta. During the years Lewin was carrying his valuable cargoes between Britain and India Anglo-French rivalry rose to a climax when Clive defeated Dupleix at Arcot in 1751, putting an end to French ambitions. Six years later, after Siraj-ud-Daula the nawab of Bengal had attacked and captured Calcutta, where a hundred and twenty civilians confined in a guardhouse — the notorious "black hole" — died of suffocation, Clive not only recaptured the town from the nawab, but also seized Chandernagore from the French who had, characteristically, sided with him. The campaign was brought to a conclusion at the battle of Plassey, when eight hundred Europeans supported by two thousand sepoys defeated an army fifty-thousand strong of the nawab, who was afterwards put to death. After routing a Dutch naval force in the Hooghly river in 1760 Clive returned to England for a well-earned rest.

Thomas Lewin, the eldest son of the old Sea Captain, after attending school at Richmond for several years had been sent to Portugal with a view to a career in the wine trade, but was soon recalled and put aboard a vessel bound for Madras, when his father managed to procure for him, through the good offices of one of his influential cabin passengers, a writership (or, as it would now be called, a clerkship) on the Madras establishment of the East India Company. In those days entry into the Company's employment was solely by virtue of private patronage, each member of the board of the directors, themselves senior Company men, having the right to nominate his quota as vacancies for writerships occurred, such nominations going either to his own relations — hence the web of family relationships among the Company's servants — or those of his friends, or being sold at a high premium on the open market. Clive had already returned to India, this time — since he now had the the financial muscle to control the Company's board of directors in London — as the governor of Bengal. His main achievement on this tour was to secure for the Company from the Mogul in Delhi the right to manage and collect the land revenues levied throughout Bengal as well as in some districts of the Carnatic, thus giving it for the first time, through its officials known as collectors, legal jurisdiction over the inhabitants of those vast tracts. It was the thin end of the wedge. Clive also (his own personal fortune being safely invested) sought to curtail the opportunities for similar self-enrichment available to officials of the Company by way of franchises and perquisites; fortunately for them with only limited success. In 1769 he returned home to Shropshire and a few years later, still only forty-nine, committed suicide.

Thomas Lewin served his apprenticeship "with much propriety and attention" in both the Civil and the Military Departments at Fort St. George. He was a personable young man, dark, handsome, of medium height and with a pleasing figure. He was well read, a good linguist and a fine musician and possessed besides the social graces and winning, courteous ways that recommended him not only to his superiors but to the ladies of the station. As a historian of the period has put it:

> His excursions into the fashionable and venal gallantries of the day were, it would seem, not few, and were attended with quiet respect for those he favoured, and with princely liberality.

His personal qualities also drew him to the attention of

the acting governor of Madras, John Whitehill, whose patronage was to prove a mixed blessing.

In 1773 parliament at Westminster had passed an act intended to make those responsible for the management of the East India Company's affairs more accountable. A supreme court of justice and a council of state consisting of four members were established, the court of directors was reorganized, and provision made for the appointment of a governor-general for the Bengal Presidency having the right of supervision over the affairs of the junior presidencies of Madras and Bombay. Whitehill somehow incurred the displeasure of the first governor-general, Warren Hastings, who caused the court of directors to remove him from office.

Meanwhile Thomas Lewin, by then secretary to the council at Madras, had been ordered to England with despatches relative to the circumstances under which the Company had blundered into a war in the Carnatic, giving him in addition certain private information it was felt prudent not to commit to writing in the formal report. He had duly embarked in His Majesty's sloop of war the *Nymph* bound for the Cape of Good Hope, thence taking passage aboard a neutral ship — for England was then at war with half the world — for Europe. In the same vessel sailed his younger brother Richard, like his father before him in the Company's naval service, who had been newly appointed resident at the Cape with instructions to gather information concerning enemy shipping movements and to give assistance to ships of the Royal

Navy and the Honourable Company putting in at the Cape. Arrived there, the brothers disembarked, Richard to start on his new duties, Thomas to take passage in a Dutch vessel bound for the island of Texel off the coast of Holland, on his way to England. Among the passengers who sailed in her was a young woman with whom Lewin's fortunes were for a time to be pleasantly linked.

The daughter of the port captain at Chandernagore M. Werlée, Noël Catherine at the age of fifteen had married a Company official George Grand and gone to live with him in his garden house a short distance from the town of Calcutta. Not long afterwards she had caught the eye of Philip Francis, one of the four members of the council of state and a practised womanizer, now known to have been the author of the political pamphlets written under the pseudonym "Junius". Since his arrival in India six years before he had been an implacable opponent of Warren Hastings, and matters had come to a head when Hastings, goaded into challenging him to a duel, severely wounded him. This unsavoury character now proceeded to lay siege to Mrs Grand, who was then and later celebrated for her beauty.

> Tall and slight with that languor in her carriage peculiar to Creole ladies; her eyes well open and affectionate; her features delicate; her golden hair, playing in numberless curls, set off a forehead as white as a lily.

Her beauty was matched by her silliness, and it was said of her that she "had all the desirable qualities necessary for one possessing perfect mental vacuity". Since she gave Francis sufficient encouragement he bided his time and, on an evening when he learnt that Grand would be out dining with a friend, effected an entry into the garden house and was about to accomplish his desire with her when the jemadar in charge of the household servants burst into her boudoir and found the pair *in flagrante delicto.* The aggrieved husband returned his erring wife to her parents and, since Francis cravenly declined his challenge to a duel, brought an action against him and eventually recovered £5,000 in damages. Francis had meanwhile set up Noël Catherine as his mistress with her own establishment at Hooghly, but the liaison lasted only a short time, and when he left for England to mastermind the impeachment of his old enemy Hastings she did not travel with him. This, then, was the fellow-passenger with whom Thomas Lewin was to share the tedious voyage home, and before their ship berthed at Cadiz — whither it had been diverted on war being declared between Britain and Holland — they had become lovers.

The purpose of Lewin's journey home was not only to be forgotten but literally flung to the winds, for when the Dutch ship in which the pair were travelling was waylaid in the Atlantic by two French warships they had the pleasure of tearing up his report and throwing the fragments out of the porthole of his cabin so as to prevent them from falling into enemy hands. From Cadiz they travelled to Lisbon and thence in a Portuguese ship to England. For some time they lived together in London, having rented accommodation in Fitzroy Square; they then proceeded to Paris, where they lived in considerable style and moved in the best circles. They were present at a ball at Versailles and saw Marie Antoinette dance a minuet with the future King Charles X. They conversed with the Marquis de la Fayette recently returned from campaigning in North America, and drove out to the royal hunt in the Forest of Marly in the phaeton and four Lewin had hired. Though they soon drifted apart, their association was an idyll Lewin was to remember until the end of his long life; while for Noël Catherine her introduction into Parisian society turned out to be the first step in an ascent that would in due course transform her, despite her silliness, into La Princesse Talleyrand.

During this pleasant interlude Thomas Lewin's career with the East India Company was put in jeopardy when the parliamentary committee appointed to investigate its affairs, including Whitehill's responsibility for the Carnatic involvement, failed despite repeated orders to secure Lewin's attendance as a witness in the proceedings. The chairman accordingly reported his default to the House, upon which Lewin was declared guilty of breach of privilege. "Having withdrawn himself from the kingdom, the House of Commons on May 8, 1782 resolved that he had absconded in order to avoid being examined, and addressed His Majesty to issue his proclamation for apprehending him." In fact Lewin had decided to keep out of the way until Whitehill had returned to England, in order to obtain his authority before releasing confidential information acquired when acting as his secretary. Naturally when the Company's affairs were in question its officials closed ranks against over-inquisitiveness on the part of parliament. The nature and extent of the evidence he was to give having been clarified by Whitehill, Lewin surrendered himself to the sergeant-at-arms and was brought to the bar of the House. As advised, he formally prayed forgiveness for his failures to attend the committee when summoned and was reprimanded by the speaker and ordered to be discharged on paying the customary fee, for which he was no doubt in due course reimbursed by his grateful employers. From their point of view his conduct had been exemplary, and the episode served rather to advance than to prejudice his career.

The cloud hanging over him having thus been dispersed, and no longer being in thrall to the charms of Noël Catherine, Lewin was now free to pursue his matrimonial designs; for he was thirty years old and had determined when he returned to his duties in Madras to take a wife with him. On a visit to relations in Yorkshire he had been entertained by General John Hale, a distinguished soldier who as a colonel had been present at Quebec at the death of General Wolfe, whose dying request had been that his old friend should have the honour of carrying news of the victory to England. He had retired to the estate at Gainsborough brought as her dowry by his wife, a lady who bore him no less than twenty-two children. Among them were twin daughters, only fifteen years old at the time of Lewin's visit and still dressed in the bib and tucker of childhood, who were so alike that they were required to wear different-coloured ribbons on their arms by way of distinction. Lewin was captivated by them without having any preference between them and eventually — for no particular reason he could later recall, except that he could not marry them both — chose Mary to be his bride; although she was never consulted. They were married early in 1784 and shortly afterwards took ship for Madras.

During this second tour the strain of arrogance in Thomas Lewin's character began to undermine his career, though for a time it seemed that he was set fair to climb the ladder of preferment. Tenacious of what he considered to be his rights, he did not hesitate to urge them on his superiors in India or, if thwarted, to appeal over their heads to the dispensers of patronage at home. At Ellemboor, where he was a member of a committee investigating certain charges of corruption, the Lewins' first child was born, a daughter they christened Mary Hale. Next year he submitted a memorial to the court of directors in England complaining of his being kept out of employ, in terms so disrespectful as to earn him a rebuke. Nevertheless he was appointed resident at Megapatam and, on that residency being abolished, chief of Cuddalore, where his wife bore him a son whom they christened Thomas after his father. Since his wife's health had begun to deteriorate in the Indian climate, Lewin applied for permission to take his family home, and they arrived in time for their third child, Richard, to be born in his grandfather's house at Bexley. Its name changed from Marrowbone Hall to The Hollies, this was to remain the family seat for many years.

Two more children were born — Anne in 1789 who died two years later, and Harriet in 1792 — before Lewin returned to Madras for his third and last tour, unaccompanied by his wife. Two years later he solicited for the vacancy that had occurred in the board of revenue, which being refused he addressed another memorial to the court of directors. Further disgusted when he was forestalled in obtaining the secretaryship to the government at Madras by an applicant less qualified than himself, due to nepotism on the part of Lord Buckingham whose relation he was, and unhappy at the prolonged separation from his wife, he returned home for the last time in 1795, his daughter Charlotte being born the following year. When a few years later he sought to return to Madras, although he had already amassed a considerable fortune, the Company refused his request on the ground of his prolonged absence contrary to standing orders. He never returned to India.

He had spent the years 1771 to 1795 in the service of the East India Company, interrupted by two leaves in Europe of several years' duration. Thereafter he lived in England in retirement for nearly fifty years, his brood of children increasing until there were eleven of them, seven sons of varying ability and four remarkable daughters, not counting Anne who had died in infancy.

After the death of the old Sea Captain at the age of ninety in 1810 the family settled at The Hollies, though there were holidays by the seaside, and Lewin found occasions for visiting London, either on business or to attend dinners of the Beefsteak Club, of which he was an assiduous member, and for less reputable reasons. Inevitably in such a large family there were tensions and misunderstandings, but on the whole they all got on pretty well together, their chief communal solace being music. There were frequent musical evenings when father played the violin or sang, such of the children as had learnt to play an instrument joining in, the rest listening or going about their own affairs.

The discordant element in the family was Mrs Lewin. As a consequence of having been pushed into marriage as a child without love on her part she was cold, even harsh, towards her own children. Harriet, the most notable of them all, looking back on her childhood could not recollect ever having received the smallest caress or mark of tenderness from her mother, who professed herself averse to being kissed or fondled by her children after they had reached the age of six. "Poor woman," wrote Harriet in her *Reminiscences of Early Life*, "I believe her heart had become, as it were, dried up for want of suitable channels during the ripening season of womanhood."

Despite bearing him a dozen children she showed an equal coldness towards her husband, who treated her more as a pet slave than an equal and never confided to

her his intimate thoughts. Although during the course of
their married life she had from time to time been attracted
to men nearer her own age — in early days in Madras she
causing her husband such uneasiness on that account
that he was constrained to write to her father the general
complaining of her conduct — she never transgressed
the line separating esteem from impropriety. Harriet in
her reminiscences was surprisingly indulgent to her
father's memory, calling him "perhaps one of the more
faithful husbands", because he committed fewer
infidelities than could be expected from a man so coldly
treated by his wife. Soon after his final return from India
there had been a connection with a person living in St.
Martin's Court in London and nothing else, so far as
Harriet knew, until 1826 when at the age of seventy-four
he was led into an intimacy with another married woman
in London, aided and abetted by her husband, a liaison
lasting several years that was only brought to an end by
reason of the old man's failing powers. By this time his
daughters were grown up and could guess what was going
on. Charlotte, then over thirty and still unmarried, saw
fit to present to him on behalf of her brothers and sisters

> a gentle memorial of the very heavy and distressing
> suspense those dutiful children have long been suffering
> under the suspicion thrown over the respectability of
> their venerable Parent owing to the concealment of his
> Abode in London and other concurrent circumstances
> not necessary now to particularise.

Harriet put the matter more explicitly at a personal

interview some years after her marriage, by expressing, as the old man noted in his diary, "much apprehension lest a spurious offspring should be the result, but I assured her there was no fear of such a thing".

Chapter Two
Uncles and Aunts

1

Mary Hale Lewin, the eldest child of the Thomas Lewins, was born in Madras in 1785 and brought home by her parents along with her infant brother Thomas when she was three. Nothing is recorded of her childhood spent mainly at The Ridgeway, the house near Southampton the Lewins then occupied, except that in 1804 she caught a bad cold consequent upon her tumbling herself and her pony into the river Itchen at Bishop's Stoke. Later that year her father persuaded her to break off her engagement to a lieutenant in the Navy owing to his lack of prospects and expressed the wish that she should bestow her hand on a certain Charles Marsh, a barrister practising in Madras, whose claims had been urged on Lewin by his old friend Sir Thomas Strange, a judge of the Madras High Court. Unwisely as it turned out, Mary acquiesced. After some years in India the couple returned to England with their young children, and as Mary's health declined so Marsh's financial difficulties increased; for it had long since become apparent that she had been induced to marry an arch rogue. On her death in 1825 still under forty, Marsh decamped to America leaving his debts and his children behind him, to be looked after by his late wife's family. Their son Hippisley in due course obtained a cavalry cadetship and sailed for India where, despite giving early signs that he had inherited his father's failings, he began to make his way, settling down with a companionable wife and seeing action in the Afghan campaign of 1842.

Thomas junior was educated at Harrow School and later articled to a firm of London lawyers engaged in parliamentary business. Never on good terms with his father, there was nearly a complete rupture when he was faced with the choice between giving up the lady he loved and being disowned. He did not hesitate for long and, like the historian Edward Gibbon before him, thought it prudent to sigh as a lover but to obey as a son. Two years later he sailed for India to take up the appointment of Master in Equity of the Supreme Court at Calcutta, a position whose perquisites enabled him to amass a comfortable fortune, which he returned home to enjoy. He stood at his father's bedside with his sister Harriet and his brother George when the old man died in 1843 at the age of ninety, having outlived both his wife and his former mistress Princess Talleyrand, whose death in 1835 he had duly noted in his diary. By his will he left the bulk of his estate to be divided equally among his children, and at once Thomas declared his intention of buying from the others their interests in The Hollies. Having renovated the rambling old house, he thereafter divided his time between solitary residence there — for he never married — and his gloomy chambers in Raymond Buildings, Gray's Inn, looked after by a mercenary but honest female housekeeper. When he died suddenly on holiday in Scotland at the age of sixty-seven Harriet expressed her feelings about her eldest brother in a letter to her sister Frances, who was known in the family as Babbie:

> You will have sorrowed over his loss, I feel persuaded, as indeed we must all do, although to speak frankly he seemed to me to enjoy life as little as anybody of my acquaintance. I do not call to mind any one subject or pursuit in which he took any interest or pleasure, and as to sensual enjoyments, I do not believe they ever counted for much with our dear Brother. His meals were habitually solitary, he had no taste for sport, and I have been led to suppose that he was chaste in his life. He had neither literary nor artistic pleasures either, and very few people to love, and still fewer to exchange thoughts with... Religion (so-called) occupied the greater portion of his time, and in this occupation he found ample food for disquiet...

Richard John, the Lewins' second son, was born in 1788 shortly after his parents had returned to settle permanently in England. Having joined the Royal Navy at fourteen, he saw much service at sea including a cruise in the Mediterranean lasting twenty-one months and a voyage to the China Sea, and later following family tradition enlisted in the East India Company's naval service. An irreverent, contemptuous, harum-scarum youth, he alienated his mother by half-serious, half-humorous interference in her high-handed dominion over her daughters, and once had to beg his father to plead with the authorities when, being wholly unpractised

in the art and dexterity of single combat, he challenged
an acquaintance to a duel for having proclaimed him "a
scoundrel and a coward", only to fall victim to the other's
unerring marksmanship. Luckily for him, the wound was
only superficial. In 1826, having had enough of what he
called a scrambling and necessitous life which had
undermined his health, he married a wealthy widow who
was, as his mother sourly reported, even older than
herself, adding:

> Her money contributes to his Luxury and indolence of
> mind, procures him all the comforts his declining health
> requires, and he has been so often shipwrecked in love,
> has had one narrow escape from beggary by imprudence,
> and so many pangs, that I think he felt no regret in
> abandoning the sea (the youthful part, at least) and
> bearing away for a safe Haven.

In fact, the ill-assorted couple kept on the move, staying
for some time in Portugal, then embarking on a leisurely
European tour that took in Gibraltar, Marseilles and
Naples. In Paris Richard's lungs became affected, and
they returned home to seek the best medical advice
available in Bath; to no avail, for his health continued to
deteriorate, and in 1827 he died in Plymouth without
leaving issue.

Little Anne, born in 1789, had an even shorter life
span, dying of whooping cough at the age of two, a loss
that so afflicted Mrs Lewin that her husband, alarmed by
the report her doctor gave of her condition, took her
across the Channel in the hope of diverting her mind.

That winter in Paris she conceived another daughter, in due course christened Harriet, whose career and those of her sisters Charlotte (born in 1796) and Babbie (born in 1804) it will be convenient to consider after brief details have been given of their five other brothers. Frederick Mortimer, born at The Ridgeway, spent some years in Madras in the Civil Department of the East India Company, retiring in the prime of life to devote himself to country pursuits, especially foxhunting. Harriet described him as "an honest, peppery chap, whom I took to very kindly, because he is frank, hearty and a gentleman". He lived on bad terms with his wife who from being good-looking in her youth early became what Harriet unkindly described as "a scrag". She bore him seven children, one of whom was tragically killed at the age of eight when she fell under the wheels of a bathing-machine at Brighton.

William — "Billyrag" to his father — eight years younger than Frederick was the last Lewin of his generation to make a career in India, serving in the Honourable Company's Artillery. First stationed at its Dum Dum headquarters near Calcutta, he later saw active service in the Chittagong area after Bagyidaw the King of Burma had ordered his army commanded by Maha Bandula to march into Bengal and capture Calcutta, an ill-judged adventure that provoked the First Anglo-Burmese War of 1824, which has been called the worst-managed in British military history. William was of a religious cast of mind and described in his unpublished *Autobiography* written a few years later how he had "visited

[his] men in hospital, read to them, and exhorted them to pursue the way of holiness".

In his high-mindedness he was representative of the new liberal spirit that, with the social reforms introduced in India during the first half of the nineteenth century, was beginning to inform the *raj*. Western ideas were being taught in the schools, Christian missions were proliferating. Efforts were being made to exterminate the *thugs*, the sect dedicated to ritual murder in the name of the goddess Kali; the practice of *suttee*, or widow-burning, was made a capital offence; and the first steps were taken towards the abolition of slavery throughout the country. Posted to Madras where his family was well known, William married after a long engagement Jane Laprimaudaye, who was to bear him six children; and his health showing signs of breaking down he was transferred to the Khasia Hills of Assam, which was considered a healthy place, then in an unsettled state following the withdrawal of an invading Burmese army. For the next ten years he lived with his family at Cherrapunji, the combined civil and military station from which the district was controlled and administered, and where a sanatorium had been built. This was before it had been discovered that Assam provided a suitable terrain for growing tea. When he died there in 1846 at the age of forty, his wife and young family returned to England, to be cared for by the Lewins at The Hollies.

The tenth child and fifth son of Thomas and Mary Lewin was George Herbert, born in 1808, whose career will be described in the next chapter.

Edward, born in 1810, had entered St. Peter's College, Cambridge, but threw up his studies when an opportunity arose for him to set up a tannery business in Sweden with money advanced to him by his father, in which — after the marriage of his sister Babbie to Nils von Koch — he induced Nils' younger brother Jean to become his partner. The venture proved less lucrative than anticipated, perhaps because Edward being of an indolent temperament was disinclined to exert himself in its affairs, spending much of his time running a school a few minutes' walk from the tannery and in carrying out his duties as a director of Swedish state schools. Harriet summed him up in a letter to Babbie:

> He is a sort of dreamer, but has another side, namely, a keen eye to self-interest, which prevents him from being a romantic dreamer. In short, he is a mixture of imagination and calculation. He is far from being unreserved, and I do not find in him the endearing qualities of our dear brother John Dick of blessed memory. However, it is not difficult to discover the cause of Edward's incompleteness. He has never ripened thoroughly: *voila!*.

The sour note in this description may be accounted for by the tensions that had been set up between brother and sister owing to their rivalry for the affections of the Swedish singer Jenny Lind, an episode shortly to be recounted. By that time he had abandoned the tannery business and returned to England, where in due course he became a sub-collector of post offices in Ipswich, an undistinguished position he held until he retired on a pension, by then old and cranky and blind in one eye. He had married Matilda Rivaz, a young woman without fortune whom Harriet thought well fitted to manage his slender means and to impart to his domestic life its chief charm and value, and succeeded in ripening sufficiently to father five children on her.

Mary Lewin was in her mid-forties, Thomas senior fifty-eight, when their twelfth and last child was born, a son who was christened Emilius. Although as a child he was declared the show boy of the family, his promise faded when he began to manifest signs of instability. Whilst under the tutorship of a clergyman he had fancied that he had a vocation for the church and worked hard for a university degree; but his enthusiasm waning he decided after all to try for a fellowship at Balliol, failing to achieve which he made plans for emigrating to Canada, but this also came to nothing. By his early twenties it was impossible for his family to disguise from themselves what ailed him, Harriet reporting to Babbie:

> He is odious to look upon, dirty, unshaven, with a perpetual horse laugh. He professes a deep attachment to me of all human kind, and listens to all I have to say with composure. Consults me about Suicide, which I seriously think it likely he may perpetrate.

Since he had by then become decidedly crazy he was placed under the care of a retired medical man living with his wife at Hampton; but this experiment having failed, he was confined permanently in a lunatic asylum at Kensington, where he died in 1844 aged thirty-three, perhaps by his own hand.

2

When Mary the eldest of the Lewin daughters made her unfortunate marriage with Charles Marsh and left the family circle for Madras Harriet was thirteen, Charlotte nine, and Babbie still a baby. To Mrs Lewin, who was held in the neighbourhood to be making a hash of their education, her daughters were proving something of a handful: self-willed, disrespectful and unruly. Harriet and Charlotte were young for their age, much taken up with girlish speculations about the few beaux who succeeded in evading their father's vigilance. What the girls lacked throughout their childhood was any outward manifestation of parental affection, being subjected instead to the cold despotism of their mother and the alternating negligence and fault-finding of their father, who was apt even when they were in their teens to put them over his knee and flog them for some minor offence. Any suitor bold enough to make application for the hand of one of them was given short shrift — none was considered good enough for a daughter of his — an obduracy that made the girls, with the example of Mary's forced marriage before them, all the more determined if necessary to fight for their own happiness.

Charlotte, who was known in the family as Couty, for

all her girlish flirtatiousness was to lead a sadly unfulfilled life. Foreshadowing the adult woman who had sternly addressed her aged father about his concealment of his Abode in London, she had been bossy as a child and apt to "set down" her brothers and sisters when she considered they were getting above themselves. Something of her discordant temperament can be detected in the portrait of her drawn when she was a young woman, the narrow, somewhat foxy eyes giving the lie to the frivolous curls clustering round her forehead, as if the elements that made up her character were at odds with one another. Couty saved herself from the spinsterhood for which nature perhaps intended her by marrying on the brink of middle age her first cousin Thomas, the son of that Richard Lewin who had sailed with Thomas senior in the *Nymph* to take up his duties as resident at the Cape. Bride and groom were both thirty-eight years old at the time. Soon a baby was born to them, the fat and ugly Johnny on whom they doted to the exclusion of all other interests in life, as Harriet described in a letter to Babbie who was also attempting to nurse a baby at the time:

> Of course you would not be up to nursing a wean. How could you think of it? There's Maam Cout, now, who was ever a better rig than you in the forehand, and she can't manage it, although the farce is kept up of putting the babe to the breast, periodically; but 'tops and bottoms' are the strict anchor there, and the child grows and may really, I think, become a fair sample. Anything to equal the absorption of father and mother is seldom met with.

But Johnny was destined to die at the age of five, a tragic blow from which his grieving parents never really recovered. No more children were forthcoming, and for the next thirty years the pair gave to each other what comfort they could, for they remained devoted to one another. To her nephews aunt Charlotte was consistently kind and despite her eccentricities was a favourite among them.

Her husband Thomas roused himself from his apathy and indolence sufficiently to undertake the modest responsibilities of Chairman of Turnpike Roads until the opiates on which he had come more and more to rely as his health declined progressively undermined his faculties, so that he lived sequestered from the world. Eventually he became bent double due to his afflictions, so that he had to suck up his drink through a quill. Charlotte, never one to bother much about her appearance, grew thinner and so haggard that Harriet once described her as "a mop-stick in petticoats"; and yet somehow managed to keep her ragged flag flying, showing herself in old age as censorious and meddlesome as ever and becoming so querulous and captious that people tended to give her a wide berth. But she could be frisky at times and at the age of seventy was seen swigging her ale in fine style. Having survived her dropsical husband by three years, she passed away peacefully in 1875.

In contrast to Charlotte's angular temperament Babbie led the contented life suited to her placid and affectionate nature. Handsome rather than pretty as a girl, with upswept hair and corkscrew curls, she attracted several suitors and was put into an uncharacteristic fluster when William Prescott, a young London banker, made a struggle for her hand just when a Swedish gentleman on a visit to England, Nils von Koch who was secretary to the royal council and court at Copenhagen, was laying ardent siege to her. She had for long esteemed and admired him, finding him good and wise, well adapted to her, and showing a sweet disinterestedness towards her; and though she was still not quite sure she loved him, it only needed Prescott's importunity to push her into Nils' arms. They were married in England in June 1832, she then being twenty-nine, and sailed for Sweden ten days later with her brother Edward in tow bound for his tannery. Though Babbie was never, as she put it, "anxious for brats", she soon to her surprise found herself *enceinte*. This unexpected first pregnancy ended, to Nils' disappointment, in a miscarriage, but undismayed she soon, in order to please him, "hoist another", which proved to be a healthy boy. She was in the years to come to hoist several more, so that she was constantly, in Harriet's words, "all over babies and nurseries"; but owing to miscarriages and early deaths only managed to rear three children, all boys, Thomas, Rickert and Oscar. Although, as she reported to her brother William in Cherrapunji, she was "sunk in the wife and mother", she led a contented life in her adopted country and was much beloved by her relations in England, whose feelings for her were summed up by her nephew Thomas Herbert: "She kept apart from worldly striving, and her high, pure thoughts were in keeping with the high, pure air of the country in which she lived and died, as her sister used to say, in Lat. 60° N". It was due to the circumstance of her living abroad that for nearly forty years she was the recipient of a series of letters from Harriet, which she carefully preserved for the benefit of posterity — Harriet, who far outshone all her brothers and sisters.

Even as a child hers was such an imperious spirit, which neither her mother's coldness nor the strict régime imposed by her father could quench, that she was known in the family circle as "the Empress". Under a hated governess whom she led a sad life she learned French, English grammar, arithmetic, drawing and the piano; but in her nature the feminine and masculine strains struggled constantly for domination, and at the same time as she was acquiring these ladylike accomplishments her preference was for such outdoor, tomboy pursuits as climbing trees or hayricks, riding horses bareback, and secretly taking her younger sisters out on the river in a rowing boat. In winter there were skating and snowballing, and in summer the children would bathe naked in the sea, segregated into separate coves according to sex.

In her *Reminiscences of Early Life*, begun in 1833 and never finished, there are several clues to the way her emotional nature was to develop. In the summer of 1801 when she was nine years old her uncle Richard and his family stayed in a house at Itchen Ferry near The Ridgeway, and the two families met frequently. The eldest daughter was some three years her senior and when Harriet went over to play with her used to make her strip and romp in the nude. "I could not see the fun of 'playing at bathing', as she called it, but her will was despotic and I submitted." Three years later Mrs Lewin's two younger sisters spent the summer at The Ridgeway, and with one of them — a lovely young woman of twenty with soft and winning manners, who was in delicate health — both Charlotte and Harriet fell headlong in love. They used to compare notes on the favours extended to each by this angelic being, and it was by this aunt Jane Hale that Harriet was first induced to read poetry, receiving from her hands a copy of Cowper's poems, which she read with pleasure, implanting in her a lifelong love of good literature.

Being tall for her age, she began to develop a stoop, and for some time had to endure the humiliation of wearing an elaborate strait-jacket, the memory of which still haunted her in middle age.

> The throat was enclosed by the iron spring, which was clasped behind by a steel stud; the arms were pinioned in the shoulder straps. The centre, made of sheet-iron and covered with red morocco leather, pressed against the back, and was secured in its place by a belt round the waist.

Handsome in youth, as were all the Lewin sisters, she had light brown hair turning early to grey and eyes of an unusually bright blue. Like Charlotte's husband Thomas she possessed the faculty of water-divining by means of a hazel twig.

In order to secure the husband of her choice Harriet had to overcome not only the customary objections of her own parents, but the protracted opposition of her intended's father, a London banker of German origin who considered his son should aim for a wife with more than Harriet's relatively modest expectations. But she had set her heart on marrying George Grote, with his ardent passion for her, his remarkable qualities of mind, and his perfect whiskers, and proved her determination by waiting for him for three years during which time he became her tutor, leading her up the Steep of Learning so that she might be a fit companion in his most exalted pursuits. At last old Mr Grote relented, but not, apparently, her father Thomas Lewin, who was not informed until the ceremony was over that the couple had been married in Bexley church, Harriet being given away by her sailor brother Richard. The bride was twenty-eight years old, the bridegroom twenty-six.

Less than a year after they were married Harriet had a miscarriage from which she seemed unlikely to recover and which deprived her of the possibility of bearing further children, a "dire mishap" she never ceased to grieve over, confessing in a letter to Babbie written more than thirty years later that she had ever since "been navigating stormy waters under a jury mast and with a battered hull". At other times she expressed regret that she had ever been born a woman as denying her proper scope for her potentialities; though with feminine inconsistency she also felt she would have been a great actress if she had gone on the stage. She was an ardent feminist, outraged at the injustice that denied married women all right to property. This early calamity did, however, save her from being submerged in a world of babies and nurseries on which she had commiserated with Babbie and allowed her to devote all her time and her considerable abilities to her rôle as George Grote's consort.

For early on she had detected that he had in him the makings of a great man. So long as his father remained alive Grote worked full time at the family banking business in Threadneedle Street, a colleague of his being the William Prescott who had been the unsuccessful rival of Nils von Koch for the hand of Babbie. On his father's death he plunged into Radical politics, taking an active part with John Stuart Mill and Jeremy Bentham, who were friends of his, in the Reform agitation and being elected one of the members of parliament for London. Harriet reported him in 1830 as taking the most vehement interest in the Paris revolution, so that she never remembered seeing him so radiant, so inspirited; and in 1833 he was in a continual state of exaltation on a visit to what had once been the residence in Buckinghamshire of the great parliamentarian John Hampden. In 1841 Grote retired from political life in order to give his full time to writing a history of Greece which, published in eight volumes over a period of ten years, was acclaimed as a work of scholarship ranking with Gibbon's *Decline and Fall of the Roman Empire*. The Grotes had rented a cottage at East Burnham in Surrey in 1838 (though still maintaining their London house in Eccleston Street off Belgrave Square) and here in the shade of the Burnham Beeches he wrote most of his great work, while Harriet fell naturally into the rôle of country squire. It was here when the composer Felix Mendelssohn was staying with them that, lying in the woods listening to the woodland sounds around him, he received inspiration for his *Midsummer Night's Dream.* Out of the considerable profits of Grote's *History of Greece* they built their own cottage on a piece of land nearby which they called History Hut. They sold it in 1858 and thereafter their country retreat was a rented house called Barrow Green at Oxted, once the residence of Jeremy Bentham and afterwards of James Mill. They had already in 1848 shifted their London quarters from Eccleston Street to Savile Row. They finally moved their country residence in 1865 to Shere in Surrey, naming their house The Ridgeway after the house where Harriet had been born.

There followed authoritative works on Plato and, posthumously, Aristotle, and somehow George Grote managed to combine his work as a historian with a full public life, becoming president of University College, London, vice-chancellor of London University, and a trustee of the British Museum. Towards the end of his life he turned down a peerage when it was offered to him, on the ground that the necessity of attending sittings of the House of Lords would be incompatible with his other responsibilities; to Harriet's mortification, because he chose not to consult her before declining the honour. She was somewhat mollified when on his death two years later he was granted burial in Westminster Abbey. They had been married for fifty years.

It would be difficult to overestimate the contribution made by his wife in sustaining this multifarious career, for Grote was a retiring man who fought shy of the titled and the great. Without Harriet he could never have made his way, as he did, not only in English society, but French and German as well; for they were true Europeans, travelling extensively throughout the Continent and speaking several languages. The imperiousness for which as a child she had earned her nickname the Empress remained her dominant characteristic, and she treated friends and acquaintances alike as if they were her subjects. Tall, square-built and high shouldered, her manliness increased with the years, providing Sydney Smith — a clergyman noted more for his wit than his piety — with one of his famous *bons mots*: "I like the Grotes," he observed: "he is so ladylike, and she is such a perfect gentleman", and enabling him to make a bad pun on the word grotesque. When someone in her presence compared her with Madame de Staël, she demurred, preferring to consider Madame de Sévigné her prototype on account of her love of reading, her habit of good society, and her having remained an honest woman. "The household virtues," Harriet would declare, "are everything."

The few occasions when the Grotes were touched by the breath of scandal arose rather from breaches of etiquette than impropriety. Denied fulfilment as an actress herself, Harriet remained stage-struck and twice became emotionally involved with a star performer — first a dancer, then a singer — whose career she had sought, unwisely, to foster. There was Fanny Elssler, born in Vienna in 1910 the younger daughter of a servant of the composer Joseph Haydn. At the age of sixteen while a member of the *corps de ballet* at the San Carlo Theatre in Naples she had borne an illegitimate son to the king's brother, whereupon she had been "acquired" by the sixty-six year old Chevalier von Gentz, an eminent German diplomat and writer who, having in his dotage become besotted with her, undertook her liberal education while keeping her as his child-mistress. She was nearing thirty, the mother now of an illegitimate daughter (father unknown) and at the height of her fame as *première danseuse* of the Academie Royale de Musique in Paris when Harriet, and soon afterwards George, fell victims to her *sorcellerie*, an infatuation so complete that they sometimes felt they had indeed been enchanted. George was at the height of his parliamentary career in the 1830s when Harriet conceived the notion of introducing this dark-haired paragon of the *demi-monde* into London society in order, as she put it, to make an honest woman of her. Fanny's dramatic renderings of the tarantelle and the wild legend of Giselle had so captivated her that she even sought to emulate her in the privacy of her own drawing-room. Her younger brother George once related how he and a friend, calling one evening unexpectedly at the Grotes' house in Eccleston Street, found the room brilliantly lighted as for a reception

> and Mr Grote sitting as a solitary spectator in a chair, while his wife in a short pink skirt and wings was in the act of bounding forth from the back drawing-room to show Mr Grote a *pas seul à la Elssler.*

The precise nature of the Grotes' involvement with Fanny cannot now be recovered, but in old age Harriet found the memory of the circumstances "so revolting and fraught with such painful incidents" as to give her a fit of the spleen, and put her so out of patience with herself "for having ever descended into such a foul stratum of immorality" that she destroyed all record of the affair, including the passionate love poems George had addressed to Fanny when under her spell.

Although denied children of her own, Harriet's maternal instincts did not go altogether unsatisfied. For two and a half years she had the care of Fanny's bastard daughter Theresa, of whose settlement George was a trustee, until 1846 when Fanny abruptly removed her from their care and shut her up in a convent in Vienna, where her temper and character were ruined by bad discipline and a want of love. Meanwhile when George's brother Arthur, twenty years younger than himself — a Bengal civilian who was to show great kindness to Harriet's nephew Thomas Herbert throughout his career in India — was left a widower with three young children to rear, Harriet had immediately taken the elder two under her care and brought them up to all intents and purposes as her own.

The Grotes got to know Jenny Lind, "the Swedish nightingale", through Babbie and Edward who had become acquainted with her in Stockholm and had started her off on her career as a singer by arranging for her to travel to Paris in 1841 with a servant-companion they provided for her. She was already a European star when the Grotes first met her in Frankfurt five years later, and through their influence she obtained her first London engagement at Her Majesty's Theatre. We catch a glimpse of her arriving in Eccleston Street in a four-wheeler cab looking scared and bewildered, her face brightening as she recognized her two friends, Harriet and the composer Felix Mendelssohn who was in England to conduct his new oratorio *Elijah*, standing on the pavement waiting for her. Between performances Jenny often stayed at the Grotes' country house at Burnham Beeches. There were picnics in Wimbledon Park when Jenny listened in rapture to the nightingales singing in the copses; a memorable *fête champêtre* at her theatre manager's villa in Putney; and an evening in private with Queen Adelaide at Windsor. Edward, absenting himself from his Swedish tannery, looked after Jenny during the provincial tour that followed her London season, for she spoke little English and was helpless on her own in a strange country. His attentiveness aroused Harriet's jealousy and caused an estrangement between brother and sister. "Either she sticks to me," wrote Harriet to Babbie, "and *éloignés* him, or she sticks to him and cuts me: that is if he persists, which I trust he will not do. At any rate Edward will become alienated from me unless I sanction his perpetual presence, which I cannot do." Given her dominating personality, it was inevitable that Harriet would win the tug of war, and for some years she remained on close terms with Jenny; but various factors — the singer's triumphant tours in Europe and America, her affairs of the heart, and finally her marriage, besides Harriet's belated realization that she was being made use of — gradually loosened the tie. In the end Harriet came to regard the liaison with such a will-o'-the-wisp as "fraught with those liabilities to bitter regrets and disappointments which I fear must ever attend similar ties". George was wise enough not to get his fingers burnt a second time.

Chapter Three
Tom Lewin's
Schooldays

1

The precise nature of George Herbert Lewin's infirmity that led to his death at the age of forty-nine cannot now be identified, but from early manhood he had manifested an instability of behaviour that caused concern to his family. He had a hot and angry temperament, often being what his sister Charlotte called "grumptious". When he had at last sailed into calmer waters his brother William recalled that in early youth he had fallen into bad habits, and his brother Edward that George's had been a hard struggle and his experience of life full of bitterness. When his eldest son Thomas Herbert applied to his aunt Babbie towards the end of her life for some account of his father, she deferred embarking on such a painful subject for so long that she appears never to have written it.

Some idea of the nature of his troubles can be gathered from the high-minded letter of admonition William wrote to him in November 1829 while on home leave from India and when George at the age of twenty-one was reluctantly serving his articles with a respectable firm of London attorneys Messrs Amory and Coles. Mr Coles had written to their father informing him that George's conduct was such as to render it expedient to dismiss him and that he had only refrained from doing so out of regard and consideration for the family. George was irregular in his attendance at the office and so negligent when he bothered to turn up at all that any business of consequence had to be entrusted to someone else. Thomas Lewin senior managed to negotiate a short extension of his son's period of probation in a last effort to bring him to his senses, but warned him that, if he did not seize this last chance, he would utterly eject him from his support and leave him to his fate. Coupled with the charge of inattention to his duties William also accused him of extravagance due to the demands made on the allowance George received from his father by some immoral connection he chose to maintain in order to secure what his brother described as licentious gratifications; from which it appears he was keeping a mistress. The portrait of him as a young man that has survived shows a sensitive face framed in poetically disordered hair and blond sidewhiskers with eyes gazing idealistically into the distance: such a face as might well captivate an impressionable young woman.

His father's threat to cut him off appears to have had the desired result, for in January 1833 Harriet reported that he was going on tolerably well in the law, and by 1836 he was working for a clever and dashing attorney called Heathcote who had a good practice, with whom he hoped to enter into partnership. But in the longer term his salvation was undoubtedly Mary.

She was one of the three daughters of James Friend

who came of a family long settled at Birchington-on-Sea in the Isle of Thanet which forms the sandy heel of Kent. The first of the line to emerge from the mists was Daniel ffriend born towards the end of the sixteenth century, who was followed by three undistinguished generations of farmers or small tradesmen. The Friend family's fortunes became linked with those of the neighbouring Taddy family when James Taddy (1747-1828), who had founded a snuff-manufacturing business in the Minories in east London, took into partnership his three brothers-in-law: William Tomlin of Birchington, John Hatfeild a banker of Norwich, and John Friend of Brooksend, Thanet. John Friend's eldest son James married Isabella Bankes, one of the daughters of John Bankes of Otley in Yorkshire and Clapham Common, another daughter Elizabeth Anne having married Robert Sackett Tomlin of Dane Court, St. Peter's-in-Thanet. When James Friend died in 1819 at the early age of thirty-seven, only two years after his father's death, his younger brother George, also married to a Tomlin and a partner in the business which now included the manufacture of tobacco as well as snuff, became the guardian of his four minor children, one of whom was Mary. The family home was in Clapham, so they were neighbours of the Bankes family. In 1831 when Mary was nineteen her guardian was killed falling out of a cart in the Whitechapel Road not far from the Minories while trying out a new horse between the shafts.

In the eyes of his family George Lewin married beneath him. It was not only that in their progress from yeoman status to gentility the Lewins were a generation or two ahead of the Friends, but the latter were unashamedly "in trade". William made the point when he referred to Mary's father as "a citizen of famous London Town", and Babbie more explicitly when in December 1836 writing from Stockholm she reported on their future sister-in-law (whom she had not then met) to her brother Frederick in Madras:

> George I love, and he has his merits, but it is no use to talk to you about him. I fear for his happiness in married life. He has made up his mind to marry a girl for her money, and she has not enough to cover his deficiencies, & this I fear will gnaw him, although she is a good girl and of respectable family, but a sugar baker's daughter.

It appears from this that the partnership's business interests had by then been expanded so as to include sugar-refining. The same note of condescension blended with goodwill is detectable in what Harriet wrote to Babbie shortly after the wedding, giving her first impressions of Mary:

> She is a good, nice girl, quite a lady in her manners, tolerably personable, and very wholesome. I consider [George] particularly fortunate in having got such a wife. I hope he will run steady now. She is devoted to him, and I think they may be very happy together.

An early portrait of her shows a young woman with dark eyes and rosebud mouth set in an oval, softly feminine face whose expression suggests sweetness and good nature.

A son was born to them at The Hollies where Mary was staying for her first confinement on 1 April 1839 and christened Thomas Herbert, his uncles Thomas and Edward Lewin and his maternal aunt Elizabeth Friend standing as sponsors.

Five other children were to follow: Mary Jane born in 1841; Friend, usually known as Bob, in 1843; Harriet in 1844; William in 1847; and Isabella, known as Bella for short, in 1849. With this growing family to support George did run steady, and his circumstances which had already been augmented by Mary's dowry of £10,000 were further improved on his father's death in 1843 from the legacy of £4,000 bequeathed to him. This was £1,000 less than the legacies received by his three elder brothers, but his father's will also discharged George from all advances of money he had from time to time made to him.

There is a brief glimpse of young Tom in a letter Harriet Grote wrote to Babbie in 1845, when he was six years old:

> I have rigged out Tommy Lewin (George's son) in his first boy's suit, to poor Mary's great delight, good woman, but what is to become of her children brought up by a mother so incapable of disciplining them, God only knows!

This disinclination to discipline her children remained one of Mary's most endearing qualities; instead she trusted to the power of her love for them to keep them on the right road; and they responded with an equally ardent love for her she never forfeited, and which in the case of her three boys came to resemble the passionate rivalry of three suitors for preference in the beloved's affections. Soft in her ways though she may have been and reluctant to enforce her will on her children, she was soon to show that she had hidden reserves of strength to call upon when they were needed, for in 1851, two years after the death of their eldest daughter Mary Jane at the age of seven and a half, her husband was stricken with an illness so severe that his brother Frederick reported succinctly to Babbie, "George seems dying". His diagnosis was premature, for George lingered on for another five years, bedridden, in a somnolent condition and substantially *non compos mentis*, placing an appalling burden on his wife who now had the sole responsibility for bringing up their young family on a reduced income and with their father a chronic invalid in the house.

As soon as they were old enough the boys were sent off to boarding-school, and as he was the eldest Tom was the first to go. The wrench of being parted from his mother, perhaps the most agonizing parting he ever suffered, cries out through every word of his first, misspelt letter to her, written in unformed handwriting irregularly across the page:

> Dear Mama i am quite well but not a fall happy if your tofe me come down and see m

His first school was an academy for boys run by Mr Grix at Surrey House in Littlehampton on the Sussex coast. "He was a fine handsome fellow," Lewin remembered many years later, "and kind in his way. Won the mothers' hearts I should think." From him he had early training in the art of humbug, being encouraged to write to his uncle and godfather Thomas Lewin — the one, as Harriet had noted, who found ample food for disquiet in the study of religion — a letter containing some expository remarks upon a chapter in Isaiah. He remembered himself at the time as a child wearing tight, threadbare little trousers who was always getting himself into scrapes, and retained the bitter memory of being sent to bed at ten o'clock one morning as a punishment for some misdemeanour, a wretched white-shirted mite (for his outer clothes had been taken away from him), lonely, cold and miserable, sitting on the window-seat and gazing longingly at the other boys playing merrily in the meadows below. Now and then his mother would come to visit him, like an angel from another world.

After four years he was moved on in 1854 to Mr Hopkirk's academy at Eltham in Kent, a preparatory school for boys destined for a military career. There were several of his cousins among the pupils such as Johnny Rivaz (a relation of uncle Edward's wife) whom he liked, and the Henry Lewins (descendants of Thomas Lewin senior's younger brother Richard) whom he disliked except for little Henry who was taking higher honours. Also at the school was a boy called Harry Graves whom Lewin came to consider his best friend, partly because he became one of the world's failures, dependent throughout his life on Lewin generosity for survival.

Lewin was bored by the monotony of school routine and hated the discipline, in reaction to which he stoutly maintained his reputation as a scapegrace, being often cruelly flogged by the master — a form of punishment known in those days as bum-brushing — though he usually had to admit that he had well deserved it. He was also beginning to develop more promising talents. He enjoyed his music lessons, learnt to draw tolerably well and began to read good books for pleasure, particular favourites being Dickens' *David Copperfield*, the novels of Scott, and fairy tales and fantasies like *The Arabian Nights*. At this young age the books that made the most lasting impression on him were James Fennimore Cooper's tales of pioneer and Red Indian life on the American frontier such as *The Last of the Mohicans* (1826) and *The Deerslayer* (1841), which provided a model for the life he was later to devise for himself on a different frontier. From these he graduated to Herman Melville's fictionalized travel-books *Typee* (1846) and its sequel *Omoo* (1847). He used to complain that at neither of his schools was he taught grammar properly, though he came top of his class in English composition and reading aloud; and even if he never mastered the mysteries of arithmetic, he did well enough in such regular subjects as geometry and French to pass the entrance examination to Addiscombe, the East India Company's military seminary near Croydon in Surrey.

During the holidays he became once more an unruly member of Mary Lewin's rampageous brood, on one occasion at Broadstairs joining Bob in tormenting Harriet, the best and most unselfish sister in the world, with a rhyme of his own composition:

> O beast, beast, beast,
> Why do you always cry?
> If you do not refrain,
> Though you give me pain,
> I'll hit you slap in the eye.

It was not in Harriet's nature to bear malice, and a good many years later she was to perform a service for her eldest brother that would alter the entire course of his life. It was while staying with the family of his uncle William who had died at Cherrapunji, at their house in the north London suburb of Walthamstow, that he fell in love with his first cousin Jane, affectionately known as Jeannie, who was eleven years older than himself. He remembered the occasion of its occurrence with exactitude as when he and her elder brother Edward were sitting in a medlar tree surreptitiously smoking pipes. There was talk of the two families joining forces and living under one roof, but nothing came of it because Mary Lewin apparently thought William's widow was too good for her. But thenceforth Jeannie became an important figure in Lewin's life, and he later confessed that everything he had done in the world had been somehow directly or indirectly under her influence. To

Jeannie and her younger sister Fanny he was always known as Tombo.

2

The patronage system whereby new staff were recruited for service in the East India Company without needing any particular qualification inevitably led to a lowering of the quality of intake, and from early in the nineteenth century various means of improving the situation were tried out. In 1800 Marquess Wellesley, elder brother of the 'Iron Duke' and then governor-general of Bengal, founded the College of Fort William at Calcutta for training candidates for service in all three presidencies, providing three-year courses in a wide spectrum of subjects. Opponents of the innovation based their objection on the ground that such an education tended to aggravate the "disease of indianization" that had afflicted the Company's servants during the preceding century, and accordingly the curriculum was restricted to the teaching of Indian languages and the Company's administrative procedures. The view prevailed that candidates should first be indoctrinated with a reverence for the religion, constitution and laws of their own country before being exposed to the alien cultural environment to which they would be subjected in India. This was the justification for the founding, in 1806, of the East India College at Haileybury in Hertfordshire, an educational establishment for potential civilian employees of the Company, followed three years later by the founding of its counterpart, the Military Seminary at Addiscombe.

Up to that time officer cadets destined for the Company's Bengal, Madras and Bombay armies — nominated like the civilians through patronage — were trained in the respective cavalry and infantry regiments to which they had been posted, the high-fliers being later transferred to artillery or engineer units. With the increase in specialization arrangements were made, in the case of these two technical branches, for the Royal Military Academy at Woolwich to allocate a quota of its vacancies to cadets of the Company, a similar facility being later extended to cavalry and infantry cadets at Marlow, later removed to Sandhurst. This proving too expensive, the Company (after an unsuccessful experiment at Baraset outside Calcutta, which was forced to close owing to ill-discipline) decided to establish its own military academy in England, for which a suitable building was chosen at Addiscombe. Here for three years cadets studied mathematics, classics, English, Hindustani, French, fortification, civil and military drawing, surveying, chemistry, geology and fencing. After 1833 between forty and fifty young ensigns passed out each half year and proceeded to join their regiments in India.

It was through the influence of his uncle and godfather Thomas that Tom Lewin was nominated for a cadetship by Sir James Hogg, MP, a director of the Company. In those days he liked to make himself out to be the bad boy of the class, always being punished with extra drills for some misdemeanour or other. His most frequent offence was talking in the ranks, but once he was given four drills for keeping a candle burning in his "kennel" after lights-out at ten thirty and, more seriously, he was reprimanded and given fifteen days' drill for "gross irreverence and disrespect" for having loudly applauded — sincerely, he claimed — at the end of a theological lecture. His youthful high spirits come across most vividly in the description he gave his cousin Jeannie of how he and his fellow cadets, returning at the beginning of term by train to Croydon, the railway station for Addiscombe, had passed the time smoking their pipes, ragging the guard and singing a chorus to the effect that "we were bound for Addiscombe & we would have a spree, to a tune something similar to the latter part of My Earrings compounded with Yankee Doodle".

He found the work hard but applied himself to it seriously, spending part of the holidays studying under a crammer, and was much put out when he was told that his poor showing in mathematics gave him no chance of getting into the artillery, on which he had set his heart. It was the more disappointing because in other subjects, including algebra and geometry, he was better than his fellows. Heights and distances he found difficult despite his talent as a draughtsman, but his appreciation of poetry and good literature will have helped him to pass the English exam without difficulty.

Nothing in his letters to Jeannie, the only ones to have

survived from this period of his life, suggest that he took any interest in the Crimean War which was being incompetently waged during his cadetship. His chief anxiety was about his mother, who was not strong and suffered from dreadful headaches and had on her hands, besides four other children ranging in age from seven to thirteen, a husband who was suffering from what was then known as "softening of the brain" and clearly dying inch by inch. It must have been a relief when after five years in a somnolent condition he eventually died of pneumonia in March 1856, aged forty-seven. Although his family was left with adequate if not ample means, his fox-hunting uncle Frederick who was now head of the family proposed that Mary should take in lodgers, though this proved unnecessary; and he had his own worries, for while he stood at his younger brother George's graveside news reached him of the death of his wife Diana. "No one I am sorry to say," Tom wrote to Jeannie, "seemed to care much about dear Papa's death, and Uncle Frederick least of all."

Tom did care, having held his father in affection and respect, and in a letter he wrote to his mother from Chittagong eight years later he revealed what his feelings about him had been:

> There is his portrait looking down at me now from the wall. They say I'm like him — but I know I am not half so good. I shall never have his gentleness and a certain charm of manner which was entirely his & particularly dangerous to women.

The matters in prospect now were his final examinations, his passing out from the seminary as an ensign of the East India Company, and his embarking for India, whence news had come of some disturbance in the Bengal army. On the eve of his departure his main worry was still the thought of leaving his mother to cope alone with her fatherless family, especially his two younger brothers, unruly boys whom he then regarded with disapproval tinged with jealousy: "I don't know what she'll do when I go, for though I say it myself, I can see quite well that she loves me better than any of the others". As for Bob he was "a dreadful fellow, as bad as I was I daresay when I was his age, but then I had my father to keep me in order".

It was a moment of misery for mother and son when from the crowded rail he saw the English shore and her slight figure growing dimmer and more distant as the ship pulled away.

Chapter Four

Ensign in the Mutiny

1

Not until the ship carrying Lewin and his fellow cadets to India called at Malta was it learnt how serious the disturbance was, that virtually the entire Bengal army was in open mutiny and the whole of Bengal aflame with revolt. What stirred them most was the news that a batch of cadets who had gone out from Addiscombe a few months before had been massacred at Allahabad as they sat at mess.

> The fun of our voyage was gone. The glories and wonders of Alexandria and Cairo; the crossing of the pathless desert sands, strewn with skeletons of animals and shapeless masses of rock, over which we jolted heavily in our mule-drawn vans; the dry burning heat of the Red Sea and the moist clinging warmth of the Indian Ocean and Ceylon; the strange new human creatures that swarmed round the ship, importunate for alms, as we stopped for coaling; all passed before our eyes like a dream, as obstacles and delays in our now tedious journey. The fever had seized us; the desire to fight, the wish for vengeance was in our blood. We wanted one thing only — to reach quickly the land where our comrades and friends had so treacherously been murdered.

In retrospect it can be seen that the Indian Mutiny was

not a nationalist rising in protest against alien domination. India was not then a nation, but a medley of races speaking scores of different languages scattered among the territories ruled by the East India Company and a mosaic of principalities, many at enmity with one another. Moreover the whole fragmented subcontinent was riven from top to bottom by the great Hindu-Muslim divide. Of the four armies maintained by the Company — the Bengal, Madras and Bombay armies and a fourth then being mustered in the Punjab — only the Bengal army mutinied, the others remaining true to their salt; so that the disturbance was confined to the central sector of northern India. Even in the affected areas the agricultural peasantry, which formed the vast majority of the inhabitants, did not side with the mutineers but, as is the way with simple people, gave what help they could to the European families fleeing from the slaughter.

What happened was the reflex reaction of a society ossified in outmoded tradition to the too sudden imposition of progressive reforms that, striking at the roots of cherished prejudices, threatened too many vested interests. New land settlement laws designed to ameliorate the lot of the peasantry enraged the corrupt and oppressive *zemindars* whose wealth and influence were thereby curtailed. The abolition of age-old customs repugnant to the Western mind, and the encouragement of new attitudes hostile to the caste system, by threatening to sweep away ignorance and superstition, outraged the powerful Brahmin priesthood which, noting the increase in missionary activity, wrongly interpreted these events as evidence of a deliberate policy of imposing Christianity on the people of India.

It is naïve to attribute the Mutiny to specific "causes". Given the prevailing conditions and the pressures being insensitively applied, a violent reaction of some sort was inevitable. But it is possible to identify certain factors as relevant to its timing, location and ferocity. In the winter of 1842, for example, during the retreat from Kabul Pathan tribesmen had destroyed not only General Elphinstone's army but also the myth of British superiority. During the next few years the First and Second Sikh Wars, though resulting in the annexation of Sind and the Punjab, had merely underlined British vulnerability. But the unwitting instigator of the Mutiny was undoubtedly the Earl of Dalhousie, during whose viceroyalty (1848-1856) great advances were made towards modernizing India. Trunk roads were built, the electric telegraph introduced, coasts and harbours improved, and the first railway lines in Asia laid down. Along with these technological advances went an attempt to dismantle several of the country's power structures. The decision was taken that the Mogul dynasty should come to an end with the death of the present emperor Bahadur Shah, an eighty-year-old nonentity who wielded no tangible power but kept alive in some Indian hearts the myth that their king still reigned, however nebulously, in Delhi. Of more immediate concern was the enforcement of the doctrine of "lapse" in all princely states recognizing British paramountcy, whereby the customary law allowing the adoptive heir of a ruler to succeed in the absence of a natural heir was overridden and replaced by the directive that in such circumstances the territories of the deceased ruler would automatically lapse and become part of British India. In this way Satara came under the Company's jurisdiction in 1848, Nagpur in 1853 and, more significantly, Jhansi in 1854.

Even more dangerously, Dalhousie in 1856 — just before he left India, exhausted but satisfied with his wide-ranging reforms — forced the king of Oudh to abdicate on the grounds of his undoubted corruption and misrule and gave his former kingdom into the charge of Sir Henry Lawrence as British commissioner with head-quarters in the capital, Lucknow. Oudh was the principal catchment area for recruits, consisting mainly of high-caste Hindus, for the Company's Bengal army, which in any case harboured the seeds of its own destruction. Organization, discipline and efficiency were alike deplorable. Its senior officers were not only over age, overweight and over-confident to the point of purblindness in the loyalty of their men, but also deaf to their legitimate grievances, which they treated with paternalistic contempt.

It only needed a spark to set the tinder alight and so lead to a general conflagration, and this, too, was soon forthcoming, though whether through negligence or misguided design is now beyond conjecture. The facts are scarcely credible. Authority was given, by whom will never be known, for the cartridges manufactured at the Fort William arsenal for the new Enfield rifles to be wrapped in paper greased with a compound of cows' fat and lard made of pigs' fat. Since a sepoy had to tear off this paper with his teeth before loading his rifle, contact with the offending substance would involve for the Hindus loss of caste or for the Muslims defilement; as neat a method of degradation as could be devised. It only needed the truth about the grease to be leaked to the army by workers at the arsenal for the stage to be set for catastrophe.

Though perhaps even then the situation could have been saved if handled differently, but the truth about the grease was withheld from the British officers (including the commander-in-chief) who — believing that the whole thing was a "fable" put about by mischief-makers — acted in a way that might well have proved effective had that belief been well founded. In face of their men's knowledge of the true facts it proved disastrous. The story is one every schoolboy used to know: how eighty-five troopers of the 3rd Light Cavalry at Meerut refused to handle the cartridges, for which they were court-martialled and sentenced to ten years' hard labour; and how at a parade of the whole garrison lasting through the heat of a summer's day they were stripped of their uniforms, had fetters rivetted to their ankles, and were marched away to the civilian gaol. Next day, Sunday 10 May 1857, the weather was oppressively hot, and that evening, as the bell tolled for evening service at the garrison church and

the British soldiers and their families began to assemble,
the sepoys rose, men of the 3rd Cavalry hastening to the
gaol to free their comrades, those from the two Native
Infantry regiments augmented by a mob from the bazaar
rampaging through the cantonment, looting, burning,
and butchering every European — man, woman and
child — they could find. When none were left alive the
mutineers took counsel among themselves and decided
to make for Delhi forty miles away, leaving behind them
a smoking ruin and a horror of mutilated corpses.

That was the prelude. Soon the rebels had the upper
hand over a huge area stretching from Allahabad in the
east to Agra in the west. They occupied all the larger
towns in between except Lucknow, where the small
garrison under Henry Lawrence held out in the Residency
against repeated attacks, and Cawnpore which eventually
surrendered to the Nana Sahib on 27th June. General
Havelock, ordered to relieve the town, defeated the
rebels sent to oppose him, who retired into the town
where two hundred British women and children were
being held prisoner. Through the treachery of Nana
Sahib, heir of the deposed Peshwa of Oudh who had
thrown in his lot with the mutineers, these were murdered
out of hand, for which no quarter was given to the rebels
when the place was relieved by Havelock on 17 July. In
August Sir Colin Campbell, who had commanded the 1st
Division in the Crimea, arrived in Calcutta to take overall
command of operations against the rebels, while
reinforcements were assembled and sent up piecemeal

to Allahabad, to be directed wherever they were most urgently needed.

Such was the situation when Ensign Lewin's ship sailed up the Hooghly and docked in the middle of October. Homesick Lewin may have felt when, after reporting to the fort adjutant, he first set foot in the bleak cadets' quarters in Fort William, but he was not alone in a strange land. Not only had a dozen of his Addiscombe friends as well as a schoolfellow or two travelled in the ship with him from England, but he soon received an invitation from Arthur Grote, the much younger brother of his uncle-by-marriage George Grote and a civilian in the Company's service, to stay with him and his wife at their house at Alipore, a residential suburb to the south of the city not far from the fort. He also made enquiries about Jeannie's elder brother Edward serving in the artillery and learnt that he was with his battery at Lucknow, "wherever" (as Tom wrote to his mother) "that may be". He was soon to find out.

"Army! — regiment!", the adjutant had snorted. "There is no Bengal army; it is all in revolt. You will be sent off to the front at once, and perhaps attached to some Queen's regiment."

This proved to be the 34th, the Border Regiment, then under orders for Cawnpore, which Lewin joined at Chinsura a short train journey to the west. After a sound night's sleep in a tent, lying on the bare ground wrapped in his cloak, he paraded with D Company at 5 a.m. which marched off, the band playing in front of them, to the railway station where they entrained for the railhead at Raniganj a hundred and twenty miles to the north-west, reaching the place at 6 p.m. Next day with a subaltern called Cochrane, a veteran of the Crimea, and fifteen men he set off by jolting horse-*dak* along the Grand Trunk Road making for Allahabad. The whole country around was under martial law as evidenced by the corpses he saw hanging from makeshift gibbets along the way, and the men were ordered to keep their rifles loaded. At Benares they joined a detachment of the 82nd Regiment under Captain Marriot and proceeded on their way by a different mode of transport.

> Nothing is to be heard [he wrote to his mother] but the slow creaking of the long line of bullock waggons, and now and then from the adjacent jungle the wail of a jackal, which is instantly taken up and re-echoed by hundreds more. This sounds as if the forest were full of [Red] Indians, as in Fennimore Cooper's novels that I used to read at school.

The passage provides a reminder of Lewin's youthfulness — he was only eighteen — as does the letter he wrote next day to Jeannie, in which he boasted a little about travelling through a country full of disaffected peasantry and mutinous soldiers, of keeping alternate watch at night with Cochrane, and of his uneasiness in Allahabad bazaar surrounded by "scowling natives", where he had gone to fetch new trousers from the *derzi*. Though his baggage entitlement was restricted to 150lb. he was as yet hardly roughing it, having engaged a bearer at Benares and now added to his personal staff a *kitmutgar* (a table servant) and a *syce* to look after the grey pony he had bought for fifty rupees. Bored by the onward journey to Cawnpore, he let his propensity to schoolboy pranks get him into trouble by taking over from the Indian driver the handling of the bullocks drawing the cart in which he was travelling, which ended up in the ditch and he under the beasts' hooves.

That summer General Havelock's relieving force had fought its way into Cawnpore against heavy odds, to find that the two hundred European women and children held prisoner by the Nana Sahib had been butchered on his orders. The British had left a detachment under General Wyndham dug in on high ground outside the town commanding the ferry over the Ganges consisting of a bridge of boats over which ran the road to the north. Up this Havelock had led his main force in an unsuccessful attempt to relieve his compatriots besieged in the Residency at Lucknow. Among the reinforcements sent up to strengthen the ridge overlooking the ferry was Lewin's regiment, the 34th, some detachments of the 82nd, 88th and 20th Rifle Brigades, a small contingent of loyal Madras troops with four 9-pounder guns under General Carthew, and a section of British Artillery with two 9-pounders: in all about 1500 men. When the new commander-in-chief Sir Colin Campbell passed through with a strong force to the relief of Lucknow his orders to Wyndham had been to strengthen the defences of the entrenchments overlooking the river in order to keep the road open, and to fight off any attack made by the state army of Gwalior under the Nana Sahib's lieutenant Tantia Topi, which was assembling round Kalpi on the Jumna river in the province of Bundelkhand fifty miles to the west.

When Lewin, still bruised and sore, got down from his bullock-cart on the morning of 18 November to find himself near some low whitewashed huts his attention was caught by groups of British soldiers standing about talking excitedly beside a large tree-stump overlooking a well in the courtyard. A serjeant told him that lying heaped at the bottom were the bodies of the women and children who had been slaughtered. The courtyard was still strewn with torn pieces of their clothing, and the walls of the huts and the bark of the tree were splashed with blood. In one hut — for this was the Bibi Ghar where they had been held prisoner — Lewin came across a Bible and in another saw scratched on the wall the words: "Oh Lord, our God, save us in this our time of trouble". The soldiers were in an ugly mood, boding ill for any mutineer that fell into their hands.

On the same day as Lewin arrived at Cawnpore General Campbell, having finally succeeded in relieving Lucknow, had begun the evacuation of the women and children and the sick and wounded — to the number of about 2,000 — a place of safety, and they were already on the road making slow progress towards Cawnpore with a strong escort commanded by the general, thence to proceed by boat down the Ganges to Allahabad. The rebels in the north had not yet been defeated, and General Outram had been left behind to hold the fort until Campbell could return with reinforcements. The frontier of Wyndham's outpost outside Cawnpore was equally insecure. Intelligence had been received the previous day that a force of rebels in the south had advanced to within fifteen miles of them, and two days later that Tantia Topi with 6,000 sepoys of the Gwalior contingent and fifteen guns had sealed off the town from the west and north-west. Then, on the 22nd, came worse news of the capture of Bani Bridge on the road to Lucknow, cutting communications and threatening Campbell's evacuation of the non-combatants. Clearly an attack on Cawnpore was intended, and Wyndham decided though greatly outnumbered to get in his blow first, incidentally giving Lewin his baptism of fire.

A composite force 1,500 strong paraded behind the entrenchment under General Carthew at 4 a.m. and stood in rank for two hours before being marched off, led by the bands which played from time to time until a halt was called and "the music" was ordered to the rear. There was murmuring in the ranks of the 34th, which had the right by seniority to be first into action, when the 88th, the Connaught Rangers, marched past them to the front of the column; then the order was given to tighten belts and jerk the shoulders to settle accoutrements, and the men knew that a fight was imminent. Lewin later confessed in a letter to his mother that the thought gave him a sinking feeling in the pit of his stomach and made him catch his breath, and glancing at his comrades he noticed that some of them were looking queer enough; but there was little time for reflection. The left wing of the regiment moved off silently, while the rest with Lewin among them had just received the order to advance when

Bang! a mighty round shot whizzed over the column. I was on the right wing. Bang! again, and this time they got the range and the grape-shot tore through our column. The word was given, 'Extend into skirmishing order to the left. Double'. Away we went, the cannon banging right at us, and shells bursting over our heads. You can form no idea how terrible is the sound of round shot: it seems like Death personified.

We were now running through a little copse, advancing under whatever cover we could find towards the enemy's guns, until at last we came to an open place and I saw stretched before me a large plain broken by shrubs and rocks, every nook and corner of which was filled with red-coated sepoys firing at us, and I was lost in astonishment that I was not hit; but we rushed on straight at them, and just then a fellow tumbled down close to me; I thought he had tripped and stopped to help him, but found he was doubled up in a heap with his face a pool of red blood. The first blood I had ever seen. Then I began to feel angry, and I waved my sword in the air calling out, 'Come along, my boys. Remember Cawnpore!' but with a somewhat feeble voice, trying to fancy myself brave; and not succeeding very well in the attempt.

At last we came to a stop under the shelter of a house and were here in comparative safety, for which I was heartily thankful, as I was terribly blown.

After a short respite the advance continued into the

hail of bullets until three of the enemy guns were overrun and taken. Lewin then found himself with some of his men skirmishing towards a village. A soldier fell from a shot fired from the flat roof of one of the houses, whereupon some of his comrades, breaking open the door, rushed on to the roof and pushed the sniper down to the others waiting below who

> sprang at him like tigers, and in went the bayonets, gliding through the flesh as if it were butter, and he (poor wretch) doubled himself on the steel and seemed to hug it to him with a groan. Up rode the adjutant. 'Damn it, men, don't be cowards,' he cried, and though the men swore savagely, we went on again.

Soon afterwards, the attack having lost its impetus, the order came to retire on Cawnpore. Early next morning the sound of heavy guns heralded an attack on the entrenchments, and the colonel gave the order: "The Grenadier Company of the 34th will hold the houses, and, skirmishing to the front, endeavour to pick off the enemy's gunners. The rest of the Regiment will hold the right approach". So off they went through narrow mud lanes and took up position astride the road while round shot and musket balls whistled over them. During the day they fought off two rebel cavalry charges before receiving the order to retire and made their way back through the deserted lanes to the entrenchments where after a supper of biscuits washed down with rum and water they slept in their cloaks.

D Company's task next day was to guard a bridge

across a small ravine where they hastily threw up a barricade of broken carts, bricks, planks, railings and anything else they could lay hands on, suffering several casualties from round shot while the work was in progress. In the afternoon, under pressure from the rebels who threatened to outflank their position, men from the other companies began to retreat across the bridge, pursued by the enemy who occupied a church on the left from which they brought a gun to bear on the bridge at close quarters, pouring in round after round of grape-shot. Others crossing the ravine and taking advantage of every available scrap of cover concentrated their fire on the barricade and subjected Lewin's company to a prolonged fusilade of bullets, causing many casualties among officers and men, including General Carthew to whom Lewin offered a drink from his flask. He was much impressed by the colonel who stood amid the tumult, smiling and calmly lighting a cheroot. As evening fell, since the men were getting out of hand, the order was given to retire, and the survivors made their way back to the entrenchments carrying their dead and wounded with them, the colonel with some old soldiers forming the rearguard to hold the enemy at bay.

That night Sir Colin Campbell with a small staff, having hurried forward in advance of the force escorting the non-combatants from Lucknow, galloped across the bridge of boats with news that help was at hand, and the situation was saved. On 29 November the enemy's heavy guns were silenced by the Horse Artillery from Lucknow.

Then, while the men of the 34th withdrew behind the entrenchments to lick their wounds, the new arrivals totalling 5,000 infantry, six hundred cavalry and thirty-five guns engaged the Gwalior contingent commanded by Tantia Topi, 7,000 strong supported by mutineers from the native regiments and auxiliaries furnished by the Rani of Jhansi, in all some 20,000 fighting men. On 6 and 7 December Tantia Topi was decisively defeated, and the back of the rebellion was broken. But though the position around Cawnpore was now secure, the rebels in the north were still unsubdued and, with the whole of Oudh "up", Campbell believed that he needed strong reinforcements before he could ensure their defeat, and these would take time to assemble. Meanwhile he kept his troops at full stretch, keeping communications with the Punjab open and clearing the Doab, the country north of Cawnpore between the rivers Ganges and Jumna.

The 34th had meanwhile taken up quarters in the Masonic Hall in Cawnpore town, and there they celebrated Christmas. Lewin shared a room with a fellow cadet Dudley Sampson who being orderly officer for the day, which happened to be Christmas Day, had to get up betimes to inspect the men's breakfasts while Lewin cuddled up warm beneath his bedclothes. Their breakfast, at which they sat garlanded with jessamine and marigolds their servants had hung round their necks, consisted of quails, beef stew, a curry and some chops, with guava jelly to finish with, after which they attended divine service in the ruined church whence the rebels had recently been shelling them at the bridge. In the afternoon Lewin and Sampson went for a canter on their respective mounts, and for dinner in the mess that evening there was turkey and an attempt at plum pudding; afterwards the officers drank punch and sang songs. Before they left Cawnpore Lewin had to attend a parade in the courtyard of the Bibi Ghar to witness four of the rebels being hanged.

At the end of January the 34th were sent to join the Madras Artillery detachment at Bani Bridge, an entrenched village on the road midway between Cawnpore and Lucknow, their task to furnish guards for convoys taking guns and supplies to the Alambagh, the walled pleasure garden south of Lucknow where General Havelock lay buried, and to keep open Campbell's line of communication with the south. Sharing the same tent with Lewin were three friends from Addiscombe days, making a quartet of jolly cadets until he received news that his cousin Edward, Jeannie's brother with whom he had sat smoking in the medlar tree, a fine officer adept at languages, had been killed by a round shot at Lucknow.

Whilst the build-up of men and materials in the Alambagh continued, Campbell found himself threatened by an attack from Bareilly in the district of Rohilkhand, whose inhabitants like those of Oudh were active in their support of the rebels. To forestall such an attack, and as a feint to deceive the enemy into believing that his objective was Bareilly rather than Lucknow, he sent a flying column under General Hope Grant to clear the area of rebels estimated to be 15,000 strong. The field force comprised, besides the 34th now reduced through casualties to only four hundred and fifty bayonets, the Connaught Rangers, the 53rd, the 9th Lancers, a wing of the 7th Hussars and two batteries of Horse Artillery, in all about 3,000 men. It was tiring but not particularly dangerous work, marching twenty-five miles a day across tilled fields and grasslands under a hot sun, attacking villages and destroying forts, meeting little sustained opposition except at the forts and a village called Meiganj, and at the end of it all their most notable bag was the Nana Sahib's secretary and one of his servants captured at Fatehpur who were duly hanged, and a little loot. Perhaps it was the presence in the column of his fellow cadets that brought out Lewin's latent rebelliousness, but the four of them resented being made to carry the regimental colours while the regular officers marched unencumbered:

> so at the end of a twenty-three miles trudge I cast my weary burden on the ground and said 'Damn the colours! why don't you carry them yourselves!' Fox of the 34th promptly reported me to the colonel, and I was severely wigged, but after this the regimental officers took their turn. Heigh-ho! I was born for scrapes.

The flying column made its circuitous way back, making short work of a body of rebels who sought to dispute its passage and, after brushing aside a few skirmishers, arrived at the outskirts of Lucknow shortly before General Campbell returned to the Alambagh to direct operations for its recapture. The mutineers with those who had

rallied to them numbering some 100,000 had had ample
time to prepare its defences and were firmly entrenched
at strategic points in the various buildings and strongholds.
The royal city of the kings of Oudh straggled over a large
area to the south-west of the river Gumti whose twisting
course marked its boundary on that side. Coming up
from the south Lewin looked down from higher ground
and "saw spread out in front of me like a panorama the
city of Lucknow with its gilded domes and minarets,
embowered in trees, among which we could see several of
the enemy's batteries swarming with men, all dressed in
white and working away like bees". For the next few days
his rôle was often to be that of spectator, because the
34th, being much reduced in strength and perhaps
having lost its edge after months of strenuous campaigning, was assigned only subsidiary tasks in the
recapture of the city.

They made camp in the Dilkusha Bagh in which stood
the summer palace, and from here on 9 March Lewin
watched the Highlanders closely supported by the Punjab
Rifles rush the parapets surrounding La Martinière
College in a crook of the river and start fanning out to the
left towards the city. Having been given nothing to do, he
called for his pony and galloped off into the fray, and
though temporarily unseated when his pony shied at a
dead commissariat camel lying in the road reached the
school buildings unscathed. From the top of the centre
pinnacle he saw the general and his staff sitting on the
steps consulting a map and further off the attacking force

storming through mud houses, gun emplacements and entrenchments, sweeping all before them as they made for the Kaisar Bagh in which stood the royal palace.

Amid its splendours, in a pink marble room hung round with mirrors which he shared with two other cadets, Lewin wrote to his mother on 20 March after the fighting was over. He described his surroundings as

> an immense garden scattered over with marble kiosks and statues; the rooms are filled with chandeliers of all colours and shapes — some of Venetian glass, and I should think very valuable. The endless suites of rooms are luxuriously furnished and lavishly gilded, but the enemy have played sad havoc with all the velvet and gold: everything is more or less smashed and cut, and even the pictures on the walls have been pierced with bullet and bayonet holes. From the gilded roofs and domes hang little golden bells and pendants which tinkle a fairy music in the wind, and the whole garden swarms with pigeons which, I am thankful to say, are very good eating.

The Residency had been reoccupied two days before, and by now the rebels had evacuated the city, taking with them such stores as they could carry and many of their field guns. Lucknow was back in British hands, but there was still a formidable force of rebels at large in Oudh and Rohilkhand.

When three weeks later, shortly after his nineteenth birthday and peacefully at rest in comfortable quarters in Jaunpur, one of the bases for operations against the rebels still at large in southern Oudh, Lewin looked back on his recent experiences it was not upon the dangers he had been through or the hardships of campaigning that his mind dwelt, but on all the scrapes he had got into since he arrived in India.

List of offences and misdemeanours of Ensign T.H. Lewin since his landing in India on October 19th, 1857, up to April 20th, 1858.
1. Walking into Major Kavanagh's Office at the Fort, Calcutta, and mistaking him for a Clerk, October, 1857. (Taken down a peg.)
2. Cutting off a turkey's head, with hungry and felonious intent, on the line of march between Benares and Cawnpore, November, 1857. (Had to pay for it!)
3. Forcibly ejecting Gentleman Cadet Moriarty from the Tent when camped at Bunnee Bridge, February, 1858. (Reprimanded.)
4. Damning the Queen's Colours at Meergunge, February, 1858. (Placed under arrest. Severely reprimanded.)

Chapter Five
Peacetime Soldier

Nearly half a century earlier the British parliament had deprived the East India Company of its trading monopoly; the India Act of 1853 had stripped its court of directors of their right of patronage; and now the Mutiny made its abolition inevitable. Its epitaph took the form of a declaration made in the name of Queen Victoria on 1 November 1859:

> We have resolved to take upon ourselves the government of the territories in India heretofore administered in trust for us by the Honourable East India Company....

It was the royal will and pleasure that thenceforward none should be favoured or molested by reason of their religion, that her subjects of whatever race or creed should be freely and impartially admitted to office in her service, and that in framing the law due regard should be paid to the ancient rights, usages and customs of the people of India, her earnest desire being to administer the country for the benefit of all her subjects resident therein. But it was too late. Never again, after so much blood had been spilt on both sides, could full confidence exist between rulers and ruled, even those who had remained loyal during the rebellion; and soon a new chasm was to open up between the old India hands, whose courage, initiative and talent for improvisation had created the India of John Company, and the faceless bureaucrats, those most adept at passing the new competitive examinations, who were sent out from home as the heaven-born of the new Indian Civil Service. It was the fate of youngsters of Lewin's generation, brought up in the old tradition, to have to try to adapt to the new system. Not all of them succeeded.

Time and again during Lewin's years in India his independence of mind came into collision with the overriding requirement of the new authority that all must conform to its printed regulations, and from each encounter he emerged even more determined than before to go his own way. Time and again his sense of frustration would bring him to the brink of resigning from the service before prudence, the recollection of where his own advantage lay, stayed his hand. Repeatedly in his letters to his mother he assured her that his only wish was to save enough money to allow him to return home, not with a fortune like his forbears, but with a modest competence; for his patrimony from his grandfather's estate to which he became presumptively entitled on his father's death was insufficient for him to live on, and he was well aware that he possessed neither the qualifications nor the training that would qualify him for remunerative employment at home. His dilemma was the more painful because throughout his service abroad Lewin remained profoundly homesick, not only hating being separated from his mother, towards whom he bore a more than usually passionate love, but also sorely missing his own country compared with which he found India a brutal place. The note of deprivation is sounded in letter after letter he wrote to her:

> Ah! how gladly would I exchange all the glamour of the East for one glimpse of dear old England with its quiet woods and vales and sweet-breath'd cattle cropping the short, crisp grass.

To all his adventures to come this feeling of nostalgia formed an unbroken accompaniment, which his many compensations served only to mitigate, never to eradicate.

Hitherto, amid the ceaseless activity of campaigning, he had had little leisure either to suffer too acutely from nostalgia or to enjoy the compensations that were taken for granted as the right of expatriates who made their careers in India. His six months at Jaunpur allowed him for the first time leisure to savour the alien environment. In northern India the pleasant sunshine of April, when the ripened crops show green or yellow in the fields and there is a scent of guavas and mangoes in the air, gradually gives place to the burning heat of May and June with temperatures rising to 120° in the shade. The khaki countryside shimmers in the heat haze and is swept by dust storms raised by the *loo*, the hot wind from the north-west which native ingenuity converts into a cooling agent for houses by screening windows and doors with cuscus tatties which when drenched with water let in cool air. Outside, the ground is cracked and hard, *pahi*-dogs stretch

out in the dusty streets, and birds sit about with beaks
open wide. Then comes the transformation.

> At last, [Lewin wrote to his mother on 30 June] the Rains
> have come and the whole face of nature is changed.
> Every little valley has become a miniature lake; every
> rivulet has swelled into a torrent, and the river itself has
> swelled into a mighty expanse of water, fed by hundreds
> of turbulent streams. It is the first time I have ever seen
> tropical rains, and the new sensation is delightful. All
> the land was parched and lifeless, its inhabitants, human,
> animal and vegetable, wilting and withering away with
> the heat, when as if a voice had cried out 'Let their be
> life' — life came. It was as if the very flood-gates of
> heaven had been opened; and after the first deluge had
> spent itself, I went out and found young green shoots
> springing out of the dried-up trees, and young tender
> grass blades pushing up everywhere out of the ground,
> of the most delicate and vivid emerald green. The birds
> had found their voices; and all the ground was covered
> with tiny frogs no bigger than a threepenny piece....
> Everywhere also one sees the ground covered with
> beautiful scarlet beetles, which have also emerged into
> life, and the temperature is delightfully cool.

In other ways, too, life was pleasant for a young
subaltern (for by now he had been gazetted a lieutenant)
assigned to a congenial station. He lived in a comfortable
bungalow with a staff of six or seven servants and kept two
horses. On a typical day he rose at five and after attending
first parade took a spear and mounting his pony Punch
cantered off after *pahi*-dogs and jackals. He rode back by
way of the station baths, where he had a swim, drank tea,
and chatted with his friends; then home for breakfast at

eight. He studied Hindustani with his *munshi* for two hours and spent the rest of the morning writing letters, making sketches, writing up his diary and going through the household accounts with his bearer. After a light tiffin of biscuits and a glass of claret and water he took a siesta during the heat of the day until five, when there was another parade and drill. In the evening, since there was no shooting in that part of the country, he would have Punch or his mare My Lady saddled and go for a gallop with the younger officers, getting back in time for a substantial dinner, for which the menu might be clear soup with rice and onions, spatchcocked chicken with vegetables, a brace of teal — breasts sliced and dressed with red pepper and lemon — and a dish of hot pancakes. He went to bed early with a clear head, for throughout his life he was an abstemious man.

Social life in the station was limited. Lewin was once a guest at a *nautch* given in the town by a rich Indian merchant on the occasion of his daughter's marriage, which rain brought to a premature end. He also enjoyed the hospitality of an indigo planter on his estate a short ride from the station. There was a scratch race-meeting at which, dressed in white jacket and cord breeches, white cap and black riding boots, he rode My Lady in the horse race and little Punch in the pony race, in each coming in a good second. Relief from inactivity came when, now in command of No. 7 Company, he took part in an operation lasting several weeks in which they scoured the countryside for remaining pockets of rebels;

but the Queen's proclamation was having its effect, and more and more of their leaders — except those whose atrocities had put beyond the pale of the amnesty — were coming in to submit.

Although his permanent posting to the 31st Native Light Infantry stationed in Central India had come through at last, the colonel of the 34th, being short of officers, refused to release him until compelled to do so by higher authority after Lewin, as was to be his way, had sent a memorial of complaint to the adjutant-general, the commander of the 31st and, for good measure, his influential Calcutta relation-by-marriage Arthur Grote. His regret at leaving the soldiers beside whom he had fought was more than counterbalanced by his eagerness to start living his own life. Making a present of his little terrier Croppy to his Irish friend in the 34th George Johnston, he set out from Jaunpur in late December on a six-week journey to join his regiment, which took him through Partabgarh, Allahabad, back to Fatehpur, then south to Banda and over the Ghats into Bundelkhand, and so to Saugor.

The city takes its name from the lake nearly a mile across, the habitat of alligators and huge turtles, down to whose shores its low-roofed houses and many Hindu temples, noisy with gong, cymbals and conch horns, clustered among feathery palms. The surrounding land was flat and marshy, shut in by jungle-covered hills. On high ground to the north-west, overlooking city and countryside, stood the six-acre fort enclosed by a curtain of thick walls in which at intervals stood twenty round towers. The 31st NLI was one of the few Company regiments which had not mutinied and for its staunchness had been officially designated as "The Loyal Poorbeahs" from the district where its sepoys were recruited. It was then commanded by Major Hampton whom Lewin described to his mother as "a very quiet dark man of the old school — smokes a Hookah and has a native wife". Since many of the officers were away either on staff appointments or sick leave, Lewin was soon required to shoulder responsibilities beyond his rank, but for the most part he found garrison life tedious. Every fourth day he took command of the guard in the fort and even off duty, in compliance with an order of the commander-in-chief, had to wear full uniform with his sword banging at his heels. For relaxation there was boating on the lake, and for companionship a bull-terrier puppy called Grabby, a present from a brother officer who had gone sick; and in the cool of the evening the band played in the Mall.

Some excitement seemed to be in prospect when news came that a remnant of the Gwalior rebels under Tantia Topi had been on the rampage and crossing the border into Bundelkhand was now encamped at Rathghar thirty miles away. A squadron of the 3rd Irregular Cavalry had been sent out to reconnoitre, and Lewin was ordered to scrape together as many as could be spared from the regiment and start at once for the trouble spot. Operating alongside the 31st was the 43rd Queen's Regiment, which hampered rapid movement by requiring a long waggon-train to carry the beef, bread and rum without which, Lewin noted, the British soldier could not move anywhere. For their part, the 43rd gave themselves airs and looked down on the native troops, for despite the proclamation which sought to amalgamate them the two services, the Queen's and the Company's, remained at odds with one another. The joint operation which lasted a week proved a frustrating business. After marching twenty or thirty miles each night in pursuit of the rebels, they would find when the sun rose that they had melted away into the jungle; and little was achieved.

By this time Lewin already stood out as having exceptional qualities. Twice he had been invited to apply for a transfer to another regiment, once by a colonel of a Sikh regiment in whose mess he had dined, then by the commander of the Irregular Cavalry which had taken part in the recent abortive operation. One day at the baths in Jaunpur the district judge, hearing him talking to his bearer, had remarked: "He will go far. He talks the language like a native". While stationed at Saugor he passed the examination in colloquial Hindustani, upon which he was confirmed as company commander besides becoming entitled to an extra allowance of Rs.50 a month. When the regiment was ordered to new quarters at Kalpi, Major Hampton thought sufficiently highly of him to give him an independent command, in charge of two companies on detachment duty at Hamirpur.

Since most of the diaries Lewin is known to have kept throughout his years in India have disappeared, the elements of his character as it now began to settle into its permanent form can only be pieced together from stray hints given in his letters home. Salient among them were his independence of spirit at times verging on rebelliousness and his growing ambition to make something of his life, in pursuance of which he was not above pulling strings. He cannot have been unaware that with his enquiring intelligence and his interest in the arts, his gift for languages and his powers of observation and expression, he was above the ordinary run of cadets from Addiscombe. Able to get on with his contemporaries as well as to impress his superiors, his was yet something of a solitary, reflective nature which was disinclined to wear its heart on its sleeve. Still holding Jeannie in affectionate remembrance, his strongly emotional nature was centred on his mother living in Clapham, now forty-nine years old, whom he missed more and more as the months went by. The station afforded no outlet for sentimental attachments, its two European spinster ladies being so determinedly engaged as to offer no encouragement to wide-eyed youngsters like Lewin. Naturally his eyes began to turn towards such dark-skinned girls as came his way: a pretty face glimpsed in the bazaar, quickly hidden behind a scarlet *dupatta* as he passed by with Grabby at his heels; a *nautch* girl at some entertainment to which he had been invited, dressed in a glistening *sari*, her eyelids darkened with *sarmak*. But whatever casual contact he may have had with local women, it was out of the question for a young subaltern to emulate his commandant and take to himself an Indian wife.

At Hamirpur, which he reached on 22 April, he shared a tumbledown bungalow with six others, officers of the Queen's 48th Regiment or the half-battery of artillery which with Lewin's two companies formed the garrison of the place. The only other bungalow was occupied in solitary splendour by the magistrate-cum-collector representing the civil authority. At that season the men suffered considerably living in tents under the broiling sun. Lewin's duties consisted mainly of filling up forms — muster rolls, pay abstracts, command certificates and the like; his main relaxation was swimming in the Betwa river nearby. After a month of this it was a relief to go out with a small force after a rebel leader who had turned dacoit and with a following of five hundred was reported to be levying unofficial tribute on the villages roundabout. The encounter was, as usual, inconclusive, the rebels on being attacked making off as fast as they could, leaving behind them only two or three dead. Next month with a large field force he pursued another band of rebels, attacking their camp on a rocky hill before first light and losing one sepoy shot through the chest; his bag this time comprised clothing and weapons scattered on the paths by which the enemy had fled, some miscellaneous articles of bedding, and a hundred pairs of abandoned shoes. Nevertheless his report on the incident, which lost nothing in the telling, was forwarded by Major Hampton, the Officer Commanding at Kalpi, to the Assistant Adjutant General, Cawnpore Division, who forwarded it to the Right Hon'ble the Commander in Chief, who in turn forwarded it to the Secretary to the Government of India,

Military Department, for the information of his Excellency the Governor-General in Council, who directed it to be published, noting that he considered the affair to reflect great credit upon Lieutenant Lewin and all engaged on the occasion. Under the new regime in India bureaucracy was already taking over, even in the army.

In camp on the march to rejoin his regiment now in quarters at Shahjahanpur, a large town situated between Bareilly and Lucknow, he wrote to his mother complaining that his men were being made to move at the beginning of the rainy season. He viewed with regret the termination of his first independent command, having found that responsibility and power gave a new zest and flavour to life. But he was doubtful whether soldiering was his true vocation because, though by an effort of will he could make his body face danger, he had no delight in the perils of war and found the sight of blood and death abhorrent. It also still rankled with him that the government not only had been niggardly in the matter of the bounty dispensed to those who had taken part in suppressing the Mutiny, but had also demanded from him Rs.500 on account of official tentage allegedly hired to him during the campaign, though all too often his bed had been mother earth, his covering the sky. He contemplated applying for special leave in England on private affairs, giving as his reason that his being entitled to a small inheritance on his coming of age next April urgently necessitated his presence at home.

Meanwhile, he settled down again to garrison duties, studying hard for the higher examination in Urdu and

Hindi, which he passed with distinction in December, thus qualifying himself for staff appointments. Since there were no quarters for officers, he and his friend George Johnston bought three small native houses in a tope of mango trees not far from the lines, which they had whitewashed, painted and cleaned. By laying deerskins on the floors by way of carpets and hanging family portraits and fixing stags' heads on the walls they made the place, which Johnston named The Groves of Blarney, as homely as they could. A large black snake and two scorpions which came to assist at the house warming were given a hot reception.

He had an enjoyable week's shooting in the jungles round Bareilly in December, but failed to bag his first tiger because his elephant bolted on sight of it. He attended a farewell dinner for the colonel of the English regiment stationed at Shahjahanpur, at which more men got drunk than Lewin ever remembered to have seen before. A day or two afterwards he took part in some theatricals performed in honour of the lieutenant-governor of Bengal who was visiting the station. The play was *A Man Can't Marry his Grandmother*, and Lewin played an old gentleman with powdered hair and small queue dressed in claret-coloured coat and black knee-breeches.

Early in January 1860, having left Grabby in the care of George Johnston, he caught the train for Calcutta and sailed for England on a year's leave. He had served in India for two years and three months and arrived home in time for his twenty-first birthday.

Chapter Six
A Policeman's Lot

Invigorated by a year spent in Europe, Lewin was back in Calcutta in February 1861, staying with Arthur Grote and his family at Alipore. He was in an unsettled frame of mind, having determined to find employment that would enable him to save as much money in as short a time as possible in order to retire from "this cursed country" and settle permanently at home. His fixed star remained his mother, to whom he poured out in his weekly letters his inmost thoughts and aspirations as they occurred to him. He dreamed of taking a cottage somewhere in the English countryside where they could live quietly together. His greatest fear was that she would die before he came home again. "Don't forget, darling," he reminded her, "our agreement that if it is possible whichever one of us dies first is to come & tell the other wherever we may be, if God please I will do so." In the meantime he entertained the hope that she would come out to India and stay with him for a year or two, perhaps bringing with her his younger sister Bella then in her early 'teens who, he was sure, would be snapped up directly by some dashing young fellow. Their sister Harriet, her elder by five years, was engaged to be married to Bankes Tomlin, about which Lewin pronounced pessimistic prognostications; proved wrong in the event which took place in December 1862, as he was soon forced to admit, for all indeed seemed to go "as merry as a marriage bell".

Bankes was the second son of Robert Sackett Tomlin of Dane Court, St. Peter's-in-Thanet, and Elizabeth, daughter of John Bankes of Otley in Yorkshire and Clapham Common. His and the Friend families were not only neighbours but also linked by the snuff-and-tobacco business in the Minories. Born in 1823 he had been educated under a clergyman at Enfield and at Trinity College, Cambridge, where he matriculated but did not take a degree, his main interests then and later being hunting and shooting, boxing and horse racing, dog and cock fighting, and ornithology. He had spent some years in the King's Dragoon Guards, serving mainly in Ireland in the aftermath of the Great Famine, retiring as a captain in 1851 to devote his life to country pursuits. In person he was tall, dark-haired and lanky, with drooping moustaches that hung down well below his chin.

Among Lewin's fellow passengers on the boat going home on leave had been some friends of Arthur Grote, Captain Pughe and his wife. Pughe had recently been appointed inspector-general of the new military police and at Grote's prompting now offered Lewin the post of adjutant and second-in-command of the 2nd Battalion then being raised at Rampur in west Bengal. It was a chance not to be missed. Intended to supplement the reorganized Indian Army, the new force was to be drilled, armed and regulated as a military unit and perform no police functions other than to keep the peace. Rampur was a civil station whose European society was composed chiefly of civil servants, silk merchants and indigo planters. Owing to the rapaciousness of these planters, who when the market fell sought to make the small cultivators on whom they relied for growing the plant bear the brunt of the depression, the local peasantry had resorted to violence in order to assert their rights. The seriousness of the situation necessitated the presence in the area of a military police battalion, ostensibly to keep the peace, but in reality to quell the disturbances for the benefit of the planters.

On arrival Lewin found himself in temporary command, as the commandant was on leave, and had his hands full building up the battalion, a mixed force of Hindus, Muslims and Sikhs six hundred strong from scratch. But the work did not appeal to him, and he began to look about for fresh opportunities. There were several choices open to him since, under the scheme for amalgamating the Company's and the Queen's armies, officers of the Indian service were given the option of remaining on the Indian cadre, of volunteering for service in one of the Queen's regiments or — provided they had the necessary language qualification, as Lewin had — of joining the Bengal Staff Corps. Because the second alternative offered the chance of service outside India, Lewin opted for general service and was in due course appointed a lieutenant in the 104th Regiment. It was a decision that was to cause him some perplexity in time to come. Meanwhile he continued in the military police, spending some weeks with a large detachment at Pabna, a small and usually quiet station where recently disturbances had occurred.

Soon after returning to Rampur he received official notice that, after only a brief existence, the military police was to be disbanded, and Lewin now had to choose between returning to regimental life with the 104th or joining the civil police where his emoluments would be much greater. Should he become a dog for the bone's sake, that is — as he put it more bluntly in a letter to his mother — cease to be a soldier and enter civil employ for the sake of the dirty rupees? Given his overriding determination to save money so that he could return home for good, he did not hesitate for long, and on 17 April 1862 was gazetted District Superintendent of Police, 3rd Class, at Bhagalpur in northern Bihar on the south bank of the Ganges, at a salary of Rs.500 a month (which was twice as much as an army lieutenant's pay) plus an additional Rs.100 a month travel allowance.

After little more than a month at Bhagalpur, spent travelling about his new district trying to learn what his new duties were supposed to be — and being called upon to shoot a rogue alligator which had eaten a small child, whose little bangles were found in the creature's stomach — he was ordered to Muzaffarpur on temporary duty to organize the new civil police system there, pending the arrival of the commandant. Previously the district magistrate had been his own chief of police, to whom the *darogas* in charge of the police stations, or *thannas*, in the district reported direct. Under the new system established throughout the province of Bengal police affairs in each district were made the responsibility of a district superintendent, often like Lewin an ex-army officer, each of whom reported to his divisional deputy-inspector, who in turn reported to the inspector-general of police with headquarters in Calcutta. Although there was obvious merit in thus separating the executive from the judiciary, the change inevitably gave rise to the sort of friction between district magistrate and district superintendent as had existed since time immemorial between the Company's civil and military branches. The situation was aggravated by the zeal with which the new super-intendents, lacking police experience as well as tact, went about imposing military discipline on functionaries reluctant to give up their old, easy-going and corrupt ways. In the result it was justice that suffered and the criminals who benefited, because magistrates began to show their animosity towards the police by throwing out cases in the preparation of which they could detect the slightest technical flaw.

Lewin spent two months at Muzaffarpur and then was given permanent appointment, with the local rank of captain, as district superintendent of police at Hazaribagh in the hilly country of central Bihar, a part of India associated with the life of Buddha, Gaya with its great Buddhist temple lying only some sixty miles to the north. It was a non-regulation district whose deputy com-missioner was an army major, and instead of friction a warm friendship grew up between him and his young subordinate. In August Lewin made a strenuous 350 mile tour of his district and on his return settled into a routine of recruiting, drilling and desk work which kept him busy from five-thirty in the morning until seven in the evening when his horse would be brought round for a gallop before dinner, after which he would nod over his pipe or a novel before waking with a start to find it was time to say his prayers and retiré to bed. His way of life was comfortable, even luxurious, living in a well-furnished bungalow with servants to attend his needs, horses to ride, and a buggy to drive about in when the weather was too hot for riding. To vary the monotony of the food available locally he had sent out to him from Crosse & Blackwell's or Fortnum's in London hampers containing German sausages, hams, pressed fish, plum cake, strawberry and raspberry jam, honey, and chocolate. For his personal use he ordered from Pierse & Lubin of Bond Street perfumery soap, scent and other toilet articles, and whalebone hairbrushes from a shop in the Haymarket.

In his spare time he wrote for the instruction of his constables a little book on the duties of a policeman called *The Constable's Manual*, which he translated into Hindustani and, with the help of his clerks, into Bengali and Urdu. It is written in the form of questions and answers:

> 1. Q. What is the first duty of a Constable?
> A. Implicit obedience to his Superiors.
> 2. Q. What should he always remember?

A. To keep his ears and eyes open and his mouth shut.

15. Q. As it is against the custom of the country for a woman to expose her face, how will the Constable ascertain whether the accused is disguised among the women or not?

A. He could tell by examining their feet or if this were not permitted he should cause some other woman such as the wife of the village chowkidar to examine the woman in question.

45. Q. What is the greatest fault a Constable can commit?

A. The taking directly or indirectly of a bribe or any article of value (money or money's worth) from anyone for the purpose of being induced to perform or to refrain from performing the strict letter of his duty.

And so on. Receiving official approval, the booklet was printed in Calcutta for general distribution and thus became the first of Lewin's books to be published.

Lewin also wrote poetry, of no great literary merit, which he would send to his mother in the hope, seldom realized, that she could place them with some magazine under the transparent pseudonym Newall Herbert, in order to earn a few guineas. He also wrote some sketches and stories of sport in India, which he thought *Bell's Life* might be interested in and began, but never completed, a novel of Indian life. He also kept up his drawing, but his greatest solace was music, and he spent as much time as he could playing the harmonium he had bought in Calcutta. About music he was absolutely serious. He not only practised but studied hard, sending home for books on composition, thorough-bass and musical theory. He tried his hand at composing, completing exercises in adagio and andante, a march, the settings for two songs 'By the Firelight' and 'The Message', and two Violetta waltzes which were played by the regimental band when the regiment stationed at Hazaribagh gave a ball. He was fond of lieder, and delighted most, as he wrote to his mother, "to be all alone of an evening & play over the ones that you used to make sound so sweetly in my ears in the little parlour at home. Please God I will some day be a great musician, but I not only want practice but theory".

His artistic interests were balanced by an equal enthusiasm for sports and pastimes he could share with his contemporaries. He went on shooting trips and sent home tiger and leopard skins to be made up into hearth-rugs. He frequented the swimming-bath and rackets courts in the station, and having been made an honorary member of the local officers' mess enjoyed playing billiards or cards, both for high stakes. One night playing *écarté* with one of the officers he won a little black cob which he thought would do for his brother Bob, who was on his way to India to stay with him.

Now eighteen years old, Bob — he had been christened Friend, because it was their mother's maiden name — was the elder of Lewin's two younger brothers and had not yet settled on a career. At first Tom had not wanted him to come out, telling their mother that he had not enough interest to get him a berth worth having, but later relented. He sent him £40 to pay for his journey and kept Rs.500 in hand to defray the expenses of his visit, but urged his mother not to tell him so or he would get into mischief. For Bob was something of a problem. Yet they got on well together, the younger man entering into the life of the station with zest. He made friends with the officers and their wives, with whom he became quite a favourite, was taken out into the district on shooting trips; in short, thoroughly enjoyed himself: as well he might, Tom noted dryly, having "no wish ungratified — money, servants, women and horses". But the question of his future remained as unsettled as ever. Every opportunity Tom suggested for him to make a career in India — to set him up in a silk factory, to get him into the magisterial commission, even for them to go in for tea planting together — he turned down. The truth was he was homesick, but seemed equally averse to taking any of the jobs at home which they discussed. Stockbroking was a possibility, but Tom thought the humdrum life of the City would not suit him. Since he liked sea voyages, perhaps he was cut out to be a sailor? Nothing was decided, and so Bob stayed on, having the time of his life, quite content to keep house while Tom went off on tour with the deputy commissioner.

Bob had brought first-hand news of the young man Lewin had come to consider his best friend in the world. A few years older than himself, Harry Graves had been a school friend and so was intimately mixed up with his childhood memories. Information about his early days is hard to come by, but for some time he had been a sailor, and was now a near neighbour of Mrs Lewin and her young family in Clapham. Ever since Lewin's arrival in India there had been talk of Harry coming out to join him, but nothing had come of it, and now with the help of money Lewin advanced to him from his English dividends he was making a fresh start in life, apparently as a surveyor. On the strength of this he had persuaded a girl called Annie to marry him, and Lewin was convinced the poor girl would not be happy very long, for Harry had been born as unstable as water and was cut out for an unfaithful husband. He was now borrowing from other sources, taking his first step on the downward road that would lead, Lewin felt sure, to utter destitution and misery. So long as Harry had remained single, Lewin was prepared to share his house and his purse with him, but now things were different. It was mad of him to have married in his precarious financial circumstances, but all the same Lewin urged his mother, for his sake, never to let Harry go short of a meal if he was in need of one.

His youngest brother Will, too, was giving cause for concern. Born in February 1847, he had been for two years a Blue-coat boy at Christ's Hospital for which a nomination had been obtained through the influence of aunt Grote; then on his father's death he had been sent to Tom's old school, Mr Grix's academy at Littlehampton. He had been removed from there and sent to join Bob and two of their cousins Lionel and Mortimer at Windermere College in Westmorland run by a Mr Puckle who was distantly connected with the Lewins through the Hale family, and there distinguished himself as a gifted fist-fighter and for his performances in the school theatricals. Unable to settle down, he was brought back to London and sent to the Bruce Castle School in Tottenham, but soon afterwards — following an incident in which another boy's arm had been broken — ran away and sought refuge with Harry Graves and his new wife in Bayswater. The news of this latest escapade reached his brothers at Hazaribagh in December, and Tom in his weekly letter to his mother was indulgent towards Will, agreeing with her that the boy was good at heart and suggesting that the best thing for him would be to go to sea while he was still young so that, if he did not like the life, he could start something else.

Meantime Lewin had gone off with the deputy commissioner on a tour that took them among the Santhals, a wild aboriginal race whose language, customs and religion differed completely from those of the Aryans who had conquered them. It was Lewin's first experience of a race which had been untainted by "civilization" — a word he always used in a derogatory sense — and he found their way of life fascinating. On his return he found waiting for him an official letter from the colonel of the 104th, the Queen's regiment to which he had been appointed, ordering him to take up his duties owing to a shortage of officers. Unwilling to do so and in order to gain time, he put in an application for a transfer to the Bengal Staff Corps and notified the colonel accordingly. He was in truth as confused as his brother Bob about the direction his career should take.

It was now the rainy season when the criminal elements, secure in the knowledge that the forces of law and order were taking their ease in their quarters, became most active. A local band of dacoits some forty strong began to prey on travellers journeying along the Grand Trunk Road, whom they plundered and murdered indiscriminately. Lewin devised his own method of dealing with them and, dressed in native costume and taking with him only ten picked men, would set off to track them down. For six weeks in pouring rain, covering twenty miles a day and sleeping rough, eating nothing but rice and chupattis, they pursued the band and, catching up with them, arrested sixteen, the rest managing to escape. Shortly afterwards, learning from a terrified villager the identity of the leader and the location of the gang's hideout, Lewin laid on a night operation. With great caution they approached the Dripping Well at Makha, a spring which issued out of a cave on a rocky hillside where the dacoits were sleeping, and reaching it undetected rushed the place at first light. In the *melée* that followed the leader was shot dead and three of the band captured. For his initiative Lewin was officially commended, the deputy inspector-general of police reporting favourably on his conduct to the government of Bengal.

Then, as so often in his life, the wheel of fortune turned, and success was quickly followed by a disaster that nearly brought his career to an end altogether. When the friendly deputy commissioner went on leave his place was taken by an official who showed himself less well disposed towards Lewin. At the same time a new assistant magistrate was posted to the district who treated all police as if they were his natural enemies. Their chance came when an ugly incident arose in which Lewin was indirectly concerned. A man who had been arrested on suspicion of robbery had died under interrogation, apparently due to rough handling by the police, which might have been prevented had there been closer supervision by Lewin's European assistant Mr Ellis. Knowing that his subordinate had not actually been present when the incident occurred — and also that he had not a penny in the world besides his pay, so that dismissal would have meant ruin for him — Lewin deferred making an official report on the case to the divisional deputy inspector of police, as he should have done, hoping that things would blow over. They did not, and when the acting deputy commissioner made his own report to higher authority he commented unfavourably on Lewin's conduct as well as on that of his subordinate, with the result that Ellis was dismissed from the service, and the secretary to the government of Bengal wrote an official letter characterizing Lewin's part in the affair as evasive and untrustworthy, and stating that the lieutenant-governor considered him unfit to have charge of a district.

Soon afterwards, sensing that he had Lewin at a disadvantage, the new assistant magistrate made some frivolous complaint about him and received an official rebuke for his pains. Incensed beyond the point of prudence, the assistant magistrate bided his time, and when Lewin failed to comply with an order he had sent him to attend before him in a case Lewin had investigated, in which the evidence of one of his constables would have been quite sufficient, he struck again and issued a warrant for Lewin's arrest. On appeal to the acting deputy commissioner the warrant was, of course, quashed, whereupon the assistant magistrate departed on indefinite leave; but some of the mud stuck, and Lewin was peremptorily removed from the district and posted to remote Noakhali in eastern Bengal.

During these manoeuvrings he had taken the occasion to review the courses open to him. These were to remain in the civil police; to comply with his colonel's order to join his regiment; to press on with his application for a transfer to the Bengal Staff Corps; to throw everything up and become a tea planter, for with another officer he was already in negotiation to take a lease of tea land in Assam; or even to emigrate to America or New Zealand and try his luck overseas. In the event he decided to allow matters to take their course, and so in late December 1863 he and his brother Bob travelled by train to Calcutta, where they were hospitably entertained by the Grotes; then, having seen Bob off in the *City of Dublin* homeward bound, he himself embarked in the *Orissa* for Chittagong accompanied by his mare, two dogs and two personal servants. He was still only twenty-three years old and, though he could not have known it at the time, was taking a decisive step towards his true destiny.

Chapter Seven
Eastern Bengal

1

For centuries eastern Bengal had been a cauldron in which a *ragoût* of different races had bubbled, boiled over, and occasionally quietly simmered. In early years Hindus from Tippera in the north and Buddhists from Arakan in the south, themselves of mixed Indo-Burmese origin, contended for its fertile lowlands. Chittagong grew up round a natural seaport which attracted trade from places as distant as Canton and Baghdad, and over its jetties came Muslim settlers who spread their faith among the earlier immigrants from western Bengal. In the sixteenth century Portuguese freebooters from Goa secured a foothold but, failing to found an empire, either entered the service of the rajahs of Arakan as mercenaries or turned pirate. The struggle for supremacy between Muslims and Buddhists came to a head in 1661 when the rajah of Arakan put to death the Mogul viceroy of Bengal who had sought refuge with him, leading to a punitive expedition which resulted in the whole district becoming a province of the Mogul empire. Chittagong was for a time known as Islamabad. For a while the cauldron simmered, Muslim, Buddhist, Hindu and Catholic living at uneasy peace with one another.

The East India Company had long cast a covetous eye

across the Bay of Bengal and twice despatched ill-managed expeditions to establish a factory there, both of which ended in ignominious failure. Where force had failed diplomacy succeeded, and in 1710 the nawab of Bengal, for services rendered, ceded to the Company along with other territories the district of Chittagong, whose administration was thereupon placed in the hands of one of its executives, called the chief, assisted by a council of advisers. With the establishment of British rule came a period of tranquillity and increasing prosperity, disturbed from time to time by raids by unknown tribes living in the eastern hills and the depredations of the polyglot inhabitants of the offshore island of Sandwip, which had become a cave of Adullam for outlaws of all races.

The conquest of Arakan by the Burmese in 1784 led to an incursion of refugees, among them many militants who began to use British territory as a base from which to launch counter-attacks against the Burmese occupying Arakan. The Burmese thus provoked sent a force into the district to exact punishment, which retired on receiving the assurance of the chief of Chittagong that the ringleaders, if apprehended, would be handed over. The job of settling the refugees, between thirty and forty thousand in number, was given to Captain Cox who died within the year, bequeathing his name to the coastal town which has grown up on the site of his refugee camp. The repeated clashes between British and Burmese over the Arakanese settlers was one of the causes of the First Burmese War. When in 1823 the Burmese sent over a force to occupy the island of Shahpuri at the mouth of the Naf river, one of the officers sent from Calcutta with the detachment of Company soldiers to dislodge them was Jeannie's father-to-be Captain William Lewin. A more substantial incursion into British territory by a Burmese army under their general Maha Bandula the following year caused panic which spread as far as Calcutta, a crisis that only subsided when, on the fall of Rangoon, the Burmese army was withdrawn across the Arakan Yomas in a vain attempt to defend their capital at Ava.

When the Bengal army mutinied in 1857 the three companies of the 34th Native Infantry stationed at Chittagong, far from home and surrounded by an alien population, announced their resolve to support the British and asked to be sent to Delhi to fight against the insurgents, which was presumably a device to secure a safe passage to join the rebels. Their request being refused, they left their billets quietly one night, taking their womenfolk with them, released the prisoners from the local gaol, and wandered off northwards, undecided precisely where they were making for. Straggling through Sylhet and Cachar they encountered a force of Gurkhas belonging to the Sylhet Light Infantry who made short work of them, those who got away falling into the hands of Chakma hillmen whose ruler, known as the Kalindi rani, handed them over to the British authorities.

It was among the mixture of races resulting from the turbulent history just outlined that Lewin worked as superintendent of police, first at Noakhali, then at

Chittagong. The Bengalis he never managed to get on with, finding them (in his own words) cringing, cowardly, lying and litigious. Scattered among the Bengali majority were settlements of Hindus, Afghans and Pathans who had filtered into the country over the centuries; and in a tight community round the Roman Catholic cathedral in Chittagong town lived the half-caste Feringhis bearing such names as Fernandez, Rebeiro, De Cruz and Gonsalvez, descendants of the Portuguese corsairs of old.

Another ingredient in the population was the assortment of peoples whose true identity was hidden under the vague and (except in one case) misleading name of Magh (or Mugh, as it was then spelt), which really meant no more than being of Mongolian descent or having some admixture of Mongolian blood. Most loosely was it applied to those of mixed Bengali and Arakan blood who had somehow managed to persuade the memsahibs of Calcutta and elsewhere in India of their proficiency as cooks. Then there were the so-called Rakhaing Maghs (the qualifying word being the district anglicized as Arakan), descendants of the Arakanese refugees driven out of their own country by the Burmese, who were now settled round Cox's Bazaar. Although they had since much intermarried with the Bengalis, they still spoke Burmese, had retained their Burmese customs and practised the Buddhist religion. Finally, the true Maghs belong to the tribe, now known as Marma, inhabiting the northern and southern sectors of the Chittagong Hill Tracts; though (to confuse matters further) the name was often used, even by Lewin himself, of any of the hill tribes whether true Magh or not as meaning hill people generally.

2

With his dogs and servants Lewin made the journey from Chittagong stretched out uncomfortably and miserably seasick at the bottom of a country-boat which made heavy weather of the voyage up the coast to the mouth of the Meghna, where they had to ship oars and wait to allow the tidal bore, four foot high, to boom past before they could proceed upriver to Noakhali. Situated at the eastern extremity of the tangle of creeks and swampy islands known as the Sundarbans, the place was dismal in the extreme. The small bungalow allotted to him overlooked the cemetery and a large tank, or reservoir, reputed to be haunted. The only other European residents were the civil surgeon and his wife and the district magistrate, an imperious and ill-tempered man who took a dislike to Lewin. It was unhealthy, too, Lewin himself going down with malaria, and in April came an outbreak of cholera which struck down many in the bazaar and also one of his constables, a youth of nineteen who died in his arms, and with the first mango-showers in May lifted as suddenly as it had descended. One morning as Lewin sat at breakfast a *pahi*-dog rushed in and made a lunge at him, then being taken amidships by his bull-terrier Grabby, transferred its attack to the little bitch he had inherited from Bob called Whisky (or, in deference to the servants' pronunciation of her name, Eskee), who was bitten before the intruder could be ejected and despatched. Soon she showed unmistakeable signs of rabies, from which she sickened and died, greatly mourned by Lewin and Grabby.

There was a great deal of work to do, since tidings of the new reforms had apparently never reached this backwater of the Indian empire, and the whole police system of the district had to be reorganized and placed on the approved footing. Lewin also set himself to study Bengali, the language of the local people. Visiting his outlying *thannas* was a pleasant change, for in order to get from village to village he had to thread through a network of streams in a flotilla of sampans rowed by boatmen; and it was restful to lie back smoking and drinking fresh coconut-milk or pomegranate sherbet while Grabby lay panting in the bows. In addition to these duties Lewin was made trade revenue officer responsible for combating the smuggling that was endemic in such a watery province. An additional hazard for the police was the risk of being made the target for false accusations. Once, on receiving a report of an armed robbery, Lewin set out after the dacoits, only to find when he reached the scene of the crime that the moneylender who had been robbed, heartbroken at the loss of his property, had hanged himself. Even before he got back to Noakhali, full of fever, an anonymous petition had been filed in the magistrate's court, accusing him of having murdered the usurer. A month later he received information that, during a scrimmage on Sandwip island between smugglers and a party of police who were searching for contraband salt, a small child had been trampled to death. Sure enough, there soon presented itself at the court-house in Noakhali a *cortège* of sorrowing relations carrying the child's corpse on a bier followed by a wailing procession of mourners, demanding vengeance on the police for having murdered her, and cash compensation. Investigation showed that the child had been killed, either accidentally or possibly as a pretext for making a complaint against the police, by the villagers themselves, but the matter was never satisfactorily cleared up. As in all such cases, the true facts could never be established, because it was impossible to sift the grain of truth from the enveloping chaff of lies told by the professional bearers of false witness who sat all day outside the court-house, waiting for clients.

Once a week, usually on Sunday, Lewin wrote to his mother in his clear handwriting, telling her of his trials and tribulations, his hopes and despairs, never failing to assure her of his tormenting love for her. "I often think," he once wrote, "that our letters might pass as love letters, for are you not the one, the only love I have had during my life?" It was only her love that made his exile, the waste of his youth and strength, endurable. Several times he told her that he could not bear to think that he shared her heart with her other children; he knew it was morbid and unhealthy of him, but he could not help it. He was constantly fearful for her health: "My darling my darling think of what would become of me if you were to die, think that all my happiness in this world & my salvation perhaps in the next is to have you to look to and to love"; and as ever his one heartfelt cry was Home, Home....

For which purpose he was trying to save every penny he could out of his salary, so that when he heard that his friend Harry Graves was sliding further downhill and might come out and join him at any time he was far from pleased. He had received a recent photograph of Harry showing a face lined with care, less free and open than it had been, the effect of his disastrous marriage which had by now produced a child. Eventually, he felt sure, Harry would become a permanent dependant, though Lewin knew that his mother would need an immense amount of coaxing before submitting to such a ne'er-do-well living in her house. But although Lewin could never push his friend from the secure niche he held in his heart, his charity did not extend to Annie and the child, whom Harry was bound to get rid of, he thought, before long, a loss that would not weigh heavily on his friend's elastic conscience.

Through his correspondence with his mother he kept in touch with all that was happening in the family. He learnt how Bob, now safely home, had lost £1,400 of his patrimony "to Tomlin" (perhaps Bankes had recommended an imprudent investment) and had now determined to become a doctor, which would involve his serving for three years under a surgeon before receiving his medical diploma or, as Lewin described it, his licence to slay and slaughter. He was glad Will had taken a fancy to their cousin Jeannie whose friendship, he believed, had done himself more good than anything else, but feared that his mother had lost all influence over him, having been persuaded to let him have his capital, though still only eighteen, which he was in process of squandering. Naïvely he added: "I never could appreciate that parable of the Prodigal Son — my heart always inclined towards the elder brother".

Indeed, he did at times tend to adopt the rôle of heavy elder brother, criticizing Harriet for her bad handwriting and spelling, and showing no sympathy when told that Bella detested school — "what girl or boy does not?" he commented — adding that she should be made to stay until she was seventeen. And his mother must discourage Charley Hatfeild, who like Bankes belonged to one of the families connected in business with the Friends, if he came after Bella. In his spare time he practised his music as assiduously as ever. He had had to sell his large harmonium (at a loss) owing to the difficulty of transporting it to Noakhali, but found the little one did nearly as well, though inferior in tone. He had with him twenty books of music, and his mother continued to send him sheet music — songs such as 'Thoughts of Thee' and 'Parting Words' — to add to his collection. His preference at this time was for the severe, classical melodies of Beethoven and, for its delicacy and lightness combined with breadth of feeling, the music of Mendelssohn. His favourite opera was Mozart's *Don Giovanni*. He was also writing more poetry than ever, conventionally maudlin verses, of which a stanza of 'Twilight' may serve as an example:

> See now, the small bright path of light,
> O'er the fast-darkening water spread,
> From the temple on the brink,
> See the small flame rise & sink;
> Women are weeping for their dead,
> Clad in their mourning robes of white.

One night he dreamt that the poet Thomas Hood had copied all his poems and published them as his own, making him feel very angry, but in the cool light of day his assessment of his talent was more realistic. To his mother he confessed how mean his little verselings seemed after reading some of the mighty utterances of Milton or plucking a flower or two from the graceful wreaths of song which Tennyson had woven. To assist his attempts he asked her to send him a rhyming dictionary. Surprisingly, his aunt Harriet Grote, who had been shown some of his poems and was a woman of discernment, thought she could get them published in one of the leading English periodicals; but nothing seems to have come of this.

At a less exalted level he completed during his months at Noakhali another *Police Officer's Manual*, this time in Bengali, containing a brief résumé of the laws it was necessary for his constables to be familiar with, which was published at government expense for general circulation and brought him in a small royalty. He continued to write stories and topical articles which were printed in Calcutta journals, work he admitted was unlikely to "inflame the Ganges", but which brought in a few welcome rupees. Among them were a series of occasional sketches which appeared week by week in *The Englishman* under the general title 'Chhota Haziree' (small breakfast) to indicate their trifling nature, and were later published in book form under the same title by the Calcutta Central Press Company in 1866. At first pleased to see his work in print, Lewin soon became painfully aware of its deficiencies.

The articles, which cover a wide variety of unrelated topics, are written in a heavily facetious vein — "A fair good morrow to you, courteous reader," one of them begins — their verbose jocularity only occasionally taking on a satirical edge. If they can be said to have a common theme, it is that of painting, the author's wish to compensate for the absence of pictures on the walls of the expatriates' bungalows in India (due to the fear of destruction by damp or the difficulty of transit) by calling to mind in each article some painting or paintings he had seen and which still haunted odd corners of his brain. These included a picture of the burial of a Comanche chief, "his war plumes waving, his tomahawk glistening, his wampum flying in the wind", which had presumably illustrated one of the Fennimore Cooper novels he had read as a boy; a Cornish fisherman saying goodbye to his wife before leaving for the Whitby fishing; a Spanish wake; a scene from the *Divina Commedia*; and one by Faed called *Baith Father and Mither* showing a widowed cobbler and his daughter, "the sweetest little lassie", still too young to know the great blank in her life — the want of a mother.

A more serious article discusses poetry, describing how the author's heart had first been touched by Wordsworth's catalogue of scenery and Southey's stilted misrepresentations of history, then by Scott's glowing words, the impassioned fervidness of Byron and the tender delicacy of Shelley. This triad had fathered Tennyson and Longfellow, the two names that stood foremost in the roll of the present with their gemmed crowns of poesy. The subject of another article is music, 'The Divine Science', in which the author praises Weber, Mendelssohn, Spohr, Mozart and Haydn, and claims that the crucial test of a great master is the faculty of moving the listener to laughter or tears: "Even the reflection of music brings back to me scenes and places, memories of long ago". In his last article there is a description of "the perfect scene", but one which was as incomplete as an arch without its keystone:

> ... for what would paradise have been without Eve, and what man's dream could be complete without a woman in it? — Someone to fill life with the pleasantest witchery of her love, making home pretty with womanly adornments, and life radiant with her loving looks and gentle tones. It is not good for a man to be alone, shut up with himself, his own joys, and hopes, and fears.

1. Thomas Lewin of The Hollies

2. Ensign T.H. Lewin in 1858

3. Mary Lewin

My bungalow at Chittagong.

4. "My bungalow at Chittagong"
5. A Frieze of Lushai girls

6. Lewin with Lushai Chiefs
7. Lushai Chiefs in Calcutta, 1873

My bungalow on the hill at
Chandraguna
Chittagong Hill Tracts

8. Early Morning in the Lushai Hills
9. "My bungalow on the hill at Chandraguna"

My Bungalow at Noakhali.

My house at Rangamati

10. "My bungalow at Noakhali"
11. "My house at Rangamati"

12. Sir John Edgar, KCSI

Amid much artificial sentiment only occasionally is a little genuine feeling allowed to break in.

On the title-page the authors of *Chhota Haziree* are shown as "Jeannie and Tom", and in a sense the book was the result of a collaboration between Lewin and his cousin. In March 1864 he had written to his mother that, if Jeannie could be got to revise his writings, "they would come out from the fire with renewed brightness, for her taste is like herself, pure and good". But even Jeannie could not make much of the sketches, which may be regarded as period pieces, a monument to Lewin's youthful versatility, and the forerunner of his later ventures in journalism.

After less than six months at Noakhali Lewin wrote to his mother about a new interest that had fired his imagination. He led into the subject by way of a description of the large dugouts called *koondas* he often encountered being poled leisurely along during his river journeys and sometimes accommodating as many as ten people, though each craft was fashioned from the trunk of a single tree:

> — these trees I understand come from the unknown country on our frontier here between the Chittagong District & Burmah the land of the White Elephant and I purpose some day taking a couple of months leave and making a voyage of discovery amongst the aborigines of those parts, about whom I have already collected some queer information.

At this stage he had no other purpose than to use the information he managed to gather about the tribes as the basis for one of the articles he was contributing to the *Weekly Journal* of Calcutta. And yet six weeks later he reported to his mother that he had applied to the lieutenant-governor of Bengal for appointment to the vacant post of Superintendent of Hill Tracts in the Chittagong Division, whose duty it was to guard the whole eastern frontier of Bengal. His application had been backed by the deputy inspector-general of police and, he hoped, by the commissioner of Chittagong, and since Arthur Grote was busy pulling strings for him in Calcutta he thought there was a good chance, despite the black mark on his record sheet over the Ellis case, of his getting the appointment. The only adverse contingency, he thought, was that the lieutenant-governor might have some friend or connection of his own whom he wanted to put in; for old abuses like the system of patronage die hard. "If I do — look out for a book upon the Wild Tribes of India — by your humble servant."

There seem to have been several reasons for this sudden enthusiasm for the hills. First, since his primary concern was still to save money as quickly as possible so that he could leave "this beastly country" and settle down quietly in England with his mother, there was the attraction of the salary he would receive: £75 a month as against the £45 a month he would get even if he obtained his captaincy. There was also his strong desire to get away from the district magistrate at Noakhali who hated him and did all he could to injure him. Linked to this was the chance of an independent command: "Only fancy," he told his mother, "up in the hills I shall be Magistrate & Superintendent & King & everything. Ah my own! I would sooner have my head on your neck than any other place in the world..."; but nevertheless the prospect was an alluring one for a man of his temperament. It also cannot have been coincidental that Lewin's application for the job had been written during a visit of inspection by the deputy inspector-general of police Captain Graham, who had himself once been superintendent of hill tracts. It is likely that Graham's tales of his experiences among the tribes were a major factor in inspiring Lewin with an overwhelming ambition to be his successor.

Meantime, while his application was being shuffled from desk to desk in the bureaucracy of Calcutta, he must continue his present police duties. Graham had declared himself highly satisfied with all he saw of Lewin's work as superintendent of police and, wishing to give him a leg up, had recommended his transfer to the more important Chittagong district, as being better fitted for the charge than the present incumbent. When the order for his transfer came through, Lewin's only regret was that he could no longer make use of the fine library, presented to the station school by a local tea planter, to which he owed his first acquaintance with the works of Addison and Steele, Rabelais, Sir Thomas Browne, Lamb and de Quincey.

3

From the first Lewin found Chittagong a pleasant change after the austerities of Noakhali. Writing to his mother in October soon after his transfer, he described the place in lyrical terms:

> The scenery here is indeed charming & reminds me forcibly of the Highlands. All the houses in the station are built upon hills and the view from our bungalow is splendid. Far away stretches a broad green plain interspersed with mango & palm trees through which stretch in many a curve the silver reaches of the river winding its way [through] the unknown hill country whence its sources flow. The horizon is bounded by a line of mountains rising up peak after peak blue & soft in the distance, their base fringed as far as the eye can reach with heavy forest jungle. Back towards the South stretches the Indian Ocean & in the harbour lie safely moored large ships that have spread their white wings from old England.

Lying in the armpit of the Bay of Bengal, the district is subject to frequent cyclones, locally known as Lady's Eyebrows from the shape of the black clouds that appear on the horizon when one is imminent, and these cut swaths of devastation through the flat, rice-growing countryside. Floods are of annual occurrence. Home of lascar seamen, its population is predominantly Muslim Bengali, but the proximity of Arakan has introduced a Mongolian strain, and the *longyi* replaces the *dhoti* as the standard male costume. The fortunate live above the teeming stench of the town in bungalows perched on the tops of the little green hills Lewin referred to in his letter. Everywhere the sound of birds is pervasive: the croak of house crows, the mewing of kites and buzzards, the barbet striking its little copper bell, the contralto flute-notes of the black-headed oriole, green parakeets shrieking as they arrow by overhead, the jungle owlet talking its own double-dutch, the Burmese-speaking cuckoo—"*yauk-hpa-kwe-kaw*"—and the koel's far-carrying cry: "you're ill, *you're ill*, YOU'RE ILL". Bounded on the west by the sea, to the south lies the pleasant beach at Cox's Bazaar, to the north the mosque of Sultan Baijid with its stagnant tank full of gross, meat-eating turtles; and far away to the east loom the blue hills.

At first Lewin chummed with the local clergyman Mr Humfrey in his bungalow called The Deanery, and on his being invalided home acquired a small bungalow of his own where he lived alone, as he preferred. He could play rackets or billiards when he felt like it and sometimes croquet with the ladies of the station, and there were whist parties and other social gatherings. More to his taste were the musical evenings at the house of the commissioner of the division Mr Bruce, when four of them — the commissioner who was a good violinist, his white-whiskered Feringhi assistant, the assistant magistrate, and Lewin bent over his recently acquired violoncello — formed a string quartet and scraped away to their own great satisfaction. In after life Lewin often recalled Mr Bruce's advice, which he found useful in other than musical contexts:

"Remember, Lewin, if you come to a passage you can't play, don't get confused, but just sway away upon G."

In addition to his routine duties Lewin was required to draw up a scheme for the fortification and defence of the station, which was duly shelved and forgotten. He was also made a municipal commissioner, giving him some insight into such matters as rates and taxes, drainage, and education. Whenever he could he got away on tour of his district, his journeyings made especially pleasant after government had sanctioned the purchase of a yacht, a yawl-rigged craft with two comfortable cabins pulling six sweeps a side. In the *Foam* he traversed the streams and inland channels of his new district, sometimes standing out to sea for a proper sail when he felt he needed relaxation.

The end of the year came, and there was still no news of the fate of his application to become hill super-intendent, though there was talk of extending his police district and making him superintendent of the hill tribes in addition to his present duties; an obviously im-practicable suggestion that came to nothing. All this time he had remained on the strength of his regiment, and understandably his colonel insisted that, if he wished to keep in line for promotion and not be passed over by a younger man, he must show his continued fitness by passing the customary examination. Lewin therefore applied to the general commanding the Bengal presidency division to appoint a commission to examine him as to his fitness for promotion. After reading hard for a fortnight, he attended before the examining board at Fort William in Calcutta in January 1865 and was found fit to be granted his captaincy, which was duly gazetted a few months later.

In Calcutta he was joined by his friend of Shahjahanpur days George Johnston. While stationed at a place in Assam nicknamed Lingering Death he had fallen seriously ill and being without means had to apply to Lewin for a loan to enable him to pay the fare so that he could proceed to England on sick leave. There he had called on Mrs Lewin and was now back in India, restored to health. Lewin's two best friends had not taken to each other when they met; George had not only sized up Harry Graves as a cad who was unfit to associate with Mrs Lewin, but had made his opinion known to Bob, who passed it on to Harry. After brooding on the matter for a long time Harry wrote to Lewin, moaning that his friendship for him was becoming cooler and dying away, and ending with fiery words of defiance to Johnston for what he had said about him. From this time forward Harry began to attach himself more and more to Will, and it was about this time that the two of them perpetrated a puerile hoax at Weston-super-Mare, in which Will impersonated Queen Victoria's second son Prince Albert so successfully that the episode was reported in the *Bristol Times and Mirror.*

During his visit to Calcutta Lewin and Johnston shared a room at the United Service Club and sat up talking far into the night, for they had plenty of news to exchange. On this visit Lewin also appears to have met a lady who engaged his interest enough for him to wish to make another visit in October to see her again. If so, the friendship did not develop, for by then his new interest was absorbing his attention. Nevertheless, it should not be supposed that his life in Chittagong — though he sometimes described it as "loveless" — was without feminine content. It is typical of the closeness of his relationship with his mother that he felt bound to reveal the situation to her, if a little guardedly: "One sin which most easily besets me — viz the love of women's society. I wonder do I get the passionateness of my nature from you or from my father?"

In the new year Lewin set off on a tour of his district, taking with him a Magh interpreter Sadu and his son Apo to carry his pistol and hunting knife. He wore a suit of grey flannel and soft yellow boots and took with him, besides a breech-loading gun with which to shoot game for the pot, no more than a white lawn shirt, a crimson silk waist-cloth and some toilet articles. They headed south, making for the foothills where some of the hill people had settled. Walking barefoot and wearing only the shirt and waist-cloth like one of themselves he visited their villages, sleeping on the hard plank floor of the *zawlbuk*, or bachelors' house, which served as the guest house as well as the club where the young men of the tribe would gather in the evening to smoke and gossip. He picked up what he could of their language, the first sentence Sadu taught him having been: "Sweet little sister, do not be afraid. Will you not speak to me?" And it must have been refreshing after living and working among Muslims whose womenfolk go about hooded in a *barqa* to be among people whose women, both married and unmarried, lived in equality with the men and met the stranger with open friendliness combined with a womanly modesty he found attractive. Moreover, the girls were often remarkably pretty.

He began to distinguish between the tribes inhabiting the river valleys and the wilder folk who built their villages on the hilltops so as to be difficult of access. The former included the Maghs who spoke a dialect of Arakanese and were nominally Buddhist while retaining many of their animist customs and beliefs; and the Chakmas, Lewin's favourites, also Buddhists, who had migrated from Arakan but spoke a corrupt form of Bengali unintelligible to the plains dwellers. The men dressed in cotton waist-cloths, the women in short jackets above skirts that opened at the front exposing the right thigh as they walked. They wore cane bracelets and bead necklaces, and earplugs into which they fitted flowers. The people of the hills were animists and went nearly naked, the men wearing no more than a jockstrap, the women a scanty petticoat and, until marriage or in some tribes the birth of the first child, a brief jacket covering the breasts. Lewin found them all friendly and honest, "the jolliest folk imaginable, always laughing and merry"; though he once declined the hospitality of a Kumi headman because he saw hanging up in his house the carcass of a dog in readiness for the cooking-pot.

Growing impatient at the delay in his application going through, he began to consider other possibilities. Over the hills that so fascinated him lay Burma, the Land of the White Elephant, and he wondered if there was a possibility of getting a posting there. By the Treaty of Yandabo ratified in 1826 the Burmese had been forced to cede Arakan and the strip of Tenasserim coast as well as Assam and Manipur to the British, thus securing India's north-eastern frontier. The Second Anglo-Burmese War of 1852 had resulted in the British annexing the province of Pegu, leaving the king of Ava with only the central and northern areas of Burma as his domain. Pegu was placed under a commissioner Major Arthur Phayre, who had already seen service in Tenasserim and Arakan. A scholar with unrivalled knowledge of the Burmese language and people, he was later to write the first history of Burma in the English language. In 1862 when the divisions of Pegu, Arakan and Tenasserim were amalgamated to form British Burma and made a province of the Indian empire, Phayre was appointed chief commissioner. It was to this high official that Lewin wrote in April 1865, asking for an appointment in the Burma Commission, though having no one to pull strings for him in that quarter he saw little hope of obtaining it.

For a time Burma filled his thoughts. Already fluent in Urdu, Hindi and Bengali, he now began to apply himself to the study of Burmese, and in June after a bad bout of malaria went for a sail in the *Foam* on his doctor's orders two hundred miles down the coast to Cox's Bazaar, a town of timber houses which was like a fragment of Burma transplanted. Both sexes sauntered in the streets wearing bright-coloured *longyis*, the women smoking big white cheroots. The air was pungent with the odour of *ngapi*, the condiment made of rotted prawns which the Burmese consider an indispensable accompaniment to good cuisine. Saffron-robed Buddhist *hpongyis* walked silently by on sandalled feet. One night he was invited to attend a *pwe* given by a troupe of strolling performers from Burma proper in an outsize marquee pitched on a piece of grassland outside the town. While the orchestra consisting of drums, clappers, flutes and other wind instruments kept up a discordant accompaniment, the players enacted in dance, mime and dialogue a scene from some old chronicle of the kings of Burma. Interrupted by obscene comments from the clown which much delighted the packed audience — composed of men, women and children who had brought along food, sleeping mats and other impedimenta, for the show would go on all night — exquisitely dressed girls with powdered faces and lacquered hair postured and swayed, making lateral movements with their heads, fluttering their hands in fluent gestures and frequently kicking backwards to clear their feet from their encumbering hobble skirts. Lewin was enchanted.

Back in Chittagong life went on as usual. In his bungalow, with Grabby for company, he practised hard at the 'cello. There were musical evenings at Mr Bruce's when the quartet tackled *The Magic Flute.* His short story 'Queen of the Rubies' was accepted for publication in *Once a Week.* He heard from his mother, now on holiday on the Continent with his sister Harriet and Bankes, that his aunt Grote had been ill. He heard, too, that George Johnston had landed the job of private secretary to the inspector-general of police in Calcutta. And he continued to gather as much information as he could about the wild tribes inhabiting the hills that formed the eastern boundary of his district.

Part II (1866-1873)

The Man Who Would Be King

Chapter Eight
A Brush with
the Shendus

1

The Chittagong Hill Tracts on the south-eastern border of Bengal are situated towards the southernmost extremity of the straggling tangle of mountainous country that separates north-eastern India from neighbouring Tibet, China and Burma, a vast territory whose inhabitants are a variety of hill tribes of Mongolian stock, each having its own language and customs. They seem to have had their origin somewhere in southern Tibet or south-eastern China and to have settled into their present locations within the last few hundred years. In the northern hills live the Daflas, Apa Tanis, Miris, Mishmis and Abors. The eastern section comprises the Naga Hills, eastern Manipur whose tribes include the (true) Kukis, and the Lushai Hills which adjoin the Chin Hills of Burma to the east. Over the southern boundary of Lushailand lies the tract known in Lewin's day as Hill Tippera, then ruled over by a Hindu rajah, and the Chittagong Hill Tracts. South of them in Arakan, which was part of British Burma, live the Lakhers, then known as the Shendus.

Comprising some 7000 square miles of wild hill country with ranges trending north-south and seldom rising more than 3000 feet above sea level, the Chittagong Hill

Tracts are cut laterally by four main rivers whose valleys provide the easiest means of access to the ranges beyond. In the north the Feni, which discharges into the Bay of Bengal opposite Sandwip island, separates the tracts from Hill Tippera. The central block of upland is traversed by the Karnafuli which, rising in the same range as the Sonai and Tipai streams, winds westwards through rocky gorges to become the principal river of the plains before discharging into the sea at Chittagong. It was navigable even by large boats which plied to the riverside posts of Rangamati and Kasalong and thence twenty miles further into the hills until balked by the Barkal rapids; at which point smaller craft could be lifted ashore and carried along the hillside overlooking the rapids and refloated, and so proceed upstream in a narrower, shallower channel as far as the Demagri falls. Further south the Sangu, known to the hill people as the Rigre Chaung, rising near the Arakan border could be navigated as far as Bandarban; while the fourth river, the Matamori or the Mori Chaung, after flowing past Manikpur in the foothills discharges into the sea opposite Kutabda island.

In Lewin's day the broad geography of the tracts was common knowledge, but reliable information about their inhabitants was hard to come by. To the Bengalis of the plains those living in the foothills were vaguely identified, on account of their method of cultivation, as Joomahs or Joomeahs. *Jhum* is the Assamese word for a hillside field, and *jhuming* is a time-consuming process that keeps the villagers busy virtually all the year round. First the site has to be cleared of small trees, bamboos and undergrowth, which are later set on fire, their ashes providing a good fertilizer. The cleared area is sown seed by seed, first with millet, maize, cucumber, marrows and other vegetables, then with rice paddy. *Jhum* huts are built nearby in which the people will sleep during the cultivating season. During the rains the growing crops must be constantly weeded and protected from the depredations of marauding monkeys, hogs and other wild animals. Harvesting begins in October, the cut paddy being laid out to dry on makeshift threshing-floors near the *jhum* houses before being threshed. The cleaned grain is carried in baskets to granaries built outside the village, where it is stored. At every stage of the process the prescribed sacrifices are made to appease the spirits and so ensure a plentiful harvest. The drawback to this mode of cultivation is that a *jhum* once harvested must be left fallow from between five to ten years before it is fit to be cleared and sown again, so that each village needs a large amount of cultivable land on which to rotate its husbandry. The same slash-burn method of cultivation was followed by the wilder tribes of the hilltops living in the far interior, who were known to the plains-dwellers by the fearsome name of Kookies.

Nor were the British much better informed about the hill people. This was largely because, ever since the district of Chittagong had passed into British hands, they had been averse to tackling the problem they posed. Unwilling to assume direct administration of the hills,

which would have involved heavy expenditure for little
return, the chief of Chittagong — an official, it will be
recalled, of the East India Company — had been content
to keep the tribes at arm's length and to deal with them
through the intermediary of the two paramount chiefs:
the Chakma chief who lived at Kasalong far up the
Karnafuli, and the Magh chief, a member of the influential
Phru family, who lived at Bandarban on the Sangu.
Under this system the two chiefs continued to exact
tribute from the villages under their control, making the
headmen (or *raojas*) responsible for its collection, a
percentage of which they made over to the Chittagong
treasury. Although the Chakmas and the Maghs were far
and away the most numerous tribes in the tracts, their
populations — perhaps 100,000 Chakmas and 50,000
Maghs — were very small in relation to the teeming
millions in the plains, whose influence on them was
already beginning to be felt. Broadly speaking, for there
was a great deal of overlapping, Magh villages dominated
the northern and southern sectors of the tracts, Chakma
villages the central sector. Interspersed with them were
those of much smaller tribes or sub-tribes, such as the
Mrus, Mrungs (immigrants from Hill Tippera), Tsaks
and Kumis in the south; the Pankos, Banjogis, Tan-
cangyas, Khyangs (from the Chin Hills) and Riangs (also
from Tippera) in the central sector; and Tipperas and a
few Lushais in the north. Somewhere in the unvisited
country to the north and north-east lay the principal
Lushai villages and over the Arakan border to the south

and south-east straddling the Kaladan river was the land of the Lakhers, both tribes much feared by the more peaceful tract-dwellers.

During the first half of the nineteenth century rumours had reached the British of inter-tribal conflict between villages — those of the Mrungs, Kumis and Banjogis were specifically mentioned — under the jurisdiction of the Phru family, members of which were at odds with one another. This local unrest seems to have prompted the Kumis living across the Arakan border to attack some villages belonging to Mru immigrants. The officer in charge of the Arakan district of British Burma at the time was the Arthur Phayre who has already been mentioned, and in December 1847 an expedition against the offenders was despatched from Akyab under the command of Phayre's assistant Lieutenant Hopkinson. After seven days' journey in boats up the Kaladan river the force struck inland, but the country proved so formidable that the men were soon overcome by the hardships of the march, and it was only due to a series of happy accidents that they managed to struggle back, having achieved nothing. That same cold season a Lakher raiding party came over the border and attacked two villages in the Chittagong tracts, one subject to the Chakma chieftainess, the Kalindi rani, a formidable old lady who was to become Lewin's implacable enemy, the other subject to the Bohmong rajah who controlled the southern Magh villages. (In the north they were controlled by another member of the Phru family, holding the title the Mong rajah.) The purpose of the raids seems to have been to take captives which would be sold as slaves, and it was rumoured that one of the buyers was the Kalindi rani herself.

The commissioner of Chittagong Mr Ricketts, who had hitherto favoured dealing with the remoter tribes at second hand through the paramount chiefs, now wanted to send an armed force into the hills making for the Kaladan, there to co-operate with the Arakan police and levies; but at that time men trained to undertake such work were not available. The following year there were Lakher and Lushai raids on encroaching Magh villages, and a year later an even larger Lushai raid on a Chakma village subject to the rani, launched in revenge for frauds perpetrated in barter deals between the two tribes. News of similar outrages between Magh and Chakma villages continued to come out of the hills until it was calculated in 1854 that during the past seventeen years there had been nineteen raids, many of them attributable to Lakhers operating from across the Arakan border, in which 107 people had been killed and 186 carried off into slavery.

Still no official action was taken except to supply arms to the Phru rajahs with authority to shoot to kill. The lieutenant-governor of Bengal, reviewing the situation in 1859, concluded that the solution lay in removing the hill country lying to the east of the cultivated plains of Chittagong from the operation of the General Regulations applicable elsewhere in India, which had never been intended to apply to untamed tribes living for the most part beyond the reach of the law. A "Superintendent of Joom Tracts" would be appointed who would exercise general supervision over the chiefs. He would interfere as little as possible with their customary jurisdiction, except to ensure that the hill people living near the plains "who are practically our subjects" — the clause reveals a certain confusion of thought — were defended from attack and themselves restrained from attacking others. In 1860 an act was passed giving effect to the lieutenant-governor's recommendations.

Before the appointment of a hill superintendent had been made there occurred near the northern boundary of the hill tracts what came to be known as "the great Kuki rebellion" when, in reaction against misgovernment by the Tippera rajah and his family (who were invariably at odds with one another), five hundred "Kukis" — in fact, they were predominantly Lushais — living near the headwaters of the Feni swept down the river valley into the plains where they burnt or plundered fifteen villages, killed 185 British subjects and, carrying off a hundred captives, melted away again into the fastnesses of their hills. Among the raiders were Chakmas and Riangs subject to the Kalindi rani and Thangluahs belonging to a minor Lushai clan living just south of Demagri near the sources of the Feni and Karnafuli. Their chief Rothang-puia — in those days his name was spelt, and no doubt pronounced by the British, Rutton Poia — was later to play a leading rôle in Lewin's adventures.

The first task of the newly appointed superintendent

of hill tracts, an eccentric character whose foolhardy physical feats had earned him the nickname the Pagla (or Mad) Sahib, was to gather information to facilitate the advance of a military expedition being sent to punish the offending tribes. In January 1861 a large body of police under Captain Raban succeeded in reaching Rothangpuia's village which, although they found it had been deserted by its people who had taken to the jungle, they burnt before returning whence they had come. Beyond proving that Lushai villages hitherto unvisited were not inaccessible, the operation did nothing to put a stop to the general state of turbulence in the hills, for it increased rather than diminished during the ensuing months. In these troubled circumstances Captain Graham took over from the Pagla Sahib as superintendent and made his headquarters at Chandragona in the foothills overlooking the Karnafuli.

In September Rothangpuia, anticipating that a more formidable expedition was likely to be despatched during the coming cold weather, came in to Graham's headquarters to tender his formal submission, offering to give assistance if a force were to be sent against the tribes living beyond where his village lay. Through him the first tentative overtures were made to open friendly communications with the powerful Haolong and Sailo clans, of whom little was known at the time. The initial response was unpromising, for the chiefs not only declined to come and pay their respects to Graham, but also sent word that, although they would refrain from attacking

Europeans, they considered they were entitled to cut up such foreign folk as Bengalis, Tipperas, Maghs and the like, in which pursuits the British, they said, had no right to interfere. Faced with this threat, Graham succeeded in persuading the rajah of Tippera to strengthen the defences intended to secure the northern boundary of the hill tracts, by setting up police posts and a stockade on the Feni; but these proved ineffective when the following March a band of Lushais, circumventing them without difficulty, made their way southwards and attacked a Magh village only eight miles from the Phru chief's residence at Bandarban.

The sense of helplessness that afflicted the Chittagong authorities is well summed up in the official history of the region written twenty years later by Alexander Mackenzie of the Indian Civil Service, who in after years became related to Lewin by marriage:

> During the whole year [1861] the frontier was in a state of constant panic: large tracts of country were deserted by the Joomea cultivators, and it seemed as if nothing that our police and troops could effect would secure them from attack. The wild and unknown country from which the savages came, the trackless jungles and rock-strewn torrent beds from which they would suddenly emerge, and into which they would, on the first symptom of attack, re-plunge, rendered helpless the best efforts of our men to pursue them, as it was also impossible to foresee their advance.

Nevertheless the instructions given to Graham by the new lieutenant-governor Sir Cecil Beaden were to maintain the policy of conciliation. He should arrange an annual gathering of the chiefs at some convenient place up in the hills at which the superintendent representing the British government should receive token tribute from them, listen to their complaints and grievances and, in return for their undertaking to keep the peace during the ensuing year, pay them an allowance on a sliding scale based on the size of the clan. Accordingly, taking with him an armed escort, Graham proceeded to Rothangpuia's village and obtained his agreement and that of several other minor chiefs to the lieutenant-governor's proposals. Messengers sent to the Haolongs and Sailos returned bringing back a document to similar effect, on which such chiefs as Vandula, Seipuia and Vanhnuaia — names soon to become well known to the authorities — had affixed their marks, since none of them could write. As a reward the following sums were dispensed:

Haolongs	—	Rs.800
Sailos	—	Rs.800
Thangluahs [Rothangpuia]	—	Rs.400

The first gathering was held at Kasalong at the close of 1863 and was well attended by the chiefs, but in future years they were allowed to send representatives to collect their danegeld for them.

These arrangements did not, of course, deter the Lakhers and other tribes living beyond the Kaladan and the Sangu from continuing their annual forays into

British territory, killing, burning and making off with their booty of slaves and severed heads.

2

When after a year his application to be appointed superintendent of hill tracts had still met with no official response, Lewin bethought himself of some way of enhancing his claim to the position in the eyes of the Bengal government. He had for long contemplated making a voyage of discovery among the aborigines living in the unknown borderland between the plains of Chittagong and Burma and had taken practical steps in preparation for undertaking such a journey during the coming cold season. He had corresponded with the Zoological Society in London which had given him a list of the specimens they would like him to bring back, and with the Asiatic Society which wanted a full account of the hill people and, knowing their propensity for head-hunting, asked him to bring them back a few skulls. He discussed the matter at length with Mr Young the commissioner of Chittagong, who put in a good word for him in Calcutta, so that Colonel Pughe the inspector-general of police not only granted him leave for the purpose, but also authorized him to spend a sum of money on presents, such as beads, looking glasses, mouth organs, cloth and spirits, likely to be acceptable to the chiefs on whose goodwill he would be dependent. It was made clear, though, that no official sanction could be accorded to his expedition, which he would undertake entirely at his own risk. It was understood that he might go into the hills for ten days or so.

In a letter to his mother written at Manikpur on 29 November 1865 Lewin was frank about what he hoped to achieve: "If I am lucky, this expedition may do me good and get me a name". As to his destination he really had very little idea. He was tempted to proceed up the Karnafuli at whose source lived Lushai tribes about whom virtually nothing was known, but this would have meant passing through Chandragona, the headquarters of the acting superintendent of hill tracts, who might well have turned him back, knowing he would be held responsible if anything untoward happened to Lewin. Instead, as he afterwards wrote, he "had arrived at the conclusion that, by going some distance southwards and then striking east I should get across to Burmah, perhaps if I went far enough, to China". This should take him into the country of the dreaded "Shendus", or Lakhers, with whom he hoped to establish friendly relations; at least he would learn something definite about them.

To accompany him he chose a Punjabi havildar Faizullah Khan, known as Fazlah, who had followed his fortunes since Hazaribagh days; two Magh interpreters he recruited in Cox's Bazaar; his personal cook Tobedhun, a (true) Magh whom he inevitably called Toby; and six Bengali constables. Personal baggage was kept to a minimum, his own consisting of bedding and mosquito-curtains, a few cooking utensils, his diary covering the previous year and a half including notes on the tribes and some sketches he had made, a volume of Shakespeare's plays, and a violin.

Starting from Manikpur towards the end of November, the party proceeded in dugouts up the Mori Chaung, branched off on to a narrow hill-stream and camped on a sandbank on the outskirts of a Mrung village within the jurisdiction of the Bohmong rajah. Next afternoon the headman with some of his elders came to pay his respects and, after being mellowed by spirits of wine handed round in bamboo cups, agreed to provide porters for the onward journey across the hills. It was on this occasion according to Lewin's later account that, on learning that the headman's name was (in Lewin's phonetic spelling) "Twekam Tongloyn", he had the happy thought of claiming kinship with him because his own name "Tongloyn" (Tom Lewin) was the same. In the modified form of "Thangliena" this became the name by which he became known throughout the hills.

A hard day's march across the hills, during which Lewin heard for the first time the joyous whooping of hoolock gibbons, brought them to a Kumi village on the Tindu Chaung, where he was given rice beer to drink. From a tall earthenware jar the refreshing brew is sucked up through a reed stuck into the top of it. Moving down to the Sangu they hired four dugouts and in these frail craft shot the rapids and paddled on until they reached its junction with the Ramakri Chaung. Still accompanied by their Mrung porters they continued in an easterly direction, wading through streams, beset by leeches, and climbing up and down steep hillsides. Waking one morning they found the footprints of a tiger near their camp, and once looking across a ravine Lewin saw a bull elephant moving slowly up the opposite slope. From the Lama Chaung they crossed a spur called the Kanka Taung, descended to a tributary of the Pi Chaung, and from thence made their way over the main range, halting for one night at a Kumi village on the Khu Chaung which lower down flows into the Kaladan. On 7 December they reached Daletme, a village of fifty houses on the Kaladan, and from there Lewin got rid of his escort of six constables who had shown no relish for hill travel, partly in order to cut down on the number of porters needed to carry the party's food, but also because he felt that the presence of armed men gave the hillmen a wrong impression of the purpose of the expedition. He sent them by boat down the Kaladan making for Akyab on the Arakan coast, taking with them a letter to Mr Young in Chittagong with which he enclosed the diary of his journey to date. He also sent the porters back to their village.

The headman of Daletme, who was old and sick and, Lewin thought, a nonentity, proved unhelpful, not wishing to put himself wrong either with the Arakan authorities within whose jurisdiction his village lay, or with the Lakhers of whom his people lived in constant fear. When he heard that Lewin's objective was the Blue Mountain further north — the only feature shown on the otherwise blank government map of the area — to reach which he would have to traverse the length of Lakherland, he declined to do more than provide him with a guide to show him the way to a Kumi village a short day's journey higher up the Kaladan, whose headman Yuong was reputed to be a man of influence. Next morning they set off by dugout while the mist still blanketed the river and arrived at Yuong's village in the early afternoon. He proved friendly, regaled Lewin with rice spirit and agreed to accompany him to a village whose chief Teynwey was said to be on friendly terms with the Lakhers, although he himself was at feud with them.

Teynwey came to the river bank with a considerable retinue to greet Lewin on landing. He was an elderly man wearing a fine homespun plaid cloth, and his grey hair was twisted into a topknot which betokened him as belonging to one of the Poi clans whose near relations lived in the Chin Hills. Half the inhabitants of his village, which consisted of some fifty houses, were Kumis who belong to a different group of clans called Mar and wear their hair in a chignon at the nape of the neck. The rest as well as the chief himself Lewin called "Kyaws", heading the letter he wrote to his mother on 15 December as being from the Kyaw village on the upper Kaladan. He was sitting at the time, he told her, in a hut twenty feet from the ground with about ten dirty savages sitting round him grunting their wonderment at his doings, for no European had ever visited their village before.

Here Lewin and his party stayed for several days while

messengers were sent to the nearest Lakher chief of importance, asking him to send someone to escort Lewin to his village. During their stay they received a visit from a lesser Lakher chief whose village was the only one of the tribe within British jurisdiction. He brought a present of chickens and eggs and was accompanied by a small retinue including four women. Being the first members of the tribe Lewin had come so far to see, he studied them carefully. The chief was a powerfully built, rough-looking old fellow with a stubble of beard on his chin and wore his long hair projecting in a knob over his forehead in the manner of the Haka Chins. The men carried guns with stocks painted red, black and yellow and from their shoulders hung powder-flasks of mithan horns inlaid with silver and ivory. The womenfolk, Lewin noted, dressed with more regard for western notions of decency than did the hill women he had so far encountered wearing knee-length kilts and often with exposed breasts. Instead they wore a short chemise of white homespun, a petticoat of dark-blue cotton stuff reaching below the knee, and over the shoulders a black plaid shawl with yellow stripes. Their black hair was parted in the middle, two braids being drawn back on either side of the head and fastened in a knot at the back. The chief told Lewin through an interpreter that many of the Lakhers would like to come and settle in British territory, but were deterred by the heavy tax they would have to pay the government. From this Lewin might have drawn the inference that the dreaded "Shendus" were not the bloodthirsty savages they were made out to be, but unfortunately his prejudice against them was soon to receive what appeared to be confirmation of the justice of their fearsome reputation.

A powwow in Teynwey's house that night developed into a feast with music and dancing at which much rice beer was drunk, and Lewin delighted his hosts with an impromptu on his violin. Afterwards in the sleeping quarters allotted to him he was so tormented by fleas and other vermin that in the morning he got the hill people to erect two shelters on the river bank, one for himself and the other for his followers. That evening as he sat cross-legged in his shelter scraping away on his violin a bullet struck him in the leg below the hip, ripped through the thigh muscle and emerged just above the knee, causing him sickening pain. What seems to have happened is that one of the hill guides who had led the party over the hills to the Kaladan, seeing Lewin's gun lying outside the shelter, had been examining it out of curiosity and by accident pulled the trigger. Fearful at what he had done, he had taken to his heels. Fazlah and Toby bound up the wounds as well as they could, but the injury seemed to Lewin so serious that he felt obliged to abandon his enterprise and try to obtain medical help. He was carried to Yuong's boat that was moored at the water's edge, rowers were hired to man it, and soon they were being paddled down the river towards Akyab, three days' journey to the south.

While convalescing from his wound under the care of Dr Lees in the bungalow of Captain Munro the superintendent of police at Akyab Lewin sent a report of his travels and also his tour diary to Colonel Phayre, by now the chief commissioner of British Burma. When he had read them it became clear to Phayre that matters could not be left as they were or misunderstandings were bound to arise. Munro would have to go up to the scene of the accident to sort things out, and Phayre suggested that it would be proper for Lewin to accompany him, provided he first obtained the approval of the Chittagong authorities.

Mr Young having telegraphed his assent, the two police superintendents started their journey up the Kaladan as the guests of Colonel Phayre in the steamer that was taking him on a tour of the district. He was, as Lewin described him in a letter to his mother, "a kindly gentle old man" — though he was still only in his mid-fifties — and he took more than an official interest in the hill people entrusted to his care. He had already decided to recommend that a superintendent of hill tribes for the Arakan Hill Tracts should be appointed, and having been impressed by Lewin's enthusiasm told him that, if this were sanctioned, he would apply for his services. It was a prospect that greatly appealed to Lewin. He had been learning Burmese for the past six months and liked what he had seen of the land and its people, describing to his mother the great bay at Akyab opening on to the Indian Ocean, the blue hills of the Chin country in the distance, delicious sands, and here and there a feathery coconut tree.

Phayre left them at Daletme a hundred and fifty miles up the river, instructing them to proceed as far as they could into Lakher country and attempt to make friends with the chiefs of the principal tribes, who should be discouraged from raiding on the Akyab and Chittagong frontiers. Having heard from Lewin that Yuong the Kumi chief was holding at least two slaves, a Mrung he had either captured or bought from the Lakhers and a Mru from the Chittagong side, Phayre wanted more information about other British subjects held captive, though at this stage there could be no question of their being ransomed.

A promising start was made when the messengers the old chief Teynwey had sent forward with presents to negotiate a safe passage to the north by chance encountered a small group of Lakhers consisting of Aylong, the second son of the chief of the Zeuhnang which was one of the largest of the tribes, and five companions. With difficulty they were persuaded to come to Daletme, and when Teynwey brought them before Lewin they were at first suspicious and frightened. Gradually he began to win their confidence and after much palaver got them to agree to his party visiting their main village Savang several days' march away, for which concession he had to pay heavily in red cloth, brass vessels and strings of beads.

Next morning, the bargain having been concluded and sealed with the ritual sacrifice of a mithan, the party, now of considerable size, prepared to move off. Besides Lewin and Munro and their personal followers and the six Lakhers there was a train of porters from Teynwey's village carrying their baggage and a small dog belonging to Munro's wife which had come along with them.

On 18 January 1866 they set off in boats and on the second day turned off the river up the Sala Chaung heading in a north-north-easterly direction until they arrived that evening at the Tawn Chaung, where they halted for the night. By now Lewin had made friends with Aylong and his henchman Yichi, who never tired of handling his possessions—his weapons, writing materials, the pipe Bob had given him, and his clothing — and comparing the colour of his skin with that of their own. Next day the party proceeded on foot through dense jungle, finding themselves that evening once more on the bank of the Sala Chaung which in that section of its course forms a great loop. Next day they struck north and after six hours' hard marching were brought up short by the unexpected appearance on the path of three equally startled Lakhers, two of them carrying Tower muskets of George III vintage and with inlaid powder-horns slung across their shoulders, the other a spear. They were not Zeuhnangs, and Aylong in parley with them ascertained that they were the advance guard of some four hundred braves out on the warpath.

Despite Lewin's later accounts it is far from clear

precisely what happened then. Aylong and his followers took their leave, but not before Yichi who was unarmed had borrowed Lewin's sword, a relic of Mutiny days. The porters, having put down their loads, now hoisted them on to their shoulders again and set off back by the way they had come, followed by Teynwey after he had failed to persuade Lewin and Munro to beat a retreat also. Which left the six of them, the two Europeans, Munro's two orderlies, Fazlah — all these well armed — and Toby, brandishing a toasting fork. Possibly by that time some of the main war party had come up, for Lakhers were apparently seen priming their guns with powder from their powder-horns, while "a hideous old grey-bearded Shendu" who had been examining one of the orderlies' guns tried, perhaps not very vigorously, to wrest it away from him. Then, warned by Fazlah that they were being outflanked, Munro gave the order to make ready and, with guns (and toasting fork) levelled, they began to retreat and, coming on denser jungle, ran for cover. Not a round had been fired by either side.

Lewin wrote several lurid accounts of the trials his party suffered during the next forty-eight hours, pursued (as they thought) by hundreds of notoriously savage tribesmen out for their blood; but it seems clear that, had they been minded to do so, the Lakhers could have made short work of them. Instead, coming on their baggage which had been abandoned by the porters, they helped themselves to the items that seemed to them worth carrying off and proceeded on their way to whatever domestic foray they had originally been engaged upon. The fugitives came upon the plundered baggage during their early flounderings, including Munro's medicine chest and Lewin's pipe, violin and diary, but retrieved only some biscuits and a bottle of gin before continuing in what they hoped was the right direction. Mrs Munro's dog had two narrow escapes, first when she growled on hearing a rustling in the bushes, threatening to betray their presence to the enemy, and Lewin had to be restrained from cutting her throat with his kukri, and then near the end of their wanderings when for lack of any other sustenance they contemplated eating her. Or so Lewin later claimed. The truth seems to be that they were not only hopelessly lost, but demoralized. Munro had mislaid his hat during the retreat, so that he suffered much from the blazing sun in the daytime, while all of them shivered with cold during their two nights spent on the hillside. On the second day, more by good luck than good judgment, they stumbled on the Sala Chaung and, following it downstream, came upon some of the boats they had left drawn up on the bank, in which they paddled gratefully back to Teynwey's village and safety.

They reached Akyab on 11 February without further untoward incident to find that, some rumour of disaster having preceded them, an armed search party was on the point of setting out to their rescue. Lewin and his people made a leisurely voyage back to Chittagong by sea in his yacht the *Foam* which he had ordered down, and when he arrived found himself more of a hero than perhaps he deserved. Wild stories had been current about his adventures which, far from discouraging, he did all he could to promote and exaggerate. In his letters home he laid it on thick, telling his family of his wonderful escape from death or bondage, how for a fortnight he had been threatened by death from violence, wild beasts, bodily illness and starvation, how his porters had been slaughtered as they fled, how his party had retreated through a "wilderness literally swarming with tigers and elephants", leeches clinging to them in dozens, nothing to drink for forty-eight hours, living on biscuits and wild plantain. Exhilarated by his own eloquence, he expressed the hope that the "government will give me command of an armed party to go again among the villains and exact from them reparation for all our hardships". He confided to his mother that when at his lowest ebb he had vowed to give £100 to charity as a thank-offering if he came through safely, ending his letter in the rôle of the Prodigal Son he had so lately disparaged: "Rejoice with me my darling — your son was dead & is alive again, he was lost & is found".

Chapter Nine
Enter Rutton Poia

1

For some time Lewin found himself in the unusual position of basking in the sunshine of official approbation. Far from being censured for his escapades among the hill tribes he was personally congratulated by Sir George Campbell the lieutenant-governor of Bengal, who happened to be aboard his luxurious yacht lying off the port of Chittagong. Sir Arthur Phayre wrote to him on behalf of the government of British Burma commending his enterprise. His friend Gordon Young the commissioner of Chittagong, who had sanctioned both his journeys, welcomed him with open arms, and the police department in Calcutta also signified its approval. It was all too good to last. All that was left for Lewin to do was to select which charities should be the beneficiaries of his anonymous thank-offering of £100 for having survived his adventures, and tentatively he decided that the money should be shared between the Lifeboat Society and some organization for rescuing poor girls from the streets.

Once more he settled down to his busy life as police superintendent, his round of duties alleviated by such amenities of civilization as Chittagong afforded. In the evenings after a game of racquets he would play his harmonium or practise Mozart or Beethoven trios and quartets on his 'cello in preparation for the musical evenings that were now held in the bungalow of the district judge Mr Alexander. He was also writing up a journal of his two journeys to be read before the Asiatic Society of Bengal, of which Arthur Grote was the president. Under the title 'Diary of a Hill Trip on the Borders of Arracan' it was printed in the *Proceedings of the Royal Geographical Society* of 10 April 1867. Apart from that he wrote little nowadays, admitting to his mother that poesie was, at least temporarily, a thing of the past. For he now had a guest staying with him whose presence, though in many ways agreeable, was sorely disruptive of the even tenor of his existence.

If he had found his brother Bob something of a handful to manage, their younger brother William proved infinitely more so. After he had run away from the Bruce Castle school at Tottenham and sought refuge with Harry Graves and his wife in Bayswater, an opening had been found for him as a midshipman in the merchant marine, but finding a seafaring life uncongenial he had got himself put ashore after a voyage that had taken his ship no further than Plymouth. When at the age of seventeen his mother was indulgent, or foolish, enough to let him get his hands on a small legacy he had inherited, he briefly set up as a man-about-town, gallivanting about in a trap of his own design which is said to have resembled a glorified milk cart. Having got through his fortune in record time, he agreed to the suggestion that he should go out to India and stay with his eldest brother in Chittagong, with some vague idea of seeing whether the life of a tea planter would be to his liking. It was touch and go whether he got there at all, for his ship ran into a hurricane on the voyage out and nearly foundered.

A good-looking, extrovert young man of nineteen, he soon settled into the life of the station, enjoying such pleasures as it offered, from riding in the local races to flirting at dinners and dances. During musical evenings at the Alexanders, when the quartet had gone through their pieces, Will would entertain the company with comic songs. Though a plucky rider, he had no consideration for his mount and in the space of a few weeks had ridden to death the pony Tom had bought for him, so that he had to get him another. In many ways Will was an overgrown schoolboy, tucking into the greengage jam with a spoon and finishing the pot at a sitting, causing Tom to expostulate in a letter to his mother: "What a boy it is for jam — he has eaten nearly all my store that came out in your last admirably selected box". In other ways he showed a greater maturity, making a set for an unmarried girl who was staying with the Alexanders, twenty-eight if she was a day and a Roman Catholic to boot; though as Tom remarked to his mother: "If she thinks she has a convert, it is something more attractive than holy water that is the bait". And yet Tom, when not exasperated by some misdemeanor or other, thought highly of Will, predicting that he would turn out a good man. Though he had his failings — who is without them?— he considered him for all his roughness of thought and expression better than Bob, because more generous and of a sweeter temper. It was also in Will's favour that Tom thought him wonderfully like their mother in looks, a comparison that made him comment to her: "You must have been a pretty girl, my dear". In fact the two brothers had a great deal in common, with the result that a rivalry grew up between them, a tension that sometimes stretched to breaking point. Tom as the elder brother was determined to keep Will in subjection and often measured strength with him, so that he was soon reporting to their mother that he had beaten him in boxing, riding, swimming, racquets "and everything else". His main weapon, though, was to keep him short of money. After a particularly violent row when he had shown him how dependent on him he was and how helpless, Will gave in, and, as Tom reported, "I made him come and kiss me before night".

It happened that the lieutenant-governor received a full account of Lewin's adventurous journey about the time that news came in of a Lakher raid on a Mrung village only half a day's march from the furthest British police outpost at Chima. It seemed to him clear that the raiders must have crossed over the watershed between the Kaladan and Sangu rivers, so that only by action on the part of the Arakan authorities could they be got at. He therefore requested Arthur Phayre to take such steps as were practicable to effect the punishment of the offenders and the release of the captives they had taken, in which endeavour he would instruct the superintendent of the Chittagong Hill Tracts to co-operate under Phayre's overall direction. Phayre demurred, deprecating any hostile movement in country of which they were at present ignorant, but proposed to appoint his own superintendent of the Arakan Hill Tracts and to establish additional police posts in the hills. The time seemed to the lieutenant-governor opportune for redefining the responsibilities of the Chittagong superintendent so as to invest him with full administrative and police powers and to give him an assistant to be stationed at some convenient and suitable place on the Sangu, more accessible to the hillmen than the sub-divisional magistrate at Cox's Bazaar who currently had jurisdiction, under the superintendent, over the southern part of the tracts.

Such was the background to the announcements that appeared in the *Calcutta Gazette* in March that T.H. Lewin, besides being promoted to a captaincy in the 104th Regiment of Bengal Fusiliers, had been appointed officiating Superintendent of Tribes in the Chittagong Hill Tracts. For this purpose he was transferred to the Bengal Staff Corps, which entitled him to place the initials BSC after his name. He had no intention of resuming military duties, but did not at once give up the idea of a transfer to the Burma service which Phayre had offered him. He thought he could play one off against the other and wrote to the Bengal government asking what they would offer him to stay, a ploy that was soon scotched when the lieutenant-governor indicated that such a transfer would not be sanctioned. By then Lewin had embarked energetically on his new responsibilities which gave him the power of a magistrate in civil cases as well as the duties of revenue officer.

This he knew was his chance to make his name, and from then on there was no more talk of his throwing up the service in 1867 and coming home. In his letters to his mother there was less mention of homesickness and fewer fulsome endearments, though he confided in his aunt Charlotte at this time that he was not yet clear of his mother's apron strings. Nor did he lose his close interest in his family's doings, noting with approval that Bob was sticking to his work at St. Mary's Hospital and had passed some intermediary examination, sending thanks to Bella for the pretty blue smoking-cap she had made him, and asking if aunt Charlotte could send him some account of the Lewin pedigree, of which he was then quite ignorant. Bankes and Harriet had settled down contentedly together and were particularly attentive to Mrs Lewin's wellbeing, several times taking her with them when they took a holiday either on the Continent or in Britain.

In April he heard that his great friend George Johnston had got engaged to Anna Verney, the daughter of the commissioner of Arakan, and later that the marriage had taken place. The news took him aback. She was a sweet girl, and he hoped she would make George a better wife than he deserved, though if he got his deserts he would soon find himself wearing cuckold horns: an indication that in his bachelor days Johnston had not been above a little poodlefaking with other men's wives. He also heard that Harry Graves was now in great trouble, so much so that Lewin asked his mother — who had recently been called upon to pay the doctor's bill for attending Annie's fourth confinement — to give him all spare income from his English investments and, if necessary, to sell out capital and let Harry, dear old fellow, have what he wanted. "God bless me," he added, "what is money compared with the happiness of those we love?"

2

Lewin was given a respite from Will's company on embarking on his new duties, which required him to take up residence in the government bungalow built for the superintendent at Chandragona in the foothills eighty miles up the Karnafuli from Chittagong. So, sending his brother off to stay with a tea planter friend in the hope that he would like the life and decide to settle down as a planter himself, he set off early in April. The bungalow stood on a small hill overlooking the river and backing on to hills that receded tier upon tier into the unexplored. Down the hill was the *cutchery*, or court-house, where he spent much of his day and the treasury under police guard. Further down were a few open-fronted shops that constituted the bazaar and the police lines housing fifty men whose duties alternated between guard duties at Chandragona and manning the three outposts sited at strategic points in the hills to discourage raiding by the independent tribes beyond British jurisdiction.

He soon fell into the pattern of a regular routine which he described in a letter to his mother.

> Now I have just done breakfast 9 a.m. & sit down to write to you a line before rushing to Kutchery where I have to try two suits for rent, one disputed inheritance, one enticing away a married woman. Afterwards drill & inspection of a bridge I am building & boats I am making. Go down and see my elephants, walk through the bazaar, hear complaints, then at dusk home up my hill dead tired. Wake in morning. One hour violoncello — half hour official letters (reading), 1 hour replying to — then breakfast — & Kutchery. So goes the round.

The climate was generally healthier than in the plains, but when the crisp cold weather gave place to hot days the perspiration dripped off him and there were nights when there was not a breath of air and the mosquitoes were a torment. The real test came with the rains when fungi appeared on his boots, mould on his bookcase, and his 'cello began to start at the seams from the damp. For days on end the bungalow was shrouded in mist and rain so that he could not see the ground under his feet and blinked, as he told his mother, like an owl in the desert. At this season he felt languid and easily became exhausted, abscesses formed on his gunshot wounds, ringworm affected his arms and legs, and he began to suffer from piles. Now more than ever he became aware of being a loveless exile, and looking into the mirror saw a sallow, wrinkled face and hair that was three parts grey. At this time he started to keep a diary again, his last one having been lost among the rascally Shendus, treating it as an outlet for thought for want of someone to speak to in the solitudes of Chandragona.

He was now lord and master over a tract of country as big as two English counties, which had hitherto been subdivided among the three chiefs — the Bohmong, the Kalindi rani and the Mong rajah — who had ruled with an iron rod, keeping all power, profit and information in their own hands, determined to oppose all orders of government that encroached on their prerogatives. Lewin saw as his first and paramount task the need to crush and extinguish the influence of these chiefs. The system of land tenure and revenue settlement, whereby the collection of an obnoxious poll-tax was farmed out to the chiefs, must also be abolished and replaced by something more in line with the wishes of the people. Something needed urgently to be done to curtail the activities of the *muktears* who made large sums out of encouraging litigation, and to place restrictions on the Bengali *mahajuns* who lent money at exorbitant interest, whereby in either case the gullible hill people were reduced to debtor-slavery for life. The people needed to be educated in order to be able to protect themselves in a world whose wickedness as yet they could not comprehend, and this meant founding schools. A missionary was needed, preferably a young unmarried man, to teach them the rudiments of the Christian religion, for though many were nominally Buddhists, they still adhered to their primitive animist belief in evil spirits inhabiting all natural phenomena which had to be placated by animal sacrifices.

The frontier force, too, needed reorganizing, since existing arrangements for the defence of the settled hills against attack from the Lakhers in the south and the Lushais in the north seemed to him inadequate.

As if in corroboration of this, in July a report came in of a Lushai raid on three Banjogi villages under the Bohmong rajah's jurisdiction ten hours' march from Bandarban, in which four people had been killed and eighty men and women carried off, their houses having been set fire to before the marauders decamped. It was rumoured that the raid had been instigated by the rajah himself in order to punish the villages for some offence against him, and Lewin at once sent to Rothangpuia to learn the truth of the matter. Since Captain Raban had destroyed his village in 1861 this Thangluah chief had sought to keep on the right side of the British authorities by acting as an informer against his neighbours, for which he was handsomely rewarded. Having felt the heavy hand of British power, he was better placed than the chiefs of the more distant clans to realize the folly of provoking an armed contest with them, but his position was rendered delicate by the fact that he was related by marriage to certain chiefs of more warlike tribes numerically far stronger than his own.

Photographs of Rothangpuia show a square, doggy face with heavy-lidded eyes and, unusually for a Lushai, a moustache. A white cloth is wrapped round his head to form an untidy turban, and a hand-woven cloak with a chequered pattern covers his body like a toga. He wears a chunky necklace and grasps a double-barrelled shotgun. A few anecdotes concerning his earlier exploits have been preserved. A story was told of how he tricked the Sailo chief Savunga with whom he had been at war. They had decided to take the *sa-ui tan* oath in order to ratify the cessation of hostilities between them, and since Savunga had a body of armed men with him, Rothangpuia persuaded him to cross the river that separated them to his own side, bringing only twenty men with him in the ferry. As soon as they had landed Rothangpuia ordered the ferry-rope to be cut, effectively making them his prisoners. The sacrificial dog had then been killed and its heart and liver removed and placed ready for eating. With pretended courtesy Rothangpuia invited Savunga as his guest to be the first to partake and when he had done so walked away without eating any himself, remarking: "Since you who are the older have eaten, it is as if we had both done so," thus tricking Savunga into taking a solemn oath while evading it himself.

Another story was told of him by a member of Lewin's household called Ramoni, who had once been a slave of Rothangpuia and used to accompany him on raiding expeditions as his weapon-bearer. On the first occasion they had attacked a Bengali village:

> They fell upon the villagers at day-dawn according to custom [Lewin wrote]; and the Bengallee men with one consent ran away. The women however stood their ground and abused their grim assailants vociferously for breaking into honest people's houses. The Lhoosai laughed at their shrill tongues at first, but later it was

found troublesome, and one young woman had to be cut down *pour encourager les autres*. The chief confided to my boy's care two women captives. All the prisoners were fastened together by a cord through the lobe of the ears, and the Lhoosai set out with their plunder on the return journey. Now, one of the captive women was young and not accustomed to walking, so after the first day's march her feet swelled, and she was unable to go further. The chief therefore ordered that she should be speared. "Well," said the narrator, "I took the spear and went towards her, and Rutton Poia said, 'Do it neatly, I will look on,' for it was the first time I had ever speared anyone. When the girl saw me take the spear and come towards her, she fell a-weeping and caught my garments and my hands, and all my heart thumped, and I could not hurt her. It was pitiful! So the chief began to laugh at me and said, 'O white-livered and son of a female dog, when we return to the village I will tell the young maidens of your courage'; so I shut my eyes and speared her. My stroke was ill-directed, and she did not die; so the chief finished the work, and he made me lick the spear. The blood of Bengallees is very salt. Since then I have not been afraid to spear anyone."

Now Lewin's messenger returned from Rothangpuia's village with the information that the recent raid on the Banjogi villages had been carried out by men of the Haolong clan, one of whose chiefs happened to be Rothangpuia's brother-in-law. At once Lewin set off in pursuit with a detachment of police, sending his assistant Lieutenant Scott by another route to try and cut off the raiders' retreat, but they failed to catch up with them. Against regulations Will had managed to attach himself to Scott's party and so much enjoyed his brief taste of action that for a while he contemplated joining the Indian police; but as usual his enthusiasm waned. Nor did he fancy the prospect of spending his life on a tea garden, and since his brother was now so often absent from Chittagong leaving him to his own devices, he made up his mind to return home and left early in August. Looking back on his visit Lewin could not help fearing that Will would somehow come to grief on his way through the world, a premonition that was to be terribly fulfilled under circumstances he could not then have imagined.

At the end of September on a visit to a Chakma village not far from the advanced police post at Kasalong, a day's journey up the Karnafuli from Chandragona, Lewin met some messengers sent to him by Rothangpuia, who wanted to assure him that his people had not been concerned in the recent raiding and that he wished to maintain his present friendly relations with the British. This was the opportunity for which Lewin had been waiting, and he put it to the envoys that such a weighty matter could only be settled by himself and the chief meeting face to face. They were emphatic that it would be impossible for Rothangpuia to come to Kasalong for the purpose, but after some demur agreed that Lewin could call upon the chief in his village. The Chakma headman earnestly tried to dissuade him from such a hazardous undertaking, assuring him that Rothangpuia was as untrustworthy as ever, but Lewin was not to be deterred.

With Jemadar Fazlah and twenty picked men he set off next morning up the river. They manhandled their boats past the Barkal rapids and paddled on through smooth water until they reached the falls at Utanchatra, where they camped for the night on the river bank. Next morning, leaving their boats under guard, they followed a jungle path into the hills, guided by Lushais from Rothangpuia's village who had gone overland the previous day, and started to climb. In a rocky defile near the summit of a ridge they stopped to parley with two Lushai scouts armed with old firelocks, who had been posted on a rock overlooking the path. At the top of the ascent they found awaiting them a crowd of forty or fifty Lushais armed with guns or spears, who stood observing them without friendliness while the guides went ahead to inform the chief of their arrival.

When the guides returned they informed Lewin that the chief would receive him on the morrow, but that he must leave his escort behind for fear of alarming the women and children. So, accompanied only by Fazlah and his hill boy Adupah to act as interpreter, he followed them along a stockaded passage, through a gateway of rough-hewn timber and into the straggling village, while the armed Lushais crowded round them. The chief's house was the largest in the village, a barn-like structure a hundred and fifty feet long by forty broad, with a platform in front raised four feet from the ground over which the roof gable projected. Lines of animal skulls among which Lewin identified mithan, deer and pig adorned the entrance. It was reassuring that the village was thronged with women, stout-legged and not uncomely, dressed in brief skirts with the upper parts of their bodies decently covered, and their children — those under ten being without distinction of sex stark naked — all peering unselfconsciously at the strange phenomenon of a white man among them; for if mischief had been intended they would have been sent away.

In the one-roomed guest house to which they were directed they made the best they could of the meal of pork and rice garnished with capsicums that was sent in to them; and Lewin and Fazlah spent the night keeping watch and sleeping, turn and turn about. At sunrise messengers arrived to say that Rothangpuia was ready to receive him and led the three of them across to his house. Entering by a low door they found themselves in a long room with numbers of men squatting along each wall with a line of earthenware pots before them, at each of which two drinkers sat sucking up rice beer through wooden tubes. An open fire burned in the centre of the room, sending up its smoke to escape through a hole in the roof. In a recess at the end of the room under a window-hole overlooking the hills sat the chief, a dark, athletic man with a melancholy expression and large stern eyes. Neither he nor the *upas*, or elders, with him gave any sign of greeting, but when Lewin and his companions were seated on a mat the chief gave a grunt which signified the opening of the parley. Asked why he had brought an armed party to the village, Lewin replied that his men were armed to defend themselves against the dangers of the road. He then indicated the bale containing the presents he had brought for the chief, which was opened to disclose scarlet cloths, cotton sheeting, beads, looking glasses and other items; but still the chief looked on impassively.

"I am glad to hear," began Lewin, "that Rothangpuia disclaims all participation in the recent outrages." No reply. "I have come in consequence to confirm the friendship between us." At this point brass cups containing fiery and evil-smelling rice spirit were handed round. "The prevention of such occurrences is my duty," Lewin continued, "and that we can punish our enemies if necessary Rothangpuia has reason to know."

The Lushais' taciturnity was broken by a big fellow called Vanhlula, who got up and delivered a prepared speech which proved to be the prelude to a general confabulation that lasted until four in the afternoon, by which time the most solemn oaths of friendship had been exchanged, ratified and sealed by the consumption of large quantities of rice beer. And though he could not then have known it, in Rothangpuia Lewin had made a firm friend to whom in the years to come he was to owe a great deal.

The commissioner Mr Young was insistent that Lewin should leave his lonely isolation once a week and come to Chittagong so that he could relax and take part in the musical evenings at the Alexanders', returning to Chandragona on Sunday. On one of these visits he discussed his proposed reforms with the commissioner, who arranged for him to go to Calcutta in November and put his case before the Bengal government. As is evident from the report of his interviews given in a letter to his mother, he did so with more force than tact.

> Its a mercy that I was not turned out of my appointment for they do not like plain speaking in Calcutta & I was very plain spoken indeed. The Lieut Govr. Sir Cecil Beaden said that he was not accustomed to have young men speak to him in that way and I daresay I was wrong but I was wrought up to a pitch of excitement about the neglectful way in which they were treating my Hill Tribes & I spoke out let the consequences be what they may. Mr. Young was very good — he was called down there too & he said that the Govt. would not get another officer so well fitted as I am for the Hills & that he himself was in everything satisfied with me. The upshot of all was that I got everything I asked for[:] men, money, roads, schools, bridges & almost unlimited powers — they conceded all save one thing — they would not hear of a hostile expedition this cold weather against those brutes of Shendoos.

He got what he wanted, but managed to tread on some exalted toes in the process.

In Calcutta he stayed at the United Service Club and was invited to tiffin one day with the Grotes to meet a party of scientific men, to whom he showed specimens of the cloth manufacture of "my people" and vocabularies and phraseologies of the hill dialects. All of which seems to have gone to his head, for he described himself to his mother as "the old Tom Lewin, bright and quick, merry and talkative, going about calling and talking to pretty women to an extent that astonishes me". One of the pretty women was George Johnston's new wife Anna, and he saw a good deal of the couple before he returned to Chandragona.

He had by now been confirmed in his appointment with the title Deputy Commissioner of the Hill Tracts of Chittagong, which gave him personal control over his huge territory. In Lieutenant Scott he had an assistant responsible under him for the country watered by the Sangu and Matamori rivers; and the deputy magistrate at Cox's Bazaar acted as his *ex officio* assistant for the area west and south of the Matamori. Under him also was an assistant superintendent of police commanding a force nearly four hundred strong, mostly hillmen. And from now on a new note was sounded in his letters home. "I am King in everything save in name," he wrote to his mother, and to Jeannie that he was as nearly as possible absolute king over thousands, his influence over them increasing daily. One thing, he told her, was becoming daily more attractive to him — power; it was almost growing into a passion, and he revelled in the almost unrestricted freedom of action he now possessed. His assumption of the posture of royalty reached its zenith a year later when he gave as his reason for planning, if possible, to take his privilege leave in Ava — that is, in independent Burma — that "I want to see the King of Burmah or his people on the subject of some of the Burmese Hill Tribes who border on my frontier". Meanwhile he was not left in undisputed possession of his kingdom.

Of the three paramount chiefs, he had established friendly relations with only one, the Mong rajah, whose name he spelt phonetically as Keo-ja-syne, living in the north at Maniksari. The other two opposed by fair means or foul every move he made in introducing any of his reforms which encroached upon their vested prerogatives, expecting him like his predecessors to be content to remain a largely decorative representative of the British *raj*. In their intransigence they were supported not only by the Bengali pleaders and attorneys and their clerks and hangers-on whose living he threatened, but also, tacitly, by the Bengal government itself whose overriding wish was for peace and economy regardless of the wellbeing of the people. First the two unfriendly chiefs tried the tactic of appealing against Lewin's court decisions, but when they found that these were for the most part upheld they put in complaints about his maladmistration to the commissioner. On Lewin being exonerated, they resorted to the expedient of presenting petitions to the government full of what he described as vile calumnies detailed with fiendish circumstantiality, in which a little truth was so cunningly mixed with a great deal of falsehood that Lewin was bound to demean himself by refuting them.

It became apparent to him that whoever was responsible for drafting the petitions was in possession of inside information, and it came to his ears how this had come about. The old Bohmong rajah who lived at Bandarban on the Sangu in the south of his district had suborned a police havildar stationed there, a hillman, not only to keep him advised of Lewin's movements, but also to intercept official correspondence and pass it on to the rajah for perusal before being sent on its way. Lewin laid his plans accordingly and one night, taking with him Fazlah and four armed policemen, secretly crossed the river by boat, made the long march to a point on the Sangu opposite Bandarban, swam across and at sunrise broke into the rajah's house. Caught red-handed with opened official letters in his possession, he was threatened with prosecution and, to avoid a prison sentence, consented to resign in favour of his brother Mom Phru, who became a loyal friend to Lewin.

The Kalindi rani, the old widow who ruled over the Chakmas in the central sector of the hill tracts, was less easily dealt with. She had earned favour in British eyes in 1857 when she had delivered up a number of sepoys belonging to the native regiment stationed at Chittagong who had mutinied and taken to the hills; since when she had proved a thorn in the side of government. Undeterred by the failure of the anonymous petitions she had instigated, she persisted in her campaign against Lewin and sent her grandson to Calcutta with a sum of money to be spent in trying to get him turned out of his appointment. "I do not know that I ever 'sowed the wind'," Lewin reflected ruefully, "but I appear to be 'reaping the whirlwind' just at present." Rothangpuia hearing of his troubles sent him a message from the Lushai chiefs inviting him to settle in their country and become one of themselves, an invitation he had to decline, though the idea appealed to him. Not long afterwards, as he was sleeping one night in his bungalow he was awoken by intruders whom he sent packing with a shot from his revolver, and he always suspected that they had been assassins sent by the rani to kill him. For a while a sentry stood guard at night on his veranda, but soon he came to rely for protection on a small statuette of Buddha given him by the Mong rajah, which he set up on a pedestal in his bedroom.

His household now consisted entirely of hill people. Although his Indian bearer who had been with him for three years left him soon after the move to Chandragona, saying he could no longer live among savages, Nurudin whom he had hired in Chittagong in an inferior capacity remained loyal to him. For the rest, there was Toby of the toasting fork, once a scullion at Government House in Calcutta, who still had charge of the kitchen; a son of the Mong rajah called Mong Yeh (sometimes Narabadi) and a little Magh boy called Khapowkee, both of whom he had agreed to educate; his interpreter Ramoni, the former slave of Rothangpuia; a youth with the suggestive name Sonarutton whom he was training to be his new bearer; Adupah a debtor-slave who had been given him as a present by the Mong rajah; someone called Morotu, and a little lad of nine who had somehow managed to attach himself to Lewin as a dependant.

Such a polyglot staff greatly facilitated his study of the various languages spoken in the hills. The most generally understood was a dialect of Burmese, of which he now had a fair knowledge, enough to justify his getting rid of the Bengalis employed as court *babus* and replacing them with Burmese recruited in Akyab. He had also made good progress with the *patois* of the Chakmas, which had a substantial admixture of Bengali words, a language in which he was already fluent. The dialects spoken by the Tipperas and the Lushais he found more difficult to master, but persevered in procuring materials for a grammar and dictionary of their two tongues, which had not previously been committed to writing. This left him little time for private reading, but he sent home for another copy of Shakespeare to replace the one he had lost during his brush with the Shendus and also for Plutarch's *Lives*. Since the hill people were great music lovers, his household will have appreciated his playing on the harmonium or 'cello, gathering round while he tried out the new sheet music his mother had sent him: 'Love's Request', 'Maid of Athens', 'The Village Blacksmith' and 'If Doughty Deeds my Lady Please'.

Even at the height of the rains he was frequently on the

move, travelling by boat wherever the rivers and streams allowed, otherwise barefoot along the hill paths, for which his feet soon became hardened, visiting remote villages, vainly chasing raiders, calling on the rajahs. At Akyab where he recruited the new clerks he stayed with Captain Munro and his young wife, having to settle a joint policy between himself and the Arakan authorities as to their future relations with the hill tribes on their respective frontiers. There he renewed his acquaintance with the little dog who had nearly met an untimely end in the course of their adventures together. And every weekend when in residence at Chandragona he would go down the river to Chittagong for a taste of civilization.

Although he found his life among the hill people of absorbing interest, assured that they had become attached to him after their fashion, he often felt lonely and depressed. He was, he wrote, among them, not of them; he could gain their respect, fear, admiration, even confidence, but their love — never. He found himself envying his bearer boy's easy relationship with the hill girls and confided to his diary what the feeling was that, in the intervals between work, swallowed up every other thought. It was not lust, for that could be satiated, but the want of someone to love, some human sympathy, something kin; a need that cried out within him with a bitter cry, making his food savourless, robbing his body of spring and elasticity. He had no difficulty in fraternizing with his people, but they were after all savages, so that even he with his loose code shrank somewhat from contact with them. "You cannot love without talking," he wrote, and with them the sort of unreserved talk he had in mind was impossible. Something of the strain under which he laboured is revealed in the accounts he gave to his mother of two dreams he had about her, the first during a journey to the Lushai country:

> I dreamt last night I was in a Hansom — coming to you & I woke in my swing cot far in the jungles with the cry of a barking deer harshly breaking the night silence.

The second occurred a few months later:

> I had a bad dream the other night that we were at a theatre together & there was a panic & I lost you. In my dream I was a small boy & I woke crying oh so bitterly & with such a terrible feeling of horror & loneliness. It was some time before I fully realised that it was only a dream & that I was a middle aged man far away from home alone among a people such as you have never even dreamt of and not having spoken English for days & days.

Chapter Ten
The Johnston Affair

1

In March 1867 Lewin returned to Chandragona after an exhausting three-week trip to the Bohmong rajah's territory in vain pursuit of Lushai marauders — marching on foot through wild jungle, creeping on all fours beneath a dense tangle of underwood, splashing waist-deep along streambeds, plopping through a morass, toiling wearily and breathlessly up mountains — to find that in his absence he had been honoured by a visit from the deputy inspector-general of police Captain Bowie, who had been deputed to overhaul his office and report on his administration generally. Bowie, who had stayed in his bungalow, had carried out his investigation and departed before Lewin got back.

It seemed an unusual proceeding, since he had been given no prior warning of the visit as was customary, but he was not unduly worried, being confident that his affairs were in order. Shortly afterwards he was distressed and puzzled to receive from his friend George Johnston in Calcutta a short note saying that Lewin's carelessness had been the cause of his ruin and bidding him fare as well as he could with that burden on his conscience. The following day a telegram arrived with the shattering news that Johnston was dead; and soon the whole squalid story emerged.

It had been Johnston's practice ever since he had become the personal assistant to the inspector-general of police to leak to Lewin such of the confidential information that came his way as he thought might be of interest to him. In this way two years earlier, before Lewin's appointment as officiating hill superintendent had come through, he had sounded him out whether he would be interested in the superintendentship of the Calcutta suburb known as the 24 Parganahs, which by bringing him under the eye of government would be likely to advance his career. It became Lewin's custom to write to Johnston "asking privately for information, advice and assistance in moving the springs of official power which," as he explained to Jeannie, "must be influenced before anything material is effected in this country; and he moved by his love for me gave me all I asked for". During Lewin's recent absence from his headquarters Johnston had sent him a personal letter, warning him that a certain person high in government employ with a grudge against him was being sent to make an official investigation into his doings and telling him how to thwart the danger. Bowie, the officer deputed by the inspector-general Colonel Pughe to carry out the task, had done his work thoroughly, but had found nothing to justify an unfavourable report until, probably due to treachery on the part of one of the remaining Bengali *babus* in Lewin's office, he came upon Johnston's letter.

Having read it, he forwarded it to Colonel Pughe, telling him he had come across it by chance amongst Lewin's office papers.

Confronted by the evidence of his having used his official position to benefit a friend, Johnston had no choice but to admit his guilt. He acquiesced in Colonel Pughe's suggestion that he should hand in his resignation in order to avoid a public scandal and should revert to a district, but remain in his quarters over the office until notice could be published in the *Gazette* that he was proceeding on leave. Having scribbled his note to Lewin and, on the plea of not feeling well, sent his wife Anna off alone in a carriage to a ball at Belvedere, he read for a while, then retired to bed. There, putting an open bottle of liquid chloroform in his sponge-bag, he fixed it over his mouth and nose, which soon induced uncon-sciousness. Anna returning home about one in the morning found him insensible, and her cries for help brought Colonel Pughe, who had also just returned from the ball. Although he at once summoned medical assistance, it was to no avail, for by the time the doctor arrived Johnston was dead.

Lewin was distraught. Bowie's malevolence, as it seemed to him, stemmed from a practical joke he and Johnston had played on him concerning some love affair of which they had been cognizant, and Pughe's unrelenting attitude from a wish to have Lewin turned out of his appointment because he was young, rash and inexperienced. At once he wrote to the inspector-general taking all the blame on his own shoulders for having instigated the correspondence, and in a wild, grief-stricken letter to his cousin — "Jeannie my sister, I am unhinged and all abroad", it began — he accused himself of being Johnston's murderer. Writing slantwise on the middle spread of the notepaper he brooded on their friendship, calling Johnston his one friend who had been more to him than his own brothers, describing him as a nervous and sensitive man, cleverer than he and physically very brave, and breaking out in a heart-rending cry that echoed David's lament for Absalom: "Poor George — my own dear boy — would God that I had died for thee oh George my brother ... As for that man Bowie, if I can take his life I will. May God have mercy on him for I will not if I am damned for it". So great was the shock of the tragedy that he was brought to the verge of a nervous breakdown, and but for the kindness and care of Mr Young in Chittagong, who took him into his own house and nursed him back to a calmer state of mind, he thought later that he might not have pulled through.

But Lewin was not one to let matters rest. He wrote a letter, charging Bowie with "conduct unbecoming", to the lieutenant-governor of Bengal who understandably returned it to him, declining to interfere and advising him to make no scandal in the matter. Undeterred, having consulted Johnston's friends, he referred the case to the adjutant-general for consideration by the commander-in-chief, demanding that Bowie be court-martialled. The months dragged on, and he heard nothing about "that murderer Bowie"; a complete official silence had descended on the case. December came, and Mr Young was sent home dangerously ill, and there was still no news; the matter (he was told) was receiving attention; and all the time it rankled with him that he could not get at his enemy. In January he was informed that the commander-in-chief had communicated his views to the government, to the effect that there was insufficient evidence to justify the convening of a court-martial. Somehow Lewin persuaded himself that this was proof of Bowie's guilt and wanted to send copies of the commander-in-chief's communication to all military clubs, after which he would "search out the Viper and give him a good kicking". Fifteen months after Johnston had committed suicide Lewin reported to his mother "No news of the beast Bowie", and gradually his fury abated; for by then other worries had assailed him, not least the failure of the Bank of Hindostan which was likely to cost him £1,000 of his savings with the consequent depression in value of the tea shares in which he had invested considerable sums as risk capital.

No official action was ever taken against Bowie, and Lewin had to rest content with the knowledge that his conduct was condemned by all who knew about it. Johnston's widow, he heard, had gone to stay with her in-laws in Ireland. For his own part, the tragedy not only left a scar that never healed, but in the official memory earned him another black mark to put beside the one he had earned over the Ellis affair.

2

Slowly he managed to pull himself together and pick up the reins once more, and there was still plenty to be done if he was to complete the work he had started. His overriding objective was to promote the welfare of his people, to achieve which he directed his efforts towards eliminating all trace of the Bengali element from among them by strengthening their awareness of their own identity. He would do everything in his power to keep them safe and simple as they were. He now knew beyond question that he had found the work God had sent him into the world to do, and that with His help he could do great good for the people. "This work is for me," he wrote, "& I for the work."

Mr Young had been replaced as commissioner by Lord Ulick Browne, whom at first Lewin didn't quite like, finding him very stiff in his manner, but his strictures were just and well-intended. When he pointed out that Lewin was acting irregularly in writing of the Kalindi rani in an official report, "she is an old woman of 60 with all the weakness & foibles of her sex aggravated — she is in the hands of an unscrupulous clique of Bengallee *omlah* etc. etc.", Lewin had retorted:

"Well, but it is all true."

"Yes," replied Browne, "it may be true, but we don't always speak so plainly in official correspondence. It may injure you with government."

After Lewin had been called upon to comment on yet

another anonymous accusation, this time "of the falsest and grossest nature", he felt bound to call for an official enquiry to clear himself, and Browne was appointed to look into it. His report not only exonerated him, but also commended him for his good work, though Browne warned him privately that he thought the government might reprimand him for sometimes acting contrary to the regulations. He was promoted from 4th to 3rd grade deputy commissioner, given a second European assistant, permitted to recruit Gurkhas for his frontier force, and sent nine more elephants to help with his various civil engineering works. He still did not see eye to eye with the government on the official policy of paying what he called blackmail to the chiefs as an inducement to keep the peace; nor could he persuade them that the only way to put an end to Lushai raiding was to send a military expedition against them in order to convince them of the reality of British power. Meanwhile by kicking up an enormous dust and making himself (in his own words) a stinkpot and an abomination in the nostrils of the Calcutta officials he had got almost all he wanted.

Indeed, his achievements were already considerable. He had reorganized his frontier force, which he now considered fit for what was required of it. He had set on foot a comprehensive scheme for the resettlement of the revenue system throughout the hill tracts. Schools had been opened and a Christian mission established. Each cold weather he embarked on an extensive tour of his district visiting the remotest villages and becoming a familiar and friendly figure to the people, by whom he was now widely known as Thangliena. The annual winter gathering of the chiefs up the river at Kasalong, when they received their allowances for good behaviour, had become a more serious event than the long saturnalia of drinking it had previously been. Presided over by the commissioner who sat in state as the representative of the British *raj*, it provided the occasion for creating a measure of trust and co-operation between the tribes and the paramount power. As a further step towards increasing his influence Lewin was granted permission to move his headquarters forty-nine miles further up the Karnafuli to Rangamati and to push forward the line of police posts nearer to "Kookiedom". For the threat posed by the untamed Lushais was never far from his mind.

He sent word to the Panko, Mru and Banjogi villages within a radius of twenty miles that he required them to build him a house there, in response to which a workforce of 300 hillmen assembled and within a week had constructed him a substantial house of bamboo fastened on to posts consisting of untrimmed timber and with a floor of saplings laid lengthwise. It was sited overlooking a bend of the river with extensive views of the hills all round, and he named it the Barn House after aunt Charlotte's house at Eltham. Seeing himself in the rôle of chieftain, he caused half an acre of ground near the house to be cleared of trees and undergrowth to form his personal *jhum*, which with the first rains he had sown with grain, cucumbers, melons and cotton; though in the first year for lack of attention the crows and wild hogs got more out of it than he did.

The police barracks, *cutchery*, treasury and bazaar were transferred from Chandragona to the new site, so that soon Rangamati became a flourishing little hill township boasting both a school and a mission house. And the people flocked to him, treating him not as a foreign ruler but as a family friend. They would gather uninvited to sit by his fireside of an evening, men, women and children, while he — wearing a smoking cap one or other of his sisters had made for him and puffing his new meerschaum pipe — would quietly revel in the new world to which he had been given access.

What he particularly admired in his people was the manliness of the menfolk for whom to lie was a disgrace; the truth between husband and wife; and the modesty of the women — though before marriage, as he explained to his mother, their ideas of morality were very loose, as with some English country folk, citing the "bundling" courtship practised in Wales. When he visited them in their villages he found their houses clean, their homespun clothing unverminous, and deplored only their habit of eating carrion and the flesh of pigs which were the village scavengers. He felt that he was beginning to gain entrance to their inner life, breaking down the barriers which difference of race and colour usually raise. More and more he became aware of the attractiveness of the girls. In April 1867 he had written to aunt Grote: "You need have no fear of my becoming enslaved by the daughters of the land", adding "although there are pretty girls here as in every other part of God's earth". A year later, after confessing that he was now grown wild and jungly so that the ties binding him to England were growing looser, he reverted to the subject, telling Jeannie:

> The only objectionable thing is that they all bother me to get married — of course meaning me to marry a hill girl; but I cannot do it, not on account of the girls for some of them are very comely, but somehow — well I don't know how but I shrink from it — I have never had any such connection since I came out & it's over late in the day to begin now.

To his mother he no longer referred to his "passionate nature", only telling her not to talk moonshine about his marrying an English girl for her money, which he thought not very probable; though if he did marry, any wife of his must live with him wherever he went, however wild and savage. Anyway, he told her, he had got over his desires for English women, all but his darling mother who was all the world to him.

It was now over six years since he had returned from his first home leave, and new regulations had come in which would soon allow him to take a year's leave on half pay. An earlier attempt to get leave on the ground of ill-health had been frustrated by Dr Duncan in Chittagong who, after giving him a thorough medical checkup, had sent him away with the words, "Go along with you — you'll never get a sick certificate — I wish I were half as well as you are". All the same, he felt worn out. He longed to see his mother again, and both Bob and Will had reached turning-points in their careers. Bob had just sat for the examination for his MD, while Will was an apprentice to an engineering firm in Oxford Street. Lewin also had his own small money affairs to attend to, having recently sold his share in The Hollies estate to uncle Frederick, since there seemed no chance of his ever being able to acquire the entire property himself. Besides, his uncle was now the head of the Lewin family, and Lewin was a firm believer in the law of primogeniture. Accordingly he booked his passage from Bombay, hoping to be home sometime in March 1869. He asked that Bob, who had finally obtained his diploma as MRCS, should check that he was still a member of the East India United Service Club in St. James's Square, and his mother to look round for somewhere for him to live during his leave, preferably at Sydenham so as to be close to the Crystal Palace for the sake of the music, the library and the gardens. He wanted to be near her but not to live at home, having become fond of solitude.

Before leaving he finished his book on the hill tribes, their manners, customs and traditions, and sent it off to Calcutta for publication under government auspices, hoping to arrange for an English edition which he proposed to dedicate to aunt Grote. He thought it might earn him some laurels and send him off on leave with a flourish of trumpets. In writing *The Hill Tracts of Chittagong and the Dwellers Therein* as in other aspects of his work in the hills Lewin was blazing a trail that others would follow, the book being the forerunner of other monographs written by later administrators concerning the way of life and customs of tribes living on the north-east frontier of India. For someone with no special training in anthropology or linguistics it was by any standard a remarkable performance, especially bearing in mind the extraordinary medley of tribes inhabiting the tangle of country he was concerned with. In order to make the subject manageable he divided the tribes, more for the sake of convenience than on a strictly scientific basis, into those inhabiting the river valleys, whom he termed the "Khyoungtha" meaning in Arakanese children of the river, and the more remote tribes who built their villages on the tops of hills, whom he termed the "Toungtha" meaning children of the hills. In the former category he classed the Maghs and the Chakmas, in the latter the wilder tribes living in the remote hills such as the Mrungs, Kumis, Mrus, Khyens, Banjogis and Pankhos. With the Toungtha he included the Lushais whose territory extended far to the north and east, knowledge of whom was then confined to the tribes living near the frontier, and the Lakhers inhabiting the country north-east and east of the Blue Mountain, of whom even less was known.

In his book Lewin not only recorded all he had been able to find out about these tribes — their ways of life, methods of building and cultivation, the clothes and ornaments they favoured, their beliefs and religious practices, the status of their women, their courtship, marriage and funeral customs — but also enlivened his pages with colourful vignettes of such scenes as the *pwe* he had watched at Cox's Bazaar, religious ceremonies at the village *kyaungs*, marriage celebrations he had attended and other personal experiences. In a concluding chapter he expressed in strong terms his views on how their country ought to be administered. There was much about the hill people, he wrote, that was loveable; they were simple, honest and merry, though whole areas of the mind were closed to them. The idea that they were well enough as they were was seductive, for inevitably the introduction of "civilization" by means of European energy would bring in its train a crowd of evils. The motive power of civilization was the desire for superfluous wealth, for the delicacies and luxuries of life, and for these the hill folk felt no need; their nomadic way of life precluded any great accumulation of wealth, and they enjoyed perfect social equality. Civilization, he asserted, would not make them happy nor improve them, but would exterminate them. Certainly they lacked some of the refinements of civilization: for them marriage was no more than a convenient connection for procreating their species and getting their dinner cooked. They did not revere women as the weaker sex, but imposed on them as much as they could, but at the same time their women, unlike their Indian sisters, lived open lives, pure and simple, honoured as wives and mothers, trusted, and their advice listened to. In them nudity aroused no extraordinary emotion: to the pure all things are pure.

[The tribes] have until lately been totally neglected, and yet a word of kindness, one sympathizing expression, and their hearts are open to you. My great and distinctive feeling with them has been that they were my fellow-creatures, men and women like myself: with the Bengallee I have never been in accord.

In India could be seen the strange spectacle of the British, though wishful to do good to their subjects, yet powerless when the interests of trade were supposed to be in danger. "When it is a question of the people's benefit or an increased or diminished sale of Manchester cottons, piff! paff! the people are nowhere." His final plea was that at least in the hills the British should govern, not for themselves, but for the wellbeing and happiness of the people, a philosophy unlikely to enhance his standing with those who had power to make decisions in Calcutta.

The commissioner, now a warm supporter of his, looked forward to his return from leave when he could complete the work he had started, and the lieutenant-governor in his annual report so far relented as to attribute the district's immunity from raids, which had occurred elsewhere in the hills, to the great personal exertions of the deputy commissioner, acknowledging his personal devotion to the district committed to his care and congratulating him on the general success of his administration. His hill people were dismayed when they learnt he was leaving them, fearing they would once again become a prey to the Kukis on the one hand and the Bengalis on the other. The women wept and the men

clung to his feet, begging him not to go. In vain he tried
to reassure them, promising them that he would return
and live the rest of his life among them, though to himself
he added: Heaven forgive me.

Chapter Eleven
'Edgar's Peculiar'

1

From his headquarters in Rangamati Lewin had so far only succeeded in making contact with the Lushai chiefs whose villages lay at the southern limit of the territory they inhabited. The more powerful clans lived in the remoter hills to the north and north-east and for many years had terrorized the plains-dwellers of Cachar and Sylhet, to whom they were known by the vague and menacing name of Kookies. Very little was known about them, and when some atrocity occurred it was often difficult to fix the responsibility on its true perpetrators, even had it been possible to get at them, because their names, mispronounced and misspelt in the reports, meant little or nothing to those in authority. An overworked official could hardly be expected to know that the names Murchailo, Murchoi Looee and Mischoee Lall were all attempts to indicate a chief whose real name was Ngursailova. A further difficulty in bringing the culprits to book lay in the fact that the boundaries defining the respective responsibilities of the Tippera and Manipur rajahs and the British had never been determined, giving endless opportunities for buck-passing.

The Lushai chiefs who divided the hills amongst

themselves all claimed descent from Thangura who lived in the first half of the eighteenth century and came originally from the neighbourhood of Falam in the central Chin Hills. Five lines of chiefs claimed him as their ancestor. To one of them, the Pallian, belonged Lalsuktla and his son Ngursailova. Another of them, the Thangluah, was Rothangpuia's minor clan. The most powerful line was that of the Sailos, descendants of Sailova who was a great-grandson of the Lushais' great originator Thangura. The Sailos had subdivided into a number of interlocking clans, the precise relationship between the chiefs of which is not always easy to determine. Of those who were destined to come into conflict with the British the most important were grandsons or remoter issue of Lalula Sailo, or those related to Rothangpuia's old enemy Savunga, or others, descendants of Rolura, who ruled over the Haolong clan.

The night of 16 April 1844 may be said to have marked a turning-point in relations between the British and their Lushai neighbours. The previous year a chief called Lalrinha belonging to the Pallian line, a descendant of the famous chief Sibuta (spelt Sheeb Boot in the old records), had been gathered to his forefathers. His son Lalsuktla out of filial piety had been desirous of procuring some human heads so that his father would have a suitable compliment of ghost-slaves to maintain his chiefly status in the village of the dead. Accordingly with his cousin Bawtaia and a party of two hundred braves had set off for the plains. Coming upon a settlement not far from

Partabghar just over the Manipur border at dead of
night, they launched a fierce attack on its sleeping
inhabitants and, having done their bloody work, made
off for home carrying with them twenty heads and six
captives. When it became known that Lalsuktla had been
responsible for the raid a detachment of the Sylhet
Infantry under Captain Blackwood was ordered into the
hills to apprehend him. When they approached his
village the chief, having as he thought been given an
assurance that he would not be molested, came out with
some of his *upas* to parley; whereupon Blackwood
forthwith had him seized and marched him back to
Silchar, where he was confined in the local lock-up.
Lalsuktla was duly tried before a magistrate and sentenced
to transportation for life to the Andaman Islands; Bawtaia
who had also been arrested was acquitted for lack of
evidence.

Resentment at what they considered Blackwood's
treachery smouldered in Lushai hearts for many years to
come. An immediate consequence of these events was a
series of raids, instigated by Lalsuktla's son Ngursailova,
against villages which had given assistance to Blackwood's
force, in which a hundred and fifty people were
slaughtered. In 1849 a Lushai raiding party attacked a
village only ten miles from Silchar, killing twenty-nine
people and taking forty-two captives, and once more a
detachment of the Sylhet Infantry, this time under its
commandant Major Lister, was despatched to bring in
the culprits. In January 1850 his force penetrated the

hills as far as Sentlang, from where he launched an attack on the village of Lalngura, a chief belonging to the Sailo family, which he burnt. Through his telescope Lister was able to observe the much larger village lying to the southwest where lived the paramount chief in the area whose name he spelt Barmooeelin, but the ruggedness of the country and his own remoteness from any supports prevented him from proceeding against it. On his return to Cachar Lister in his report gave it as his opinion that only a major expedition against the tribes would dissuade them from further raids on British territory, and that occasional forays against a single village merely served to provoke further outrages. Despite this advice the government decided to maintain their policy of conciliation, though they authorized Lister to raise a force of Kuki Levies which would be posted in stockades along the frontier at the main passes giving access to the plains.

For a while the policy of restraint appeared to be bearing fruit, for in the autumn of 1850 several of the Lushai chiefs sent representatives to Silchar to sue for peace, among them Bawtaia who had narrowly escaped transportation and Suakpuilala, both belonging to the Sailo family which was already establishing a dominance over their neighbouring clans. They wished, they said, to become British subjects and were prepared to pay tribute to the *sirkar* in exchange for a promise of protection against the Poi tribes — Chins or Lakhers — which were harassing them from the south. But Lister's instructions were clear: he must firmly reject all overtures that the Lushais should become British subjects, while assuring them they would not be molested by the British provided they kept to their side of the border, wherever that might be. In December Suakpuilala appeared in person at Silchar accompanied by a few followers and had a friendly chat with Lister, but the other chiefs held aloof, afraid of suffering the same fate as Lalsuktla then rotting in the Andamans. So for a few years an uneasy truce was maintained. In 1855 Suakpuilala again requested British assistance against some neighbouring chiefs who had attacked his village, and in 1861 his cousin Vanpuilala, son of the Lalngura whose village Lister had burnt, asked for help against the Pois who were pressing him from the south; but to no avail. Both requests were refused on the ground that the government could not interfere in the internal quarrels of tribes living "beyond British territory", and thus a great opportunity for coming to terms with the Lushais was lost.

Suddenly in 1862 violence again erupted in the form of savage Lushai raids on three villages near Adampur in Sylhet district, which were plundered and burnt, many of their inhabitants being massacred or carried off. The identity of the chiefs responsible was confirmed the following year when four of the women captives made their escape back to Cachar and named them as Suakpuilala and Ngursailova, who were brothers-in-law, and two others. The occasion for the raids was the fact that Suakpuilala's sister Vanaitangi after quarrelling with her husband had left him, for which Ngursailova demanded repayment of the bride price he had paid for her. As a compromise they had agreed on a joint raiding venture to secure slaves in discharge of the debt. The Sylhet authorities urged the immediate despatch of a punitive expedition, but the viceroy Lord Mayo, mindful of Suakpuilala's hitherto friendly attitude, again preferred a softer approach. He was also afraid that if the Lushais were provoked they would seek revenge by attacking the tea gardens, whose stealthy advance up the river valleys into the hills the Lushais viewed with the gravest suspicion. Instead, he ordered Captain Stewart, who was then the deputy commissioner of Cachar, to treat with the chiefs, offering, if they returned the captives they had taken and swore an oath of friendship with the British, to pay each of them a sweetener of fifty rupees a month. Sensing that they had the upper hand, the chiefs prevaricated. The captives were withheld, an expedition was once more mooted and again shelved, and matters were brought to a head in the winter of 1868-69 when reports came in of fresh raids, not only on defenceless villages but also, confirming Lord Mayo's worst fears, on several tea gardens. Chiefs Suakpuilala, Vanpuilala, the latter's brother-in-law Lalruma and his cousin Deonti were held to have been responsible.

Without proper preparation or regard for the approaching rainy season an expedition was hastily organized and despatched against the offending villages under the command of Brigadier-General Nuthall. The main column led by the general set off up the Dhaleswari river making for Suakpuilala's village near Aijal, but was forced to turn back due to torrential rain. A second column headed up the Sonai river and got as far as Bazaar Ghat, where they were met by a delegation with the news that the young Vanpuilala had lately died and protestations of innocence on the part of his mother Impani, who had taken over the chieftainship since his son Lalki was still an infant. The column, which had also been incommoded by the rain, was happy to accept these assurances and tramped back to base. A third detachment, sent by a roundabout route as a feint to draw off the enemy before linking up with the general's column, reached the rendezvous after a slight skirmish but seeing no sign of the general likewise made tracks for home.

The lieutenant-governor of Bengal Sir William Grey recommended that the situation be retrieved by the despatch of a large-scale expedition, not just to punish the odd village or two, but strong enough to overcome all opposition and to remain in the hills long enough to convince the chiefs that their best interests lay in keeping the peace. Once more Lord Mayo demurred, favouring the notion — with the example of Lewin's success in the Chittagong Hill Tracts in mind — of placing a well-qualified officer in charge of the disturbed area with entire control over the tribes, subject only to supervision by the commissioner. He should confer with, and take engagements from, the chiefs, demand a nominal tribute from them, and require them to refer their quarrels to him, so placing the government's intercourse with them on an improved footing. Unfortunately, such a man was not to be found in Cachar.

The deputy commissioner was now John Ware Edgar of the ICS, a convivial bachelor of notable girth who had accompanied the Sonai river column during the recent abortive expedition. At this juncture he conceived the notion of getting himself into Lushai country with the object of obtaining personal interviews with the chiefs and thus settling issues between them on a man-to-man basis.

> Accompanied by Major Macdonald of the Survey, protected by a well-armed guard and followed by a crowd of coolies bearing food for the travellers and fripperies for the Lushais, Mr Edgar started from Silchar on 20 December 1869. He arrived at Lushai Hath on the Sonai by 1 January following.

So began the satirical account of his adventures that in due course appeared in the Calcutta *Observer*. For thirty-eight days the emissary of the British Empire sat in his fortified camp listening to the conflicting tales that were poured into his receptive ears by representatives of various rival chiefs, who required cash payment for all they chose to tell him. Never once did he set foot in a Lushai village, not a single chief came to call on him, while Lushais of humbler status flocked round him, trying to fathom what he was up to and gladly accepting whatever bribes they could extract from him.

> With infinite patience and wonderful tact, displaying at
> once the good humour of an Irishman and the immobility
> of a Falstaff, Mr Edgar received and palavered.

He was lavish in the provision of big dinners and even bigger drinks, overpaid generously for every service given and every point orally conceded, secure in his strong camp guarded by eighty armed police. During these weeks nothing was obtained but worthless, postprandial assurances from people without authority to give them.

On 8 February Edgar, Macdonald and their escort left Lushai Hath and making their way up the Dhaleswari valley reached Bepari Bazaar twelve days later, having been detained on the road because they had run out of supplies. Here they sat for a month, at the end of which they were honoured by a visit from the old chief Suakpuilala, enticed by the prospect of unlimited potations of rum and curaçao and of returning home laden with presents. He was not disappointed. After inconclusive talk with Edgar he was presented

> with a pair of green pyjamas with scarlet and gold
> flowers, a purple coat with green and gold embroidery,
> an indescribable hat of green and white silk, a necklace
> of glass buttons and gold beads, and two glass earrings.
> One farewell tot of 'Edgar's peculiar', and the Sahib and
> the Savage parted with mutual esteem.

For two years while he was at home Lewin had been concerned with matters remote from what was going on in Lushailand. Looking back, he regretted that during his leave in Europe the flood-tide of pleasure had kept him so much away from the tranquil haven where his cousin Jeannie lived. The things that had eaten up his time he listed as a visit to his aunt Babbie and her family in Sweden, the studio of the art school where he had taken drawing lessons, St. Mary's hospital where Bob was now a house surgeon, the British Museum, and the all-devouring aunt Grote whose protégé he had become. He also spent much time vainly searching for some opening in other employment, for his great longing was never to return to India. He did not mention — may not even have been told at the time — that in September his youngest brother had got married.

Up to then Will had shown little inclination to settle down. After his brief apprenticeship with an engineering firm in Oxford Street and, remembering his success in amateur theatricals at Windermere College and later with Bob at St. Mary's hospital, he decided to try his luck on the stage. He made his début in 1867 in a walk-on part in Dion Boucicault's *Arrah-na-Pogue, or The Wicklow Wedding* at the Prince of Wales Theatre in Birmingham, which led to his first paid engagement in a small part in *The Flying Scud* at eighteen shillings a week. Out of deference to the feelings of his family he had adopted the stage name

William Terriss, he and Bob having coined the surname after looking through a street directory and perhaps with an eye to its resemblance to an already distinguished theatrical name. Feeling he was now ready for the London stage, he brashly introduced himself to the actor-manager Squire Bancroft who, falling victim to Will's brand of breezy effrontery, cast him as Lord Cloudways in *Society* at the Prince of Wales Theatre in Tottenham Street. On a weekend visit to Margate Will's prowess as a swimmer caught the eye of Isabel Lewis, a young actress who as Amy Fellowes had performed in small parts with the Vaudeville company; and after the briefest of courtships the couple decided to get married. The ceremony, which was informal to the point of casualness, took place at Holy Trinity Church in Portland Road, London, only Bob and their friend Harry Graves being present to see Will through his ordeal. Writing to his mother from Rangamati Lewin stood up for his brother. "A man can marry who he likes, and no one has the right to say a word, and as long as Will is happy I think it is a very good thing and may be the salvation of him, for he will have some reason to work now." To his family's dismay Will at once turned his back on the stage and with his new bride embarked at Southampton for the Falkland Islands, where he proposed to try his hand at sheep-farming.

Lewin returned to Calcutta early in January 1871 after a leisurely journey which had taken in a sight seeing tour of Italy with two friends, and, after landing at Bombay, visits to Meerut and Agra, and soon he felt his old distaste for India reviving. There was so much uncertainty about his future that he thought it possible that a short time might see him homeward bound again. Owing to his mother's anxiety for his health he had applied on arrival to be transferred to a more civilized district and, after a deal of bowing and scraping, had been offered the Garo Hills in northern Assam, which was even more unhealthy and isolated than the Chittagong Hill Tracts. Then all at once the whole picture changed when news started coming in of an epidemic of Lushai raiding on tea gardens in Cachar and Sylhet.

With Edgar's sojourn in the hills the previous winter the government's policy of conciliation had reached, in the words of the *Observer* newspaper, its grand climacteric. In the light of his report on the trip the idea of putting an officer permanently in the hills was shelved, and instead it had been decided that the deputy commissioner should pay an annual visit to the Lushais in order to hear grievances, to adjust quarrels, and to dispense largesse. Accordingly, soon after Lewin had arrived back in Calcutta, Edgar once more set out on his travels, with guides provided by the Lushais, their route taking them past the site of Lalngura's village which Lister had burnt in 1850 to a place on the Sonai called Panchinkai, which Edgar chose as his permanent camp since it was reachable from the plains by small boats. Here Mr Burland who was in charge of the police escort set his men to work clearing the jungle round the camp and building a palisade of bamboos as a protection against surprise attack, for rumours of the wildest sort were pouring in from all sides. Slowly Edgar was able to piece together a rough outline of what was going on around him, which caused him considerable anxiety; he feared for the safety of the messengers he had sent back; and the situation had become really alarming when a relief party under Captain Lightfoot arrived to escort them back to Cachar, where more reliable news of what had occurred awaited him.

While he had been sitting behind the bamboo palisade at Panchinkai two Lushai war parties belonging to the Sailo and Haolong clans, each some five hundred strong, coming from the far interior of the hills had infiltrated past him, travelling north and making for the tea gardens. On 23 January one of the parties, having attacked and burnt a Cachari settlement at Ainerkhal in the Hailakandi subdivision, twenty-five people being killed and thirty-seven taken captive, hurried on to the Alexandrapur tea garden, which was also destroyed. Among the slaughtered was Dr Winchester who was on a visit there and having his breakfast at the time, while his five-year-old daughter Mary was carried off. (The child's mother is nowhere mentioned in any of the accounts of the disaster or its aftermath.) A few hours later the adjoining tea garden Katlicherra came under attack, but through the presence of mind of its European managers Bagshawe and Cooke the assault was beaten off, though not before several of their employees had been killed or wounded. Cooke then led a rescue party to Alexandrapur, which recovered

Dr Winchester's body and brought back some wounded garden coolies for medical attention. That night they were reinforced by some police, and when the Lushais resumed the attack next morning they were met by a hail of rifle-fire and eventually made off.

For two days all was quiet, then on the 27th a band of Lushais under chief Lalbura surprised some sepoys and police at Monierkhal tea garden, shooting one sepoy and cutting down another. The survivors under the head constable, who was wounded, took shelter behind a barricade and were subjected to harassment throughout the day, while other Lushais looted the coolie lines. Next day Mr Daly the superintendent of police arrived with reinforcements, but two sorties from the barricade failed to drive off the attackers, and it was not until the night of the 28th that they eventually retired with their booty. Their losses were reported to have been heavy, but owing to their practice of carrying away their dead and wounded the exact numbers could not be ascertained. While Monierkhal was under attack some of the Lushais moved on to the adjoining Darmiakhal tea garden, which they plundered, while others attacked the nearby Nudigram estate, killing eleven and carrying off three. A small rearguard of troops and police sent to the relief of Monierkhal was overpowered, six being killed and one wounded. There was a pause of three weeks while both sides licked their wounds, then on the morning of 23 February some Lushais attacked the coolie lines at Jalnacherra tea garden, killing four and wounding three before being driven off by the police detachment that happened to be present.

Meanwhile Sylhet was also being subjected to similar attacks by the second war party of Lushais who raided Cacharipara village on 23 January, killing more than twenty and carrying off some young women. Another village not fifty yards from the frontier outpost of Chargola was attacked next day, but after an exchange of fire lasting an hour the raiders conceded defeat and retreated into the hills. On 27 February there was a fight between police and Lushais in which one Lushai was killed whose body they failed to recover, and two other Lushai corpses were later found abandoned in the jungle. A village in the Manipur hills south-east of the valley was attacked and destroyed on 25 February, forty villagers being killed and decapitated, another twenty-five carried off; after which the Lushais cried quits. So much for what the *Observer* called Edgar's policy of rupees and rum.

While these events were taking place in the north all remained relatively tranquil in the south where the chiefs were more or less honouring their oath to Lewin not to cause trouble within his jurisdiction. In the winter of 1869-70 there had been two raids, one on a village on the Kaladan, the other on a Magh village near Chima, and as an outlier of the Cachar raids a Lushai raiding party had attacked a village on the Sangu. Graham, who had been deputizing for Lewin while he was on leave, had undertaken an expedition into Lushai country, hoping to meet Edgar at Bepari Bazaar, but chief Vandula Sailo had refused him permission to pass through his territory. A minor chief Lemsailunga, a friend of Lewin, who had given assistance to Graham, had his house plundered and his village destroyed by order of the Haolong chiefs for his pains. Nor had Rothangpuia been guiltless, for early in 1871 his people had attacked and plundered a village near Subulong, carrying off three of his former subjects who had gone behind his back and referred to the acting superintendent some dispute about stolen cattle. Was he not justified in punishing his own dogs, he asked? Graham thought not and to teach him a lesson had deducted Rs.100 from the chief's allowance for the year.

Now Lewin had returned to Rangamati and resumed his benevolent despotism over his people. In anticipation of his being involved in fighting he ordered an "Express" rifle from Dickson & Son of Edinburgh and asked his mother to arrange for enough wines and foodstuffs to be sent out to him to last until he came home again. These included cases of dry sherry, whisky, rum, champagne, moselle, claret and brandy, which he asked Bankes to choose for him, and, from Crosse & Blackwell's, haddocks, whitebait, anchovies, sausages, hams, tongues, potted meat, essence of beef, soups, plum puddings, tart fruits and Stilton cheeses. When his mother remonstrated with him for being extravagant he explained that he had only ordered what was necessary: he had hardly any appetite and unless he lived well would not keep his health.

In April came a telegram requiring him to come to

Calcutta to attend a conference on the situation on the frontier, to which Edgar was also summoned from Cachar. Used to being looked down upon by the civilians in Government House as a troublesome backwoodsman, Lewin was gratified to find himself treated as an authority on the matter causing greatest concern at the highest level. "Well," he reported to Jeannie:

> as long as [the Lushais] confined themselves to slaughtering and carrying into captivity dark-skinned British subjects, the government did not think the matter worth particular notice, but now, Great Powers! that these barbarians dared to disturb Englishmen in making money, when tea plantations of Sylhet and Cachar were endangered, a perfect storm of wrath arises so that its eddies reach even as far as you in England.

His opinion was sought on a variety of subjects, he was called upon to write memos and minutes, he was haled hither and thither for interviews with the viceroy, the lieutenant-governor, with general this-that-and-the-other; but still the main question whether a punitive expedition should be mounted against the Lushais during the coming cold weather had to be left undecided. Such a step would require the sanction of the home government, though few doubted that it would be forthcoming. In one respect Lewin's advice was overruled. The majority favoured Edgar's recommendation that there should be an invasion of Lushailand comprising two columns converging on the territory of the tribes held to have been principally responsible for the recent atrocities, a northern column advancing from Cachar and a southern column from Chittagong. It was Lewin's view that, since his own people had by and large complied with their undertaking not to disturb his district, to advance through their country would amount to a breach of faith, and he considered that the invasion should be launched from Cachar only. Such scruples were pooh-poohed: since when had moral considerations had any place in dealings with savages?

Meanwhile aunt Grote had been pulling strings on her favourite nephew's behalf, but with uncertain effect; for when Lewin mentioned to Lord Mayo that he understood the Duke of Argyll had written to him about his case, the viceroy put him off with the excuse that he might or might not have received the letter; his Grace wrote to him about so many people that really.... Nevertheless, when instructing Lewin to proceed to Sylhet to set on foot the raising and equipping of two hundred recruits earmarked for service in the hills, bringing the strength of the frontier force under Lewin's command to six hundred, Lord Mayo promised him that at the expiration of a year his services would not be forgotten.

Stranded at Chuttack in Sylhet district after seeing to the recruitment of his men, Lewin found time to describe to his mother a scene with poignant associations for the Lewin family.

I am now sitting in a little mat hut with a mud floor, having finished my breakfast of rice & eggs & a glass of brandy & water. Before me stretch the beautiful blue ranges of the Cassya [Khasia] hills where Uncle William & all of them lived & where he poor fellow died. Cherra

Poonjee has hidden his topknot in a fleecy white turban
of clouds but all the blue wall of hills is streaked with
white lines of foam marking where the cascades take
their mad leap of four thousand feet into the plains
below.

On his return to Rangamati at the height of the rains
he found all was quiet. It was the lull before the storm,
and he made good use of it, straining every nerve to equip
and polish his frontier force to the required pitch of
perfection. At this time he received a letter from
Alexander Mackenzie the secretary to the government of
Bengal in response to his application for a transfer to a
healthier district, saying that the government particularly
wanted him to stay where he was until the following April,
since no man could be found so fit to take his place.
There was likely to be an expedition next cold weather,
but after that they would do their best to find him another
district. With the viceroy's promise in mind Lewin
permitted himself visions of being invested with the Star
of India or even a CB.

In such spare time as he had he studied hard for the
higher standard examination in the Burmese language
and added to his collection of fireside stories and
household proverbs of the hills. His musical activities,
because his 'cello had been smashed on the journey back
to Rangamati, were restricted to practising on the small
harmonium he had bought, which was harsh and rough
in tone. Family affairs also took second place, though he
noted with regret that in June uncle Grote, "that grand
old Pagan philosopher", had died, widely admired but

unbeloved of any save his wife, "who now sat alone and desolate with the dust and dregs of life alone to comfort her". His mind already morbidly exercised by the mystery of death, Lewin asked Jeannie to give him some account of George Grote's illness and end.

In July he received notification that the government had at last sanctioned a punitive expedition against the Lushais, and that he was to accompany the southern column as its political officer and interpreter.

3

The orders of the viceroy dated 11 July 1871 went into the matter in some detail. It was the general opinion, he wrote, that an armed expedition would probably have the effect of preventing a recurrence of the outrages and establishing the security of the frontier. His Excellency had arrived at the conclusion that armed intervention was necessary with real regret, but the recent raids had shown that the policy of forbearance, which would remain unchanged, had not been understood or fully appreciated by many of the tribes. Some leaders might have "imbibed" the idea — could this be a sly dig at Edgar? — that the British were unable or unwilling to punish them. So ran the preamble. Since the perpetrators could not be exactly identified — though Howlongs and Syloos were clearly the predominant offenders — the object of the expedition could not be pure retaliation, and much discrimination would be needed in dealing with the various chiefs. If guilt could be brought home with certainty, punishment must follow; the restoration of the captives must be insisted on; it might prove desirable to detain leading chiefs as hostages for future good behaviour; and if hostility were met with, the resisting villages should be attacked and burnt and the surrounding crops destroyed.

The main end in view was to "show these savages that they are completely in our power", to establish friendly relations with them, to make them open their villages to "our agents" and make travelling in their district safe; to show them the advantages of trade and commerce, and to demonstrate that they had nothing to gain and everything to lose by hostility to the British government. As much use as possible should be made of friendly chiefs like Rutton Poea and Sookpilal. His Excellency considered that a large force would not be required, but whilst the utmost possible economy was to be practised, this must not jeopardize the certainty of complete success. (Even viceroys must cover themselves against the possibility of failure.)

He envisaged the force being divided into two portions, the larger one advancing from Chittagong to punish the Syloo and Howlong clans, the other from Cachar to punish the villages of Lalbura and Vonolel and those of his sons. The military department would decide the strength and composition of the force and any special equipment needed, but one or two survey officers under

Major Macdonald should accompany the columns and make such survey of the country as circumstances permitted. Preparations should be made with secrecy and without bustle. It should not be looked on as a campaign, but a military occupation and visitation for the purposes he had described and to show the Lushais there was no part of their hills the armed forces could not penetrate.

For Lewin the time of preparation for the expedition was the busiest of all. His frontier police, which had been considerably increased in numbers, had to be drilled and licked into shape, and though Mr Crouch was sent to him as an assistant to take direct charge of them, the overall responsibility for ensuring that they were properly trained was Lewin's. He paid a flying visit to the Bohmong at Bandarban to arrange for him to take over the garrisoning of the frontier posts, so as to release the police at present manning them for other work during the expedition, and to furnish men to act as guides and scouts; though the Banjogis he eventually provided proved to be so timid that they had to be sent back home. He visited the Mong rajah at Maniksari to consult him about recruiting the considerable number of coolies who would be needed during the expedition in order to maintain the movement of supplies up the line of communication. Even the Kalindi rani was prevailed upon to furnish sixteen Chakmas armed with guns to act as scouts and spies. Lewin also communicated secretly with Rothangpuia in order to cement their alliance, guaranteeing his safety if he would throw in his lot with the British during the coming struggle.

On 28 October, having made a new will leaving everything to his brothers and sisters in equal shares, Lewin went down to Chittagong to report to the general who was to command the column for which he was to act as political officer. Charles Brownlow, the son of an Indian Army officer, had first made his name during the Mutiny when he had raised and commanded the 20th Punjab Infantry, a reputation that was consolidated during operations on the north-west frontier in 1863 for which he was awarded the Victoria Cross. "He was a gentlemanly, refined-looking man, in the prime of life," Lewin later wrote in his autobiography, "with a genial smile and a kindly blue eye, which occasionally shot forth an eagle gleam that to an enemy or an offender might seem ugly." At the time he was forty years old, only eight years older than Lewin.

Before he left Calcutta Lewin was approached by the private secretary to Lord Mayo who asked him to send him semi-official reports of all that transpired, to which he agreed with reluctance, knowing that he ran the risk of inadvertently saying something which might offend either his general or the Bengal government. Even more unwisely, he arranged with the Calcutta *Observer* to act as their war correspondent with the Chittagong Column and to send them anonymous articles on the progress of the expedition.

Chapter Twelve
The Lushai Expedition - 1

The Lushai Expedition of 1871-72 consisted of two independent though concurrent operations. It was hoped that the columns, besides keeping contact with one another by means of the telegraph line which unrolled behind them as they advanced, might meet somewhere in Lushailand, but that was never an important element in the military plan; and throughout the campaign Lewin had only the haziest idea what the Cachar Column, pursuing its own objectives in the north, was up to or even of its whereabouts. Its adventures may be briefly told. From its base camp at Tipaimukh on the Barak river the force advanced on 23 December towards the Senvong range where, after encountering light opposition, it burnt the Sailo villages within reach. After delays due to transport and supply problems it moved on to the Murtlang range and destroyed more villages, sustaining a few casualties in the process. Although by now some of the chiefs had come in to submit, the Lushais made a last stand on 25 January at Kungnung, and in the scrappy fighting that ensued the column sustained a few casualties, four killed and nine wounded including the column's commander Brigadier-General Bourchier hit in the arm and hand. The column's two guns were brought into action for the only time at the taking of Taikum, at which the defenders abandoned the village, bringing hostilities to a close. The column then marched east into the Champhai valley to secure the submission of the Sailo villages there before turning for home, reaching base by 6 March, its mission successfully accomplished. John Edgar the political officer with the column was held to have performed his task well, in addition to which he endeared himself to the column's senior staff officer Lieutenant-Colonel Frederick Roberts, VC, who had a positive horror of pork, by the exercise of his culinary talent in disguising the unclean meat in tasty soups and stews of his own concoction. It was one of the jokes of the column that Edgar, having brought in his limited baggage an inscribed silver-gilt goblet and claret jug which he intended to present to Suakpuilala ("Sookpilal") for services rendered, had to carry it all the way back again because the chief had proved such an unreliable ally during the campaign.

The Chittagong Column under Brigadier-General Brownlow with Lewin as its political officer began to assemble in November at Kasalong on the right bank of the Karnafuli, where an extensive base with sheds to accommodate the troops, commissariat godowns, hospital huts and an ordnance depot was under construction. From this base a road eight miles in length was being built as far as Lower Barkal, later extended a further two and a half miles beyond the rapids to Upper Barkal, and here the general arrived on 12 November with his headquarters and two companies of the 2nd Gurkhas under its commandant Colonel H.T. Macpherson, CB, VC, which was to constitute the column's main fighting force. Two other infantry units did duty on the line of communication. Next day chief Rothangpuia, who had come in from his village near Demagri with two minor chiefs of his clan, was introduced to the general with due formality by Lewin and, while professing a desire to be friendly and promising assistance, expressed alarm at the likely consequence to himself and his people of allying himself to the British against the other tribes. Having been given a broad assurance of protection if he behaved himself, he spent the next three days (as the general reported in his first official despatch to the commander-in-chief in Delhi) principally engaged in drinking rum.

Leaving the chief behind to act as guide in marking out the road now being extended to Demagri — the place was known as Tlabung to the Lushais owing to the waterfall nearby — the general with his headquarters staff, including Lewin and a company of Gurkhas made their way there by the river route, the fleet consisting of ten country boats from Chittagong and eighty canoes manned by Chakmas Lewin had recruited in his hill tracts. Up to now they had been usefully employed in various ways, but as the force advanced into the hills their fear of the Lushais caused so many desertions that the general foresaw the possibility, unless Lewin's personal influence could keep them together, of all five hundred of them melting away, bringing the expedition to a deadlock. He wrote to Mr Hankey the commissioner of

Chittagong asking him to order up the Chakma rajahs and chiefs in order to put some heart into them. Lewin's assistant, Crouch, was doing good work at Demagri, clearing the jungle, building a stockade, making paths and preparing godowns, and while these arrangements were going forward Rothangpuia arrived and invited the general to visit his village not far away. Called Lungsen, it was situated on a flank of the Ui-phum meaning the hill of the dog's grave, so called in honour of a famous hunting dog which was buried there.

The general and Lewin set off early with a company of Gurkhas as escort and were courteously met by the chief at his village boundary and taken to his house, where as they ate the breakfast they had brought with them they were regaled with cups of rice beer. A mithan was killed in the general's honour and two baskets of fresh beef sent back to camp for the officers' consumption. Altogether it was an enjoyable occasion, picturesquely described in an article datelined 1 December which appeared in the Calcutta *Observer* by "Our Correspondent with the Right Column", the anonymous author of which was, of course, Lewin himself. Although he was not above indulging in journalese when occasion demanded, his articles may well have been touched up by a sub-editor before being sent to the printing-room, as this passage describing the visit suggests:

The General stood for a long time sweeping with his glass the grand stretch of hill and dale that lay before him, Rutton Pooia standing beside him dirty and stolid, with his cloth thrown toga-fashion over his shoulders. It was a strange contrast, — the one a type of the English soldier gentleman, the other an anti-type of treacherous savagery, looking indeed more like a trapped wolf than a forest chief.

That description has no counterpart in the handwritten diary Lewin wrote up day by day during the campaign, providing a more immediate and authentic account of his doings than the newspaper articles, or his letters home which sometimes exaggerated his part in the proceedings, or his autobiography written some years later which was to some extent fictionalized at his publisher's request.

The general and his escort left Rothangpuia's village about 2 p.m. while Lewin stayed over for the night so that he could attend a council of the chief's relations and dependants, called to decide the course of action the clan should pursue during the coming hostilities. There was, as the diary states, a big talk and a corresponding drink, at the conclusion of which Rothangpuia promised his loyal and true assistance and to obey all orders. He was prepared, he said, to provide guides, scouts and fighting men (though these last the general declined), but not coolies since his people would object to such a menial rôle. In return Lewin undertook to assign fifteen frontier police to guard his village against attack by the Sailos, provided he supplied their food. In the morning the chief's wife — the sister of Seipuia and Vandula, two of the Haolong chiefs the expedition had come to punish — presented her only son to Lewin and, placing the boy's hands in his, asked him to take him to live with him when the expedition was over in order to educate him.

For all his promises of help Rothangpuia's usefulness was for the time being limited by his long-standing feud with the Sailos, which prevented him from acting as honest broker in opening communications between them and the British. Nevertheless he was a frequent visitor to the camp at Demagri, seeking medical treatment by the force's chief medical officer Surgeon-Major F.F. Allen of the 2nd Gurkhas for the fever and chronic bronchitis from which he suffered. So ineffective was he that the general felt constrained to report that hitherto his alliance had been of the most passive kind. Lewin, too, was becoming exasperated with him, and when on recovering from his illnesses he showed reluctance to provide meat, fowls and rice for the force to augment the rations that had to be carried laboriously up the line of communication, he exploded, telling him that it would be better if his tribe were openly hostile than to profess friendship and do nothing. Preserving a dignified silence in face of this rebuke, the chief left for his village where he intended to offer a sacrifice to consummate his recovery.

On 1 December two companies of the 2nd Gurkhas under the second-in-command Major D. Macintyre set out for the Sahjuk river, making for the nearest Sailo villages. After they had gone Lewin's hopes of opening negotiations with them rose when chief Lemsailunga came in, bringing two female captives with him as earnests of his good faith. Lewin had known him of old and before going home on his last leave had visited his village at a time when the chief's wife was shortly expected to be confined, and when wishing her good luck had prophesied that the baby would be a boy. A boy it was, and his parents had named him "Tongloyn" in gratitude. Since then, as already described, the chief's village had been burnt by Haolongs, his followers scattered, and he and his family become fugitives living on charity with the Sailos. Suspecting that he was unreliable, they had been keeping him under close surveillance, twice preventing him when he had tried to slip away; and when he did manage to evade their vigilance had seized his wife and little Tongloyn as hostages. Now Lewin, after a friendly talk with him, sent him off in the evening to have a meal with his followers, providing some rum to celebrate the occasion. Half an hour later word was brought to him that Lemsailunga, taking fright at the sound of bugles being sounded near by, had started up and plunged into the darkness, dropping in his haste his only garment. Men sent out to search for him next day returned empty-handed, saying they had heard from the chief's people that his behaviour had not been unusual, for he had a spirit which on occasions took possession of him, causing him to shun his fellow men. He was later seen making his way stark naked through the jungle in an easterly direction. Meanwhile agents Lewin had sent out to gather information reported that all the signs indicated that the Sailos proposed to fight.

On 8 December Lewin left Demagri and, overtaking the Gurkhas who were camped on the banks of the stream, crossed over with his hillmen and climbed the opposite hillside to the village of Liangura, a sub-chief of Rothangpuia's clan. The place was deserted except for two mithan and a pig, which were commandeered and sent back to the soldiers together with some unhusked rice they found in one of the houses. That evening Lewin laid an ambush, and as the chief came stealthily into the village his men sprang out and caught him. Late into the night Lewin reasoned with him, trying to persuade him to come over, for he was married to a sister of the powerful Sailo chief Savunga, whose large village the force was making for, and might therefore prove useful as an intermediary. Since Liangura refused to be persuaded, next morning Lewin sent some of his men to seize his wife and daughter and take them to Rothangpuia's village to be kept as hostages. When the general arrived at the village with his staff that evening he approved of the chief being placed under guard, and a few days later Lewin persuaded him to act as his ambassador to the Sailo chiefs he had heard were assembled with a large following at Vanhlula's village on the Belkai range, while himself proceeded to the *jhums* situated some 1700 feet below the village, to await developments. The message the chief brought back was unpromising: if the soldiers remained where they were, the chiefs would send representatives to treat with them; if they approached the village, they would be fired upon.

The first shots of the campaign had in fact been fired earlier that morning from a neighbouring ravine as Lewin strolled towards the village.

> I thought that someone had let off a gun by accident [he noted in his diary], but remembering the whistle of the balls & hearing a man say 'He's not hit — run', at the same time the sound of men making off among the underwood I awoke to the fact that the attention was personal.

The attack on Vanhlula's was a scrambled affair originally intended merely as a reconnaissance, but after one detachment of Gurkhas led by Macintyre had prospected the village from the north and retired with the information they had sought, the larger detachment under Colonel Macpherson sent to reconnoitre from the south lost its way. Coming unexpectedly on the village, they mistook the defenders eating their morning meal for Macintyre's men and advanced to join them, so astonishing the Lushais that they dived into the jungle, leaving three dead in the haphazard firing that ensued. During the night the Lushais set fire to the village, and in the morning two companies of Gurkhas took possession of what remained of it, unopposed. Lewin's hillmen were set to work building a warm hut for the general who was temporarily indisposed. A few days later the Lushais hit back, ambushing three Gurkhas below the camp who were bringing up letters, killing one of them at a cost of two of their own people shot by the rescue party sent to drive them off.

Having established his headquarters amid the ashes of the village the general now despatched Macpherson with three companies of Gurkhas carrying five days' rations, and Macintyre with 100 Gurkhas carrying three days' rations, each on a separate errand of devastation. Eight miles away to the east across a deep and difficult valley lay chief Lalhlira's village, which Macpherson's force destroyed before moving on a further six miles to destroy two more villages; they also set fire to immense quantities of grain stored in the granaries outside all three villages and in the surrounding *jhums*, returning to base at Vanhlula's in time to celebrate Christmas. Macintyre's force proceeding in a north-easterly direction up the valley of the Kahadung destroyed the villages of chiefs Vanhnuaia and Vanshuma with their granaries and captured fifty mithan which they found grazing in the jungle, twenty-four of which they managed to herd back to camp to supplement the men's rations. Virtually no opposition was encountered by either force, each of which was supported by guides and interpreters provided by Lewin; and although a lot of rounds were loosed off, the only casualty was one of Macpherson's Gurkhas who caught his foot in a deer trap contrived out of a sapling bent double to form a noose, which jerked him high into the air and left him dangling upside-down until some fellow soldiers cut him down with their kukris, suffering from fright and a slight sprain.

Lewin noted in his diary on 23 December that the burning of *jhums* was going on all round him, and that day

Rothangpuia came in. They had a long talk, especially on the subject of the tea planter's daughter Mary Winchester whose rescue was one of the main objects of the expedition. The chief was then sent back to his village to arrange for the road to be extended; to furnish unhusked rice as fodder for the transport elephants (which were proving a poor substitute for mules in such difficult country); and to send messengers to the Haolong chiefs who were holding Mary to find out whether, now they had seen the punishment being meted out to the Sailos, they were prepared to submit and give up the captives taken in the Cachar raids in order to avoid a similar fate.

On Christmas night the general gave a dinner for all the officers in the makeshift mess, at which the beef of a captured mithan was served as the main course. This was followed by a miraculous plum pudding, the recipe for which the *Observer*'s correspondent disclosed in his next article:

> 1 pot marmalade, 1 pot black currant jam, some guyal [mithan] suet, and a quantity of biscuit pounded fine with a table-spoonful of essence of ginger. The whole boiled for two hours produced a beatific result when served with a few spoonfuls of burning brandy.

The season of peace and goodwill having been celebrated in traditional style, the work of devastation was immediately resumed, the villages of chiefs Vanhnuna and Vankunga being destroyed the day after Boxing Day by Macpherson's force, while Macintyre's departed northwards on a *jhum*-burning foray. Proclamations drafted by Lewin and written in Bengali and Burmese, stating that no harm was intended to the people if they would send in deputies to treat for the delivering up of their captives, were posted on trees along the way, but to no effect. On the contrary, as Macintyre reported on his return, the Lushais had hailed his sentries at night, shouting from the darkness:

"Do not burn the rice."

Called on to come in and make terms, the voice had replied:

"No. Go away. Leave our country. We have nothing but powder and ball and plenty of that for you. We have formed a league with the Haolongs and will not come in to you."

Meeting some Lushais in the *jhums* and calling on them not to be afraid but to come in and make terms, the response had been a bullet. So hostilities had to continue, and now the general decided to make for the large village of Savunga, the most powerful Sailo chief in those parts, who had so far maintained a low profile. From a peak on the Thaurang Tlang nearly 5,000 feet high the general surveyed the surrounding country through his glass. Ten miles away, a little north of east, lay Savunga's village, called Buarpui after the pine trees in its vicinity. This was a cluster of between three and four hundred houses separated from the column by a confusion of smaller ranges involving ascents and descents of as much as four thousand feet, between which flowed three rivers that would present a challenge to the half-company of sappers accompanying the force. Further east, on the third and fourth ranges from where he stood, could be seen the principal Haolong villages, the direct approach to which would pass through Savunga's. Some miles to the north and reachable by an easier route from the Thaurang lay the old and new villages of Savunga's eldest son chief Lalgnura, which the general decided should be destroyed before the force moved eastwards.

The old village was found to be strongly stockaded, and in the attack which was made on it by the entire Gurkha battalion on 3 January one soldier was killed and one officer and nine men wounded. After the houses had been fired and its stores of grain destroyed the general moved up his headquarters, the march of seven miles taking them as many hours.

> Where the path did not ascend or descend at an angle of 35° [he wrote in his despatch] it followed the tortuous bed of a mountain torrent overhung by trees and precipices, and blocked up with rocks or boulders, through which we waded and stumbled for three miles, chilled by the cold clammy atmosphere, and feeling that fifty determined men might do as they liked with us, for there was no possibility of protecting our flanks.

On reaching within a thousand yards of Lalngura's new village the general ordered Lieutenant-Colonel J. Hills, vc, who commanded the half-battery of the Peshawar Mountain Battery, the only artillery unit attached to the force, to get his 7-pounder steel guns — which had been carried in two pieces by coolies — into action and to fire a few rounds into the middle of the village which could be seen to be crowded with defenders. While the Lushais were still stunned by this new mode of warfare, which they afterwards described as the firing of one gun out of another, a company of Gurkhas went in and drove them out without loss to themselves. That night some Sailos crept up to the camp under cover of darkness and held parley with Lewin, saying that chief Savunga wished to come in and submit. They were told that he might do so with safety, in which case their villages and crops would be spared; otherwise the advance would continue. Rothangpuia who was listening advised Lewin that, if his old enemy Savunga did come in, his head should instantly be cut off; but the matter was never put to the test. In the morning his village was seen to be burning, set on fire by its inhabitants, and a few days later its site was occupied unopposed and became the general's new advanced headquarters.

Since there remained only one Sailo village in that part of the hills left standing, that of Savunga's second son chief Laljika, Brownlow considered that they had now been effectively subjugated, and attention turned to the Haolongs, a clan which had played a major part in the tea garden raids and held many of the captives taken. From Savunga's their villages were in full view, conspicuous among them, three ranges to the east, being those of chiefs Benkhuaia and Sangbunga, the sons of Lalpitanga who had ruled over the northern Haolongs. But first it was decided that, since Rothangpuia was allied by marriage to the Haolong chiefs, his powers of diplomacy should be put to the test. On 13 January with Lewin beside him to strengthen his resolve and an escort of fifty Gurkhas he was taken to the banks of the Dhaleswari, which formed the boundary between the territory of the two clans, and put across the river with a few of his people, his mission being to try and persuade the chiefs to come to the general's camp to parley. As they approached a small village a short distance away on the other side it went up in flames, a sign that the defeated Sailos had retreated in that direction, and Rothangpuia declined to proceed any further, believing that to do so would precipitate a collision and so put it out of his power to mediate.

On his return to Savunga's to report his failure the chief began to show his true mettle and asked to be given another chance before the advance continued and to be allowed to take a more southerly route to try and reach the Haolong villages, only begging the general to remain on the hither side of the Dhaleswari until the 25th of the month. Brownlow was less reluctant to agree to his proposal than he might otherwise have been, because he had barely one day's rations left in camp and needed to build up a reserve of ten days' at least before he considered it prudent to make a forward move. So on 15 January Rothangpuia set off again, this time accompanied — but only, he was told, as far as it was safe for him to go — by Subadar Mohamed Azim of the Chittagong frontier police, who had long experience of dealing with the hill tribes and had already performed valuable services during the early part of the expedition. Rothangpuia's instructions were to inform the Haolong chiefs that the only basis on which the general was prepared to treat with them was the unconditional release of all captives and their undertaking to give free access to the force to march through their country.

It was with no great feeling of optimism that Lewin bid the pair godspeed, for at this stage of the campaign he was in low spirits, having had such little success in bringing the Lushais to reason that he almost believed that there was some fatality connected with his functions as the column's political officer. First there had been the case of chief Lemsailunga who instead of undertaking, as Lewin had hoped, to negotiate with the Sailos had fled naked into the jungle and was now, as it had been reported to him by his agents, disseminating among them the most hideous falsehoods concerning the expedition's merciless intentions. Later, due to a misunderstanding, some of Rothangpuia's men he had sent to parley with the Haolongs had been promptly arrested and sent back by the force's pickets. Worse still, messengers which another chief, Vanpuia, had sent at Lewin's request to the Sailos had actually been shot at by the sentries as they were returning to camp. Now, to crown everything, he heard that Rothangpuia had been delayed in setting out on his second mission owing to an outbreak of malignant diphtheria in his village, which had necessitated his presence there. Lewin was also worried about his hill coolies, for with the prophecy of rain at the full of the moon they were more anxious than ever to get home before the *jhuming* season started, otherwise their families would be hard put to it for food during the coming year. As for himself, the camp being situated on the top of a high hill, it was far from pleasant being billeted in a hut made of leaves and branches through which the wind, uncertain and boisterous, drove clouds of gritty dust and ashes over his meagre possessions. He was sick of hard fare in a savage country, subsisting for the most part on rum, chupatties and tinned mutton.

To fill in the time while awaiting the result of Rothangpuia's embassy the general on 20 January marched out with all his horses (three ponies) and all his men (the faithful Gurkhas, the half-battery of artillery and the half-company of sappers) against Pukzing on the Sirte Tlang, the single Sailo village, Laljika's, that still remained standing. Finding it elaborately stockaded and crowded with defenders, so that it could not have been taken without sustaining a certain number of casualties, he once more ordered the guns into action. Ten rounds of shell and shrapnel fired at a range of seven hundred yards were enough to scatter the Lushais, who were seen to be scampering away with their hands raised to protect their heads, and the soldiers took possession of the village without loss to themselves. They were then employed in destroying the considerable quantities of grain they found stored in the houses, which they set fire to before returning to camp. As soon as they had gone Laljika's people retook possession of what remained of their village and, as they watched the attackers marching away, fired shots into the air and shouted brave words to demonstrate their continued defiance.

Chapter Thirteen
The Lushai Expedition - 2

1

On returning to Savunga's early in the evening of 25 January after the burning of Laljika's village Lewin learnt that a message had come in from Subadar Mohamed Azim that Mary Winchester had been recovered, safe and sound after her year-long sojourn among the Lushais. On their way to the Haolongs Rothangpuia and Azim had met a party of them coming from Benkhuaia's village bringing the little girl with them. The chief had apparently calculated that, if he handed over the captive about whom so much fuss had been made, the soldiers would go back without molesting his villages. Leaving Rothangpuia to continue his mission alone, the subadar took charge of Mary and brought her back to Demagri, where she was made the responsibility of the frontier police guarding Rothangpuia's village. It seems likely that she was looked after by the chief's wife, for when a British officer arrived to fetch her away to Chittagong pending receipt of the government's instructions for her disposal, he is said to have found her wearing nothing but a blue rag round her loins, sitting on the steps of one of the houses in the village, smoking a pipe and lording it over a bevy of young savages who were disporting themselves for her amusement. The Lushais had renamed her Zoluti because she was a stranger in Lushailand. Although Lewin had not set eyes on her, he described her in his *Observer* article of 3 February as a very pretty child about six years old with fair complexion, hazel eyes and pure European features. She appeared to know no language save Lushai until the officer who had come to fetch her, fumbling in his pocket, asked her if she would like some sweets, to which she instantly replied: "Give me them".

At the same time as he gave news of Mary's recovery Azim reported that, before continuing on his journey to the Haolongs, Rothangpuia had asked that the general should postpone his advance a little longer until 28 January, so as to give him time to get clear should his mission have miscarried. Azim also informed Lewin that most of the fugitive Sailos had found refuge in Haolong villages. Another messenger sent by Azim came in next day with the information that the Haolong chiefs had agreed to submit and surrender their captives, provided they could do so at Demagri, again showing their anxiety to prevent the soldiers from entering their country. After discussing the position with the general Lewin sent back a message that they could only make terms if the chiefs presented themselves in person at Savunga's, and that the force would not retire until the captives had been given up. On receiving Lewin's letter Azim, who had been instructed on no account to place himself in the hands of the Haolongs, out of mistaken zeal — which, as the general wrote in his despatch, admitted of much excuse — set out at once to join Rothangpuia in the heart of Haolong country. He found him at the village of the chief Seipuia, Rothangpuia's brother-in-law, who had inherited with his brother Vandula the paramount chieftaincy of the southern Haolong villages from their father Lutpura.

Lewin had strongly urged on the general the advisability of the force remaining halted at Savunga's for the time being, pointing out in a memorandum not only the danger to his two emissaries if hostilities were resumed prematurely, but also the political advantages to be gained if their mission were to prove successful as compared with the results of merely punitive measures to which they would otherwise be reduced. Finding his arguments unanswerable, Brownlow gave orders for the advance to be delayed, to the confusion of his commissariat arrangements, but during the pause in operations he sent out detachments to complete the destruction of the Sailo *jhums* and, more constructively, ordered Major Macdonald to organize survey parties, with guides and interpreters furnished by Lewin and an armed escort, to map the surrounding countryside; himself meanwhile chafing like a caged lion at the necessary inaction.

All this time messages had been coming through by telegraph from the Cachar Column reporting on their progress in the north, in some of which could be detected the hand of its political officer John Edgar. A week after Mary Winchester had been retrieved the Chittagong Column was reliably informed that she was being held by Edgar's trusted friend chief Suakpuilala and would be sent in without delay. (The fact of the matter appears to have been that Suakpuilala, appreciating the kudos he would acquire if he were the one to bring in the child, had been negotiating to buy her from the Haolongs, but that events had overtaken his scheme.) Next day another telegraph told them of the brush with Lalbura's people when General Bourchier had sustained his wound. Later still a false report was received from Edgar that Suakpuilala had taken the Sailo chief Laljika prisoner and urging that the Chittagong Column should attack the northern Haolongs without delay. As the date approached on which the two columns were to try and establish communication between one another by direct signal and there was still no precise information as to the Cachar Column's whereabouts Lewin, as the *Observer*'s correspondent, permitted himself some words of mockery he was later to regret.

> By last accounts [he wrote in his article of 16 February] General Bourchier has marched clean out of the map, a military blunder which the Quarter Master General's Department will find it hard to pardon.

Since no further news had come in from Azim, Lewin sent him a message instructing him, if there was any disposition on the part of the Haolongs to delay or shillyshally, to return at once; but if things went favourably, to try and include the refugee Sailo chiefs in the peace negotiations. He also wrote another memorandum to the general, once more urging upon him the necessity of continuing to stay his advance eastwards until further intelligence had been received from his emissaries, who were still at the mercy of hostile tribes. They were soon to be sharply reminded that none of them was safe, for on the evening of 4 February as Lewin and some of the officers were sitting in the general's hut playing a rubber of bridge after dinner shots were heard followed by a scream and more shots, and dashing out they found that a Gurkha sentry had been shot through the chest by a Lushai sharpshooter. They were not in the mood to finish the rubber when they returned to the hut, and instead the general reminisced about his adventures on the north-west frontier ten years before when his regiment, the 20th Punjab Infantry, had faced in the wild Afghans a foe vastly more deadly than his present opponents.

The following morning Lewin received information that Azim had returned to Demagri, having been prevented from penetrating deeper into Haolong territory by chief Seipuia, who was doubtless afraid that he would be held responsible if anything untoward happened to the subadar. He reported that the southern Haolong chiefs — Seipuia, Vandula and those they controlled — had again expressed themselves willing to submit and give up their captives, but still insisted that this must take place at Rothangpuia's village, alleging their inability to come to the general's camp on account of the distance and their fear of the Sailos. On 8 February there was another message from Azim that Rothangpuia who had now returned to his village was confident that the chiefs would come that day bringing some captives with them, but adding that, since there was no sign of them, he personally tended to disbelieve their fair words. This was enough for General Brownlow, whose patience had already worn paper-thin. He forthwith issued orders for preparations to be made for his force — which after providing for a sufficient garrison at Savunga's could only muster some three hundred rifles besides the artillery and sappers — to make a forward movement into Haolong country.

Even so his position was not entirely easy. Although the Sailos had taken a lot of punishment they were by no means defeated. Still at large was the paramount chief Savunga who, having abandoned his village that was now the force's headquarters, was lying low with his formidable sons Liangura and Laljika, biding their time. The shooting of the sentry was not the Sailos' only exploit, for they continued to snipe at the convoys of coolies bringing rations up from the rear, and it could be expected that, once the force was embroiled with the Haolongs, they would step up their harassing tactics. So proper safeguards had to be taken, and it was not until 11 February, by which time he had built up twenty days' supplies at Savunga's so as to be quite secure in case of any serious interference with his line of communication, that Brownlow judged himself ready to advance.

Again Lewin's spirits were at a low ebb.

I am sick of this place [he wrote in a letter home]; there is nothing to do, nothing to eat, nothing to read, no news & no music. Our shanties are bitterly cold and the ground is so hard that one cannot sleep — quite a small catalogue of miseries. Our peace negotiations have fallen through so we have to advance again, & worse than all, the transport service at this critical juncture has broken down & our supplies of provisions from the rear have stopped. Our advance into the enemy's country is perforce stopped too, & this does not improve our tempers.

2

It appeared from Subadar Mohamed Azim's reports that the chiefs of the southern Haolongs, descendants of Lutpura — his sons Seipuia and Vandula and the former's sons Lalngura and Jothoma — were prepared to submit and surrender their captives, provided the force first retired to Rothangpuia's village near Demagri. Some reliance might be placed on this in view of the fact that Rothangpuia's wife was Lutpura's daughter; besides, the general thought it advisable to shelve the southern Haolong problem for the time being and first to proceed against the northern section of the clan under their chiefs Benkhuaia and Sangbunga (who happened to be married to Rothangpuia's sister), the sons of Lutpura's brother Lalpitanga.

Accordingly on 11 February an advance party of the 2nd Gurkhas with the sappers moved out under Colonel Macpherson's command and after a hard day's march in a north-easterly direction bivouacked a short distance from the villages of the subordinate chiefs Lianrikhuma and Chawngmama, which their inhabitants burnt on seeing the troops approaching. The rest of the fighting force followed next day. A day's halt having been called so that the coolies could return to Savunga's to bring up more supplies, Lewin went out with a reconnaissance party under Captain C.J. East, the senior staff officer with the Chittagong Column, to reconnoitre the route to be taken next day. As they approached the nearest of the burnt villages they saw that the site was crowded with Lushais and hailed them. It was some time before they realized from the response that they wanted to be friendly and were asking for some of Rothangpuia's men to be sent over to them.

> I accordingly [wrote Lewin in his diary] went back, got some men & commenced a conference which ended in peace and goodwill, the Howlongs in some numbers returning with us to camp. They say they are willing to give up the captives & that they wish for peace. We may go anywhere we like & they will offer no opposition — will call their chiefs to come and make submission if we wait a couple of days.

Early in the morning of the 14th some men from Lalbura's village which lay one and a half days' journey away to the east came into camp and after a short stay went off to fetch their chief, who was the head of seven villages including those of Jothoma, Chawngmama and Lianrikhuma. Later, when the force with a number of Lianrikhuma's men tagging along marched the two miles to Chawngmama's burnt village, which was called

Thenzawl after the stand of oak trees nearby, they found it occupied by some forty Lushais, who offered no resistance but retired as the force advanced. Here they made camp and before long the place was invaded by friendly Lushais who roamed about poking their noses into everything, later bringing fowls and eggs to barter for whatever trifles they could persuade the soldiers to part with. That evening Lewin was visited by representatives sent by Benkhuaia and other chiefs, and by Lianrikhuma's son who spent the night with Lewin's followers and left in the morning to bring in his old father, and soon afterwards Chawngmama's son put in an appearance.

Now that opposition appeared to be crumbling the general sent out reconnoitring parties, one to the north under Major Macintyre accompanied by Major Macdonald of the Survey in the direction of Lalbura's and Jothoma's villages on the Mawi Tlang, the other under Captain Battye accompanied by Captain East making towards the villages of Benkhuaia, Sangbunga and their widowed mother beyond the deep valley of the Kaladan. Macintyre returned after two hours having gathered the information he had gone out to obtain, while the other party "on reaching a small stream just below the camp" (as the general wrote in his despatch) "came upon a small body of the enemy, who said that their chiefs were then on the way to make their submission, and that if they were met by a large armed party they would probably get alarmed and go back. Captain East halted, and sent for instructions, on which I directed him to return to camp." Lewin in his diary gave rather a different account of this incident at the Tuldung stream:

> Two parties of Ghoorkas went out to prospect. One under Capt E. on road to Benkuias abt. an hour after departure messenger returned to say they were halted in face of a large party of armed Kookies. I went out & crossed over to the Kookies — a deep stream flowed between our men & them. They were Benkuia's men sent to guard the ford but were friendly. I sent some of them to fetch the chief & returned to camp.

Later that day Lianrikhuma came in and swore allegiance, promising to bring in Lalbura and Jothoma.

16 February was the turning-point in the campaign, for on that day Lalbura's representatives arrived at Thenzawl and told Lewin that the chief wished to submit and make terms, but was afraid of the soldiers' long-range guns, which had been brought up that day. He first wanted to meet Lewin alone, and only after they had sworn an oath of mutual friendship would he be prepared to come in and submit. In the evening representatives from Benkhuaia arrived saying that the chief was only a few miles off and had brought a mithan with him to be sacrificed if Lewin would agree to take an oath for his safety, in which case he, too, would come in and submit. Such was the reputation for honesty and fair-dealing, and power, Lewin had acquired among the hill people. He sent them away bearing a message that he would meet the chiefs next day and then sought an interview with the

general, to whom he made his recommendation in his usual forceful way.

He was firmly of the opinion, he said, that the only terms the general should insist upon were the restoration of the captives, the swearing of an oath of friendship, and pledges to commit no more raids and to allow free access to their country. To demand hostages for future good behaviour or to impose other conditions that might not be complied with or might later be evaded would, he believed, be impolitic. Although both Benkhuaia and Sangbunga had been concerned in the Cachar raids the previous year, he deprecated the imposition of any special penalty on that account as likely to alarm them and put them to flight. Remembering the fate of Lalsuktla, they were in abject fear of treachery on the part of the British. On the general's decision, he said, depended whether the chiefs remained to take the oath or absconded, in which case the whole sorry business of burning and devastation would have to begin all over again. After careful consideration of all the circumstances Brownlow decided to accept the chiefs' offer of submission on the terms proposed by Lewin.

And so it came about. At the oath-taking ceremonies the chiefs made a formal presentation of elephant tusks to the general in token of their submission to the British, and with Lewin personally entered into a solemn oath of friendship involving the sacrifice of a mithan, the smearing of its blood on feet and forehead, the eating of a piece of its raw liver, and the repetition of the formula that their friendship would last until the rivers ran back into the earth again. They handed over to him either a gun or a *dao* or a headdress plumed with the tail-feathers of the *bimraj* to signify that they accepted him as their paramount chief. They also petitioned the general that Lewin should settle on Sirte Tlang near their villages, so that they might come in and see him and talk over their affairs, which they could not do while he lived at such a distance from them as Kasalong or Rangamati. That evening the captives began to arrive, many of them most reluctant to be parted from their abductors with whom they had settled down in amity, and meanwhile the camp was thronged with friendly, inquisitive Lushais.

Submissions by chiefs Lalbura, Jothoma, Lianmanga and Lalrikhuma followed next morning, and later came *upas* from Lalhleia, Vansanga and other chiefs subordinate to Sangbunga with the assurance that the chiefs held themselves bound by the oath he had taken. Taking advantage of this mood of reconciliation the general sent out Major Macdonald with a detachment of Gurkhas to visit Benkhuaia's village, guided by men provided by the chief himself, thence to proceed on 20 February to the villages of Lalbura and Jothoma on the Mawi Tlang whose highest peak, on which a survey station was to be erected, had for long been a conspicuous landmark ahead of the advancing column. This was the day when contact was supposed to be made with the Cachar Column, but although the latter fired rocket signals and lit bonfires on conspicuous heights, nothing was seen by Brownlow's column, who were told by the Haolongs, whose jungle telegraph kept them better informed, that their sister column was in the Champhai valley some four days' journey distant from them. According to Lewin's article in the *Observer* it had been General Bourchier's "extra-geographical movements" which had precluded a junction between the two columns.

Next day they were stunned by the news received by their own telegraph that the viceroy Lord Mayo had been murdered, stabbed by one of the long-term prisoners while on an official visit to the Andaman Islands, and for days afterwards there was talk of little else round the camp-fires. It was, Lewin wrote, like the skeleton at the feast, for the viceroy had died just at the moment when the expedition he had sponsored and whose fortunes he had been following with close attention was on the point of being brought to a successful conclusion. It was reassuring to know that the crime had no political significance, having been committed by a man from the Khyber Pass sentenced to transportation for life for murder, who considered his sentence unjust; but many on both sides, remembering Lalsuktla, must have given some thought to the mysterious workings of Fate. The brief but sorrowful brigade order issued by Brownlow found an echo in the heart of every man under his command, and for Lewin there was a further cause for despondency, for it had been Lord Mayo who had given him his personal assurance that his services would be rewarded after the campaign was over. Only a few days earlier Lewin had brooded on the question of honours in his letter home:

> I wonder sometimes whether if we are successful I shall get the Star of India. It is a queer thing this desire for Stars & Garters. The monarch who first built this upon the weakness of human nature was an ingenious observer — a leg lost in battle is amply paid for by a bit of ribbon — the service of a lifetime is recompensed by some small tinsel frippery — & so long as the king has a yard of ribbon left he will always find brave & good men who will give him their lives in exchange.

Now the prospect of any such reward had receded; it had been Mayo's campaign and to him Lewin had looked for recognition.

Now the last vestiges of opposition to the force were melting away. Savunga and his two sons were treating for peace, for the Haolongs had finally turned against the Sailos, expelling from their villages those to whom they had previously given refuge, even offering to send armed men to destroy the clan if that was what the general wished. On 27 February their chiefs arrived in a body to submit, except Savunga who asked to be excused on the grounds of illness arising from his recent troubles and wanderings, though he would make the effort if the general insisted. Not that he was an entirely spent force, for soon he was going about threatening to cut up Rothangpuia for having been a traitor to his people. When the Sailo chiefs were asked the reason for their prolonged resistance against overwhelming odds they put the blame on their hot-headed young bloods who would fight in spite of their elders' advice to surrender. They had also listened to the bloodcurdling stories put about by the mad chief Lemsailunga about what the British proposed to do with them and had been afraid to put themselves in their power. Now in token of their submission they handed over offerings of tusks, cloths and two fine long-haired goats.

After more than four months in the field the soldiers, too, had had enough, especially the British officers who were beginning to hanker for the comforts of civilization, a mood Lewin described in his *Observer* article of 26 February:

> We hunger after the fleshpots of Egypt, and visions of iced Moselle-cup and a good dinner occasionally disturb our slumbers; even a bottle of beer would be welcomed as an event, and every step we take 'bock agin' brings us nearer to these fleshly joys. There are no books in camp save the Brigade Order Book and a stray volume of Swinburne, the latter having been brought (of course by accident) by a romantic officer of one of the scientific branches; but it is astonishing what popularity this latter volume has obtained, attributable, I should think, to the bountiful manner in which this glowing poet gushes and overflows in praise of flesh. If you wish to ascertain how much of the old Adam is within you, or to understand your relationship with the inhabitants of the Cannible Islands, make a campaign on tinned mutton and preserved soups.

On 28 February Macdonald of the Survey with an escort of the 2nd Gurkhas provisioned for thirteen days and Sailo guides set out for Bepari Bazaar and

Suakpuilala's country in the north, in a belated attempt to make contact with the Cachar Column. On the same day the general with his staff started back to Demagri, leaving Colonel Macpherson with the rest of the 2nd Gurkhas and the half-company of the sappers to withdraw along the line of communication, rolling up the telegraph wire and removing the stores that had been left under guard at the various depots along the route. But Lewin, who reached Demagri a day before the general, had one more task to suggest before the force retired from the hills altogether. The villages of the southern Haolong chiefs Seipuia and his brother Vandula and their cousin Vantanga which lay three or four marches away remained unvisited, and he recommended that a show of force should be made against them, having reason to believe that, immediately the soldiers approached, the chiefs would present themselves and submit. The general concurred and ordering up the two companies of the 4th Gurkhas and the two companies of the 27th Punjab Infantry from their positions in the line of communication and taking one gun of the mountain battery set out with Lewin on a weary hill march of forty miles over as bad a country as any he had yet encountered.

On the third day, after a steep climb of 4,000 feet, they reached the outskirts of Seipuia's village, which brought the chief out to meet them. After he had done all that was required of him, the general growing impatient when the other chiefs failed to appear ordered the march to continue on 12 March, which had the result of bringing in Vantanga with a batch of captives, "weeping bitterly", as the general reported in his final despatch, "at parting from their captors". Next morning brought Sanghena the son of Vandula who sent word asking to be excused from presenting himself in person on the ground of illness. Although the general was minded to call his bluff and continue the advance, he was persuaded to accept the young man's submission on behalf of his father, for the heat was becoming excessive and both the coolies and his supplies were nearly exhausted. So at Seipuia's the oaths were taken and more captives handed over, and the force started back for Demagri *en route* for Chittagong and home.

In his final despatch General Brownlow was generous in his praise of the officers and men who had served under him during the campaign. He also had a favourable word to say about his former enemies the Lushais.

> The impression left on our minds [he wrote] was, I think, that the Looshaies could bear comparison with most eastern races in physique, natural intelligence, and character. Their thews and sinews and wellturned limbs indicated health and freedom from want or toil; their faces showed a happy genial disposition, without any expression of cruelty, and very little of courage. They were all clad in home-spun cotton; the sheets or plaids worn by the men being often a dark tartan, and the highland sporran a frequent article of apparel among them.

For Lewin he reserved his most fulsome praise, ascribing to "his strong personal influence over the tribes, his knowledge of their language and habits, added to his patience and sagacity in dealing with them, that a single chief surrendered or a single captive was recovered". In his description of Seipuia's submission he used an expression — a surprising one for a general to use in reference to one of his more junior subordinates — which brings Lewin vividly before the mind's eye:

> Sypooea is a very distinguished looking and intelligent Looshai, who so far succumbed to the animal magnetism of Captain Lewin as to express a desire to accompany him and Rutton Pooea on a visit to Calcutta, which the latter chief is quite prepared for.

By using the term "animal magnetism" Brownlow was suggesting that Lewin possessed a charisma that gave him the same kind of power over the hill people as a mesmerist exercises over his patient; though in Seipuia's case it had lost some of its potency when the time came for him to put his resolve to visit Calcutta into effect.

Chapter Fourteen
Thangliena

1

In April 1872 Lewin was again summoned from Rangamati to Calcutta, this time to appear before the General Council of India which was to deliberate future policy on his frontier. It was a new experience to find that his name had gone up in the world, so that many people now wished to know him who before were ignorant of his very existence. General Brownlow was especially good to him and lost no opportunity of praising his services during the campaign, and the lieutenant-governor Sir George Campbell gave flattering attention to his views. Since it was too expensive to stay at his club, he took furnished rooms and, with his musical instruments around him and Nurudin to look after him, enjoyed this brief civilized interlude, though he could not stand the heat as well as he used to and at the end of the day was too weary to practise on his harmonium for long. He regularly played racquets and was occasionally invited by friends to a game of croquet.

The main decision reached by the council was that they should avoid assuming direct control over the tribes, but continue to exert a general political influence over them. A precise boundary line would be determined beyond which ordinary jurisdiction should on no account be extended, and this would be guarded by a chain of police posts. The country between Cachar and Chittagong along the eastern border of Tippera and reaching as far south as Arakan was to be surveyed and mapped. It was also decided that a permanent post should be established at Demagri under an English officer, for which purpose Lewin was assigned an additional assistant in the person of Lieutenant Gordon. The conference over, they travelled together by ship to Chittagong, thence up the river to Rangamati, leaving for Demagri with a detachment of the frontier force almost immediately because the rains were imminent. Not soon enough, for the monsoon broke before they left Kasalong, and they had a hard time of it making headway against the strong current, having to jump overboard and help the boatmen heave the boats through the rapids which had become foaming torrents. Camping at night on the river bank they were tormented by sandflies. Arrived at Demagri, Lewin began prospecting for a suitable site for the new post.

At this point the Karnafuli has gnawed a narrow gorge through the black rock and descending two shallow falls forms a pool of clear green water, about half a mile in circumference.

The hills, which rise in long ranges to the east, trending north and south, shielded the place from the cold winds, while the level shores of the basin offered facilities for building. On the south-western side of the basin a bed of rock deflected the river, causing it to make a bend, and thus to form a small peninsula surrounded on three sides by deep water; a strong stockade across the neck of this peninsula rendered it an easily defensible position, and here consequently were placed the police barracks, hospital and provision depot. My own house was built on a small eminence outside the stockade, commanding a good view of the bazaar on the north side of the pool, whence a path ran steeply up the Sirthay Tlang, a lofty peak of the Ohepoom range, where I proposed building a strong stockade together with a house for myself. Here also I hoped eventually to establish the headquarters of the frontier administration, Demagri serving as a trading centre and a place of disembarkation and storage.

A quantity of surplus stores had been left behind by the departing soldiers, and these Lewin made available to the Sailos living in nearby villages, who were cowed and broken by the expedition and facing a serious food shortage owing to so many granaries having been destroyed. His survey completed, Lewin took Gordon to visit Rothangpuia in his village some miles to the north, whose power and prestige had been much enhanced by the part he had played in the campaign. Then, leaving a strong guard to keep an eye on the stores, Lewin and Gordon returned to Rangamati, for work on the new post could not be commenced until the rains were over.

Rangamati was no longer the solitary outpost it once had been. Besides Gordon there were now three other Europeans in the station — Knyvett, Crouch, and Bignell — who had been assigned to the frontier battalion under Lewin's command. A flourishing bazaar stood on the site of his old *jhum*, many homesteads had sprung up in the neighbourhood, and where once jungle had covered the hillsides cattle peacefully grazed. In the lapses between the steady downpour Lewin worked in his garden in which, except for a stunted rose or two, English flowers stubbornly refused to grow. Instead, he tended his plants of Noon Knot which opens all its blossoms regularly at midday and the Sensitive Plant that cringes to the ground when touched. In addition to his official duties he was working on a grammar and dictionary of the Lushai language, hitherto unknown and unwritten, a task he often found hard and puzzling.

While staying in Calcutta he had narrowly missed running into his brother Bob, who had finally decided on a seagoing career with the Peninsular & Oriental Steam Navigation Company as ship's surgeon aboard their passenger vessels plying world-wide. He had arrived in Calcutta shortly after Lewin had left and was awaiting a berth in the P&O vessel *Pekin* homeward bound. He had been out of spirits, bored by the monotony of life on the ocean wave, and already talked of retiring from the sea. Will, too, had made a new start in life. After spending a year on a sheep station in the Falklands, during which time he had become adept at breaking-in horses and a good man with a lasso, he had had enough. Nor had Izzy enjoyed being left alone in lodgings in Stanley to await the birth of their first child. As soon as the baby was born, a girl whom they christened Ellaline, the family embarked in a whaler on passage from Honolulu and after a long voyage berthed at Falmouth. While his eldest brother had been making final preparations for the Lushai expedition Will, who was now twenty-four years old, having settled with his family in a cottage in Barnes had begun a series of theatrical engagements in London, in which the discerning had hailed him as a coming juvenile lead. Then after less than a year he abandoned the stage for the second time, having agreed to join a school friend Percy Tattersall, a nephew of the head of the firm of Knightsbridge horse auctioneers of that name, in a horse-breeding venture in Lexington, Kentucky; and once more the Terriss family set off on their travels. Will's participation in this new venture had been made possible by Lewin who, admiring his brother's pluck in facing the world again after his Falklands failure, lent him £500 as his share of the capital on the condition that "penniless Percy", as he called him, put up a like amount. "Please God the boy will yet do well," he wrote to their mother; "he has a good sensible head on his broad shoulders in spite of all his wild careerings." Their sister Harriet was causing concern due to her delicate health, which Lewin put down to her not having had children: such a fine, strong-built woman ought, he thought, to be very healthy in normal circumstances. In September 1872 at St. Peter's church in the Isle of Thanet Bella married Lieutenant-Colonel Nathaniel Stevenson of the 87th Regiment, the Royal Irish Fusiliers, the second son of a Lanarkshire laird and one of four brothers to have distinguished military careers. Much of his early service he had spent in staff appointments before he rose to command his regiment, later being given military charge of districts in Ireland and England.

In due course notification was received from Calcutta that most of the reforms Lewin had advocated before the council had been sanctioned; in particular he was authorized to make small loans to the hill people with which to purchase ploughs and cattle, in the hope of persuading them to give up their nomadic slash-burn method of *jhum* cultivation. All that he had most hoped for seemed to be coming to pass in his little kingdom.

> Numbers of our quondam enemies, the Sailos, came in to visit me, for my name had become great in Lushailand. They called me father and named children 'Thangliena' after me, it being (they averred) a name of power and good fortune. I thought sometimes of King David's psalm, 'A people whom I have not known serve me ... as soon as they heard of me they obeyed me; but the strange children dissembled ... the strange children failed and trembled in their hill forts'; and I thanked God, very humbly and sincerely, in that He had strengthened my hands and prospered my work.

And yet, while the government gave him most of what he wanted for his people, those set in authority over him had other ways of showing that he was far from enjoying their full approbation; for when the honours awarded to those who had played leading parts in the campaign were announced one name was significantly omitted from the list. The generals received knighthoods, the senior expedition officers were made Companions of the Bath, even Edgar for his work as political officer with the

Cachar Column was invested with the Star of India; but Lewin received no mark of recognition whatever. On all sides influential friends expressed their dismay at this studied insult and did all in their power to have the omission rectified. General Brownlow had the case placed before the commander-in-chief Lord Napier of Magdala, urging the claim of the officer "to whom I was so entirely indebted for whatever success the expedition may have met with". Alexander Mackenzie the secretary to the government of Bengal expressed himself vexed beyond measure, and the lieutenant-governor Sir George Campbell wanted to know what the new viceroy was going to do about it.

At this distance of time it is not possible to discover precisely what manoeuvrings went on behind the scenes which resulted in Lewin's daydream of being made a Companion of the Star of India being frustrated, but the letters on the subject he received at the time from General Brownlow which he preserved among his papers provide some clues. On reading the telegram announcing Edgar's award Brownlow wrote to Lewin on 29 May from Rawalpindi to tell him that he felt the absence of his name from the list to be as severe a blow to himself as it must have been to Lewin, because in the eyes of the world it would be seen not only as a reflection on their joint work, but also on his endeavours to procure for Lewin the just recognition of his services. He did not know what the cause might be, except for the fact that Edgar had been longer in the service than Lewin. "Besides," he added, "he plays his cards *well*, and I never met anyone who played them worse than you do — I am sure you will excuse my saying so." Nevertheless, the general assured him, he could depend upon him to do all he could to put things right.

The progress of his efforts he described to Lewin in a letter from Murree dated 25 July consisting of no less than sixteen pages written in the general's flowing, rather feminine hand. The distress he continued to feel at the insult to Lewin is apparent in every line, and although his enquiries in high places had elicited a number of possible reasons for Lewin having been refused a decoration, none of them seemed conclusive. There was the misunderstanding that had arisen when they were in Calcutta after the expedition, and both the commander-in-chief and the lieutenant-governor had taken up their joint recommendation that a post should be established on Sirte Tlang within reach of the Haolong chiefs. Lewin had then spoken of its impracticability, referring to the difficulty of doing anything until the monsoon was over, but had given the impression that, having got the post sanctioned, he no longer wanted it. Hence the general's earlier reference to his playing his cards badly, and he remembered reading Lewin a lecture (one of many) on his impulsiveness and general want of discretion, to which Lewin had listened with his usual good nature. Brownlow then briefly mentioned another possibility:

I remembered your telling me of some anonymous charges with regard to the *ladies* in your district, which you successfully refuted, and wrote to ask Hankey [the commissioner of Chittagong] if he thought that matter could have stood in your way, but he said no, and must be right or Sir G.C. would know something about it, whereas it is quite clear that the latter is very well disposed towards you.

Then there were those *Observer* articles Lewin had written, in one of which he had said something, simply with a view to throwing off suspicion of its authorship from himself, for which the general considering the remarks damaging to himself as well as to Lewin had reprimanded him. The matter had somehow come to the attention of Lord Napier, on hearing which Brownlow had within half an hour gone in to see him to express his regret that the story had been repeated. It was, he had told him, a personal matter between Lewin and himself which had been settled between them on the spot. (In his letter to Lewin Brownlow did not mention the *Observer* article in which Lewin had disparaged General Bourchier, which the commander-in-chief might well have considered highly insubordinate.)

He went on to wonder whether "Macdonald's malignant tongue and pen" had done Lewin any harm, presumably referring to the senior Survey officer who accompanied the Chittagong Column, since he had never ceased to abuse them both and was going home "to appeal to Parliament and the Throne"; though precisely what was troubling him is unclear. He may have considered that they had shown undue lenience towards the Haolongs, censuring Lewin, as did some people in the Bengal government, for "allowing them to escape their rightful punishment", and the general's next paragraph lends some support to this theory.

> Your operations among the Syloos and Howlongs appear to have been very satisfactory & though you may sometimes think it would have simplified matters if we had trounced the latter instead of treating with them we did what seemed best at the time. It is easy to be wise after the event. If the business were to be done again we might do it differently.

Undeterred by these setbacks, the general promised to continue to press for proper recognition of Lewin's services, even to the extent of making it a personal matter, and was confident that all would come right; though Lewin should build no hopes on his words.

> You know enough of the human heart [he concluded] to understand that such baubles as we seek afford us a very fleeting happiness. I can assure you that my KCB has been robbed of all the characteristics of a new toy during the first months of its possession by your ill luck and that I shall not know its full value till you have got your CSI. Believe me or not as you like. Goodbye. The length of my letter is proof, to myself at any rate, of the strength of my feelings on the subject.

From this remarkable letter it appears that the reasons why Lewin was deprived of the fleeting happiness such a bauble as the Star of India might have afforded him were complex. The veto seems to have been the result of an accumulation of factors, perhaps going back as far as the

Ellis case and the Johnston tragedy which will not have been forgotten. The fact that he was a soldier in civilian employ also complicated matters, for the CSI was a civil honour in the granting of which the commander-in-chief had no official status. Moreover, throughout his career Lewin had pursued his objectives with a blind bull-headedness that took no account of the unpopularity he was earning for himself in high places. He must now have bitterly regretted having agreed to write those newspaper articles, although apart from Brownlow the *Observer* was his only champion, informing its readers that the Haolongs would never have consented to submit

> but for the influence over them, not of our columns, but of a *political* officer, Captain Lewin — but for whose tact and good luck on the occasion, both the columns would have had to return to quarters with the satisfaction of knowing that they had left the work of the Expedition unfinished, and perhaps so much so, that another expedition to reduce the Howlongs would still be a necessity!

Or was Lewin the anonymous author of that article as well?

That can now never be known, but the muddle over the post on Sirte, the poison-pen letters making charges against Lewin with regard to the ladies in his district, and the view held in Calcutta that he had taken too soft a line with the Haolongs, these taken together were enough to spoil his chance of any public honour. The final decision rested with the new viceroy Lord Northbrook, to whom he was personally unknown, who was bound to take note of whatever Lewin's ill-wishers chose to whisper in his private ear.

Though he put a brave face on it, Lewin was mortified in the extreme and fretted for many months, but realized that to resign in disgust would be to cut off his nose to spite his face — or, as the Lushais say, to set fire to the house in order to kill a rat — for he would never again get another appointment that suited him so well. So he swallowed his pride, deriving what comfort he could from the reflection that in any case "a glittering star ill becomes a threadbare coat". Meanwhile he was quite alone in Rangamati as the rain ceaselessly fell, all his assistants having either succumbed to the climate or, finding the loneliness of the place unendurable, had beat a retreat to the comparatively bright lights of Chittagong.

At the beginning of the cold weather Lewin moved his headquarters to Demagri. Gordon and Bignell were sent with a strong detachment of the frontier battalion to take charge in the Bohmong's sector of the hill tracts, with a view to their protection from raids by the Lakhers from across the Arakan border who had been untouched by the recent expedition. Crouch was placed in direct charge of the Demagri post and chose for the site of his house a position under the hills to the south of the pool, overlooking the path that led to Rothangpuia's village; while Knyvett remained in charge at Rangamati.

Before Lewin could settle properly into his new home

he had first to make a journey to the south of his district in order to determine how to link the line of India's eastern frontier from Demagri to Arakan with that of British Burma. In a letter to his mother addressed "In the woods" he described how he had come seven days' journey from any human beings and still had six more to go. Laying down the frontier of an empire, he wrote, does not fall to everyone's lot. He had chosen fifteen picked men to go with him, well armed, and taken along ten hill coolies to carry their food, while the special officer of the Survey called Cook who accompanied him for part of the way in order to map the country came with a guard of military police and a host of coolies to carry their baggage and his heavy surveying instruments, his party making a grand total of ninety souls. They left Demagri at the end of November and made good progress until the surveyor decided that his instruments could be conveyed no further; and since his food was running out, he called a halt on 17 December and, leaving Lewin and his small party to complete the task, made tracks for home.

The virgin jungle they now entered was uninhabited except by wild animals, which were plentiful. One morning a rhino trotted for a while along the path in front of them before disappearing into the jungle, and several times they came upon clearings trampled smooth where a herd of elephants had danced. For two days and nights a tiger kept pace with them, mewing round their camp at night like a great domestic cat, and once a twenty-foot python as thick as a man's thigh slid across the path. Lewin's Christmas dinner consisted of boiled rice washed down with water because his last bottle of Holland's was exhausted, but he still had enough tobacco to fill his pipe. Averaging about twenty miles a day they covered a hundred and fifty miles of unexplored hill country, scaling heights, skirting precipices and fording rivers, and at last reached the southernmost outpost of Chima in the Bohmong's country. They had roughly demarcated the frontier all the way from Demagri and now marched into Gordon's headquarters on the Sangu, their clothes worn and ragged but in the best of spirits, and ravenously hungry. Having inspected the posts, Lewin made the journey back to Demagri, mainly by river, and soon had settled down again to his normal routine.

He was now busier than ever, for in consequence of the recent reorganization a new district had been added to his old one, and though he had several assistants they were his subordinates and required close supervision. In a letter to his mother he described the manifold activities that all needed to be done at once:

> to inspect my sepoys and arrange about guns & powder & clothing or talk of leave of absence or pay then there is the hospital where I poor physician have to prescribe as best I can for 15 or 20 poor sepoys besides I have dozens of houses to build or building, trees to fell, ground to clear, to manage the providing of food daily for 600 people and 12 elephants from a distance of 180 miles — and on the top of all to write & copy the frequent clever reports that Government require from day to day upon Frontier Policy, codification of law,

vaccination, education, survey of the country, frontier defence & God knows what beside. I am quite at my wits end my dear.

He now had little time for private writing or for playing music, or indeed to himself at all, for there always seemed to be some Lushai chief with scores of followers squatting on his veranda placidly drinking and smoking and refusing to go away.

In March 1873 he had to drop everything and set off in pursuit of a band of Lakhers who were reported to have crossed the frontier with evil intent, but on his approach they made off too fast for him to catch up with them. Soon after his return he had to go out again and meet another survey party which had entered the northern part of his district, whom he provided with provisions and a guard and set on the road back towards Cachar led by one of his assistants. Next he was off again to the frontier, diverging at Kasalong to inspect the Gurkha colonies he had founded on uninhabited land to serve as a buffer between the Mong rajah's people and the independent tribes to the east. On his return to Demagri he found waiting for him a paper from government suggesting that he should assume responsibility for additional Lushai territory, a notion he quickly dispelled, explaining how impossible it would be for one man to be in so many places at once, but proposing instead that the frontier should be made a separate charge from the hill tracts, with the idea of taking charge of it himself.

Since 1867 he had been making a collection of folk

lore, songs and old wives' stories of the hill people, many of which he had incorporated into his monograph *The Hill Tracts of Chittagong and the Dwellers Therein*. The proverbs were issued in 1873 as a pamphlet published by the Bengal Secretariat Press in Calcutta under the title *Hill Proverbs of the Inhabitants of / The Chittagong Hill Tracts* consisting of 278 sayings written in Burmese script with an English translation, a preamble and occasional notes. In the preamble he explained that the proverbs served the people as a system of mnemonic wisdom and repartee. They had not been taken from books or musty records, but from the lips of men and women, old and young, belonging to the Khyoungtha, the "sons of the river", on the hillside, in the forest or beside the earthen hearths of their hill homesteads. Some of the proverbs, such as "He got angry with the rat, and set fire to the house" or "The unsuccessful fisherman blames the river", have obvious English equivalents. Many are concerned with the relation between the sexes and throw light on the social habits of the people, for example:

> Man's life is ambition, woman's life is man.
>
> If you want a good pot, sound it first; if you want a good wife, know her first.
>
> If you love your wife, neither tell her your secrets nor make friends with young policemen.
>
> For sweetness, honey; for love, a wife.
>
> In flowers, perfume; in woman, beauty.

Others provide oblique comments on village life:

> Dry vegetables smell in the pot: cold people thaw at
> a feast.
>
> A thorn under the nail is unbearable; so is it to have
> a relation in slavery.

He had placed Nurudin in charge of the household in
his shanty in Demagri and even bought a cookery book
with the help of which, when Toby his Magh cook had
gone off on leave, they together concocted some curious
dishes. For the faithful and brave service Nurudin had
given her son during the campaign Mrs Lewin had sent
him a double-barrelled, breach-loading gun with five
hundred loaded cartridges, three hundred shot and two
hundred bullets. Now Lewin had appointed him bazaar
superintendent, with the result that, with his servants
unsupervised, the household fell into sad disorder. More
than ever he had to rely for his sustenance on the stores
which had been sent out from home — mock turtle or
oyster soup, Scotch broth, anchovies from Fortnum &
Mason, black puddings, haggis, bacon, German sausages,
mushrooms, Brussels sprouts and asparagus' — though
he supplemented these tinned supplies with whatever
peas, beans, carrots and turnips he could persuade to
grow in his vegetable garden.

In the rainy season he was sometimes overcome by his
utter isolation and loneliness, reporting to his mother in
July with some exaggeration that he had not spoken

English for nearly three months. To while away the evenings he read translations of Tacitus and Herodotus and with only two cats for company felt that he only wanted an attendant parrot to be a nondescript sort of Robinson Crusoe.

2

From the first Lewin had it in mind to build a house surrounded by a strong stockade on Sirte Tlang, a ridge some miles to the north-east of, and at an elevation of a thousand feet higher than, Demagri, where eventually he hoped to establish the headquarters of the frontier administration. Rothangpuia willingly set his people to work, and soon a house built to Lushai specifications — which came to be known to Lewin's assistants as Uncle Tom's Cabin — crowned the hilltop commanding magnificent panoramas of the surrounding hills. It was constructed of rough unhewn logs plastered outside with mud, the inside walls being covered with bamboo matting. "I must needs confess," he wrote later, "that the wind whistled at times very keenly on my lonely hilltop, and I gazed enviously at the crested falcon which perched on a dead tree near the house, wishing that I had a warm suit of feathers like his, instead of some thin old English garments which kept out neither wind nor weather." His household still consisted entirely of hillfolk who, without Nurudin to keep them in order, lost Lewin's clothes, broke his lamps, dropped his concertina into the river and, crowning misfortune, allowed a case of wine and beer newly arrived from Calcutta, which they were unloading from the back of an elephant, to fall on to a conical black rock, smashing the lot.

Over the years he had become more and more aware of the beauty of some of the hill girls, admiring especially their skin: "It is almost a gold colour; they are like statues of transparent gold through which shines out the life light". Tradition has it that his household included a Lushai girl. Her full name has not been handed down and might have been Darthuami, Darthluangi, Dartangi, Darlaii or something similar, for she was known as Dari for short. It was remembered that her name was so often on Lewin's lips that the sepoys thought it was the Lushai word for girl, and so it took on that local meaning among the soldiery. Dari was a village girl, not a chief's daughter, and since in old age she lived at Lungsen, which had been Rothangpuia's village, it is likely she was living there when Lewin first saw her. It is said, too, that she bore him a son, who died when he was just able to walk.

The house on Sirte Tlang held a strange fascination for Lewin, and when he wrote of the place in his autobiography some years later his prose took on an unaccustomed lyricism as he recalled an afternoon when he had stood on the hill close to the house, at his feet the valley falling sheer for hundreds of feet, but able to see nothing but the mist that came billowing up from below before gradually thinning away.

That same evening there was a glorious sunset, so I scrambled down a neighbouring ravine and watched the rushing torrent cast its masses of topaz-coloured water over the dark rocks, foaming, raging, roaring and tumbling headlong down with such an uproarious outpouring of living strength that I shouted aloud in sympathy with the wild water.

In the evening he had watched as the light faded away from the faraway purple hills of the Haolong country and, below in the valley, the flickering hearth-fires of the houses in a distant village, and there had come faintly to his ears the lowing of mithan as they lumbered in from the jungle where they had browsed during the daytime, each making for the courtyard of his master's house where a lick of salt awaited it.

With such a household it is not surprising that books and music for the time being lost their importance for him, and he now dismissed them as only the scrollwork and ornamentation of life; as well, he reflected, ask a man to live on gingerbread. Reading through the poems he had written in earlier years he thought them not good enough to be published and not for the first time concluded that his poetic days were over, for his writing had now taken a more serious turn. He was engaged in the tiresome work of preparing the vocabularies for his *Progressive Colloquial Exercises / in the / Lushai Dialect / of the 'Dzo' or Kuki Language / with / Vocabularies and Popular Tales (notated)*, which was published in Calcutta in 1874. Though he acknowledged that it was imperfect and incomplete, he intended it as a manual for the use of government officers and to pave the way for education among the tribes. It consisted of ninety exercises and three stories — 'The Consequences', 'Story of Lál Ruánga' and 'The Story of Kúngóri' — having the Lushai text and an English translation side by side and accompanying notes. Though the work has now been largely superseded, it was a considerable achievement for an amateur untrained in linguistics and proved of great value to government officers and missionaries needing a primer from which to learn the basics of the language. It still possesses a special usefulness in that it preserves evidence of idioms and usages that would otherwise have been forgotten. Although certain elements of the grammar of the language eluded Lewin, he was truly a pioneer and provided the groundwork on which later scholars have built.

Lewin also completed in manuscript *A Grammar of the Aracanese dialect of Burmese for use by government officers among the Hill Tribes of the South-East Frontier of India* which remained unpublished, and his work in that field is reflected in the translation he made into Burmese, for the instruction of the people of the Chittagong Hills, of Müller's translation from the Pali of Buddha's *Dhammapada*, or *The Path of Virtue*.

When his *Hill Proverbs of the Inhabitants of the Chittagong Hill Tracts* was published he asked his mother to send a review copy to the *Pall Mall Gazette*. "In this world," he wrote to her, "notoriety is everything: a rose that is born to blush unseen had just as well been a buttercup, a daisy or any other lowly flower"; in which conviction he sent two copies of the book to General Brownlow asking him to forward one of them to the commander-in-chief, and a specially bound copy to the commissioner of Chittagong Mr Hankey. In return for the copy of her *Personal Life of George Grote* published earlier in the year which his aunt Grote had sent him he sent to her also a copy of his *Hill Proverbs*. Her book interested him so much that he asked his mother to get him copies of Grote's eight-volume *History of Greece* and also his books on Aristotle and Plato, second-hand ones because they would inevitably be destroyed by the damp.

Writing to him that aunt Charlotte was growing feeble his mother must have speculated on the destination of her money when she died, for Lewin reacted strongly. His aunt was loveable and good and gracious in many ways, and her being their own flesh and blood was sufficient cause why they should be tender and reverent to her in her old age. It disgusted him, he wrote, when relations waited for someone to die in the expectation of inheriting their money, like a crowd of greedy vultures such as he had often seen in India, waiting in dull silence for the death of some nobler creature so that they might fill their maws. It was strange, though, how aunt Charlotte put her faith in Bob. He had recently returned from a voyage to Hong Kong where his vessel had been held up for repairs and was now staying with their mother, and there was talk of his putting up on the door a brass-plated sign reading 'Dr Lewin', but he was not to retire from the sea just yet. If he wanted money, Lewin wrote, he could draw on him either as a gift or a loan, whichever he liked.

Will, Izzy and Ellaline had also returned home, the Kentucky venture having proved as unsuccessful as the sheep farm in the Falklands, and were back in the cottage in Barnes where in September their first son Thomas had been born. A week earlier Will had resumed his acting career, appearing at Drury Lane in an adaptation of Scott's *The Lady in the Lake*, and his performance had attracted the favourable notice of one of London's leading drama critics Clement Scott. At last Will seemed to have turned the corner. All was well, too, with Harriet and Bella who in 1873 within three months of one another had each produced a baby. Mrs Lewin had gone to Dumpton Park in East Anglia where the Tomlins lived, to help Harriet through her first confinement; the best thing that could have happened to her, commented Lewin. Nor did he forget his best friend Harry and on his birthday, 18 July, raised a solitary glass and drank to his health and happiness.

It was a sign that Lewin was still emotionally tied to his mother's apron strings that, although at thirty-three his hair had now turned grey as his father's had done, he continued to have nightmares about her. One night at Sirte he dreamt he was at home and because the maid servant Jane could not look after his things he had put his arm round his mother saying "Never mind about that sulky bit of goods, come for a walk", and walking along the bank of a canal she had tripped and fallen head foremost into the water and he woke screaming for Bob to help him. Thoughts of her dying still haunted him, once prompting a declaration that vividly betrays the confused state of his emotions:

> Comfort and honour and fine covering for back and belly — the bodies of young girls and the homage of men — these things can Mammon give us, but health and a quiet conscience or the long-suffering, never-dying love of a mother, these are God's gifts above all price and given by Him to rich and poor alike, even as he sends rain on the just and on the unjust.

3

By mid-August Lewin was beginning to look forward to the cold weather when he planned to visit Rangamati for a change from his lonely life. He was tired of the rain and the sleet, the wind that chilled him to the bone and the damp that destroyed his books, and fussed over his much-enduring harmonium like a hen clucking over her chickens. He had not touched his 'cello for a year because it was so damp in his bamboo house that he dare not string it up. Besides, the scores of *Lohengrin* and *Tannhauser* his mother had sent him were too advanced for him to manage. Outside the house everything was wrapped in dense mist so that he could hardly see a yard in front of him, and it was so cold that he had to dress warmly in flannel and have a fire at night. And yet, he reflected, take away the flies, the leeches and the loneliness, and his kingdom was a beautiful place after all.

And he had great plans for the future. He had applied to the American Baptist Mission in Rangoon for a missionary to come and work in his hills, for the English missionary societies he considered no good as they would do nothing except to the sound of a trumpet; and if the AMS could not help, he would seek the aid of the bishop of Calcutta. The lieutenant-governor had approved his proposal to make an expedition into the far Lushai country in the coming cold weather, when for two months he would be swallowed up off the face of the earth, but had urged on him the necessity of avoiding risk and "complications", so he would have to take a good guard with him. As for his long-term schemes for reorganizing the administration of his district, the government would settle nothing, so he would have to pay another visit to Calcutta in order to press his case. Mr Hankey, who had just returned from home leave and was still in Calcutta, would be useful in assisting him in dealing with the authorities. Just before leaving he had an official visit from Colonel Raban — in his younger days the destroyer of Rothangpuia's village — who came to inspect the frontier battalion under Lewin's command and, finding everything in order, had gone on his way again. As the time approached he began to worry that the government might stop his eastern journey after all, because his district work was increasing so rapidly in extent and importance, and he had so many strings in his hand and so many English officers under him, that they might be inclined to insist on his sitting still like an old spider in the middle of his web and managing everything from Rangamati. If so, his dreams of residing in the hills at Sirte would vanish away like the morning mist. Certainly, to Calcutta he must go.

Besides, his visit would provide the opportunity for him to put into practice a notion he had long had in mind, of taking the principal Lushai chiefs to Calcutta so that they would begin to see their little world in its true perspective and also to enable them to pay their respects to the great ones of government. They needed a lot of persuading, no doubt remembering the fate of another chief, Lalsuktla who, having entrusted himself to an English *sahib*, had been snatched away and exiled to the Andamans. After all, they had nothing to gain from the visit, but if Thangliena insisted... In November the chiefs began to assemble at Demagri, seven of them with a select number of their followers, the whole party numbering twenty-seven altogether. First to agree had been Rothangpuia who had reason enough to trust the *sirkar*, and his example was followed by Lalngura, Vanhnuaia, Lalchema, Lalnghura and two other chiefs; but nothing would now induce Seipuia, although he was Rothangpuia's brother-in-law, to go along with them.

"It is true that we believe all you say, Thangliena. We have known you a long time and your tongue is straight. But you say the governor-general is more powerful than you are. Is that the case?"

"Yes," replied Lewin, "he is very great, certainly more powerful than I am."

"Well, then, suppose he orders Seipuia to be speared?"

They left on 1 December by river for Chittagong where they boarded a steamer which took them across the Bay of Bengal to Calcutta. Throughout the voyage the chiefs maintained an impassive demeanour, only betraying the nervousness they felt by their reluctance to let Lewin out of their sight. In Calcutta tents had been pitched for them on the *Maidan*, and when they had disembarked and Lewin had seen them safely into carriages under the care of Nurudin, he was about to enter another carriage to take him to the comforts of his club when he felt his coat-tails firmly clutched from behind. Nothing he could say would persuade the chiefs to allow him to leave them, so willy-nilly he drove with them to the *Maidan*, where another tent was pitched for his own occupation.

A photograph taken outside a house in Calcutta shows eighteen of the party, many of them holding the shotguns which had been presented to them, and none of them looking as if he was enjoying the occasion. In a chair in the middle sits chief Lalgnura in white with Vanhnuaia sitting on his right and Rothangpuia in a chequered tartan on his left. They were not particularly impressed by the splendours of the City of Palaces. At Belvedere the lieutenant-governor's residence they showed a brief interest in a solid silver sofa in the drawing room which was supported by silver lions, and for once dropped their reserve when they were taken for a hair-raising ride at full speed in a railway engine which had been placed at

Lewin's disposal by the traffic manager of the East India Railway. They were constantly subjected to scrutiny by sightseers, curious to see the wild savages they had read about in accounts of the Lushai campaign, among them Lewin's friend of Mutiny days Dr Busteed, now working at the mint. Another visitor was the 'Indian Affairs' correspondent of the London *Morning Post*, who in his telegram filed on 2 January 1874 permitted himself a little gentle raillery.

> You will remember the 'terrible' Lushai war, when six thousand men walked up the hill, and then walked down again, doing a little in the way of village burning on the way. There were those then, and there are now, who state that the permanent results of the expedition would last about as long as it would take to rebuild the light bamboo huts we had destroyed...
>
> Last Sunday there were encamped at a short distance in front of the United Service Club, Lal Ngora, eldest son of Savunga (the Great Bear), head chief of the Sylo tribe; Van Hnuya, not a Dutchman, but a Lushai of importance and an old enemy; and Rutton Poia, our most faithful ally in the late contest... Their dress consists of a single sheet worn round the waist, which they are at no trouble to fasten, and have to be constantly hitching in order to keep them from falling to the ground. In the second place they would drink any Dublin cabbie or Highland ghillie I ever met under the table without wincing. They cannot get their native 'gee', a rice spirit, here, so their affectionate ally gives them the best Old Tom and brandy to be got in the Great Eastern Hotel. My visit was the sign for two bottles of the former to appear. I sipped a thimbleful, whilst they drank their liquor by the tumblerful, to their manifest and loudly expressed satisfaction.

After two of the chiefs had lost themselves in the teeming maze of streets and been brought back late at night by friendly policemen they seldom strayed far from their tents except when Lewin was with them. They slept little, but sat up far into the night talking and smoking, homesick for the peace and cleanliness of their hills; and after a fortnight they gladly set out for home in the charge of Nurudin, laden with presents and purchases. Lewin remained behind to discuss his reforms with the government people.

At which point there is a sudden gap in the otherwise plentiful records of Lewin's life. On 30 November 1873 he had written to his mother from Rangamati to say that in a couple of days he would be leaving for Calcutta with his convoy of Kookie chiefs, and then the correspondence lapses. Of the official documents there is a despatch from Lord Salisbury, the secretary of state for India in London, to the government of India dated 19th March 1874, praising Lewin's efforts to secure the confidence of the hill tribes; but by that date Lewin was already on his way home. The hiatus is papered over in his autobiography in general terms. After describing the chiefs' departure from Calcutta he wrote:

> Honest fellows they were, and true, in their own wild way. I never saw them or their hills again, for the home government refused to sanction the proposals made by the government of India for the reconstitution of the frontier administration, and I saw no chance of being able to carry out efficiently the work on which I had set

my heart, to which I had pledged my faith, and for which
I had worked so long.

I think, also, I was out of spirits, as I was certainly out
of health. The life which I had led in the hills was one
involving the extremest hardships and personal
responsibility. Without friends, without society, and
(until the last year or so) without the companionship of
a fellow-countryman, and now, added to this, the lack of
any recognition for my services, filled me with such a
chill sense of disappointment, that I felt it impossible to
renew work on the old terms.

Lewin's behaviour on previous occasions of disagreement with higher authority provides some basis for
guessing what occurred when his scheme for reorganizing
his district was turned down. Once before he had been
pulled up sharply by a lieutenant-governor for using
language that bordered on insubordination, and many
times in letters to his mother written in moments of
depression he had threatened to resign his appointment
and come home for good, even if it meant his starving.
Moreover, his personal record sheet was not without its
blots, including the Ellis case, the tragedy of George
Johnston, and the many accusations levelled against him
by the Kalindi rani which, though proven false, will still
have left a sour after-taste. Nor could his success in
securing the confidence of the hill tribes dispel the
official disapproval of Lewin's practice of running his
district as if it were his personal kingdom. "What is
wanted now," he had written in his book *The Hill Tracts of
Chittagong,*

is not measures but a man. Place over them an officer gifted with the power of rule; not a mere cog in the great wheel of government, but one tolerant of the failings of his fellow-creatures, and yet prompt to see and recognize in them the touch of Nature that makes the whole world kin; — apt to enter into new trains of thought and to modify and adopt ideas, but cautious in offending national prejudice. Under a guidance like this, let the people by slow degrees civilize themselves. With education open to them, and yet moving under their own laws and customs, they will turn out, not debased and miniature epitomes of Englishmen, but a new and noble type of God's creatures.

The contrary view of officialdom had been summed up in what a senior official once said to Lewin: "We don't want personal influence; we want men who will obey orders."

The truth is that Lewin and the government of India had completely different priorities. Officialdom saw its overriding task as the creation of a favourable environment in which British business could flourish, whereas the chief concern of Lewin and his like was the welfare of the people entrusted to their care. That is not to say that the British enforced their rule with unnecessary harshness, though dominion over palm and pine must of its nature involve the suppression of the rights of the governed. Nor is it suggested that Lewin was so altruistic as to deprive himself of the opportunities that came his way of investing his savings in such British enterprises as tea gardens. Moreover his concern was not for the indigenous inhabitants of India generally, but solely for the hill people of the north-east frontier who come of a completely separate racial stock and have never considered their homeland as being a part of India at all. The fact that throughout his career Lewin and his superiors had been at cross-purposes was at the root of the disagreement that resulted in his being exiled from his kingdom. So it is likely that a typical compromise was arrived at: Lewin would not be sacked, but he was forbidden to set foot in the hills again; his resignation was refused, but he was to depart immediately for a long and well-deserved home leave. In such ways are the decencies preserved in the corridors of power.

As for Dari, having emerged briefly and indistinctly from the shadows she again fades from the picture. There is a tradition in the hills that Lewin asked her to come to England with him, but that she had not courage enough to go with him to a strange land. Instead she returned to her village and resumed her old life, refusing to be treated as the wife of a high official; and some years later she married one of her own people. Many years were to pass before Lewin heard of her again.

Part III (1874-1916)

Limits and Renewals

Chapter Fifteen
Margaret

1

In July 1874 while on home leave Lewin accompanied by his mother and his cousin Jeannie went to Kissingen, a German spa, to drink the medicinal waters for the sake of his liver. While he was away aunt Grote once more busied herself on his behalf, pulling strings in the highest quarter; with her usual success, for Lord Salisbury, then secretary of state for India in Disraeli's government, unable to resist the blandishments of so formidable a lady, consented to recommend Lewin for a more salubrious station. In order to clinch things she also wrote to the lieutenant-governor of Bengal Sir Richard Temple, whom her husband had known slightly, soliciting his interest on her nephew's behalf. "He is now quite restored to health," she wrote to Babbie, "and will, I trust, resume active duty under favourable conditions on reaching Calcutta," for which place he had sailed in the s.s. *Surat* in February 1875.

No unusual incidents occurred on the voyage except that one of the passengers, a Miss Hatch, appears to have paid marked attention to him, and in the Mediterranean one of the screws broke, necessitating the vessel being detained at Suez for repairs after steaming slowly through the canal, which had been opened six years before. There he received a letter his sister Harriet had addressed to the ship's agents, which caused him some agitation, the reason for which is apparent from his reply to her:

> I almost wish you had not written to me about Maggie Elliot, for although she is the only woman I have seen in England who moved me, yet is she at the same time a bright particular star far out of my reach and only to be admired at a distance. (Do you remember the bright diamond star she wore in the soft white foldings round her neck the night she dined with us?)

For Tom Lewin had fallen in love, and when that happens to a man of his emotional composition it becomes an overmastering passion. From the first Harriet, quick to notice their mutual attraction, had done all she could to foster it, and to the last acted as confidante to both parties and self-appointed matchmaker. Years later she remembered vividly the first time she had seen Margaret, "the tall beautiful fair woman walking on Stone House lawn, with sunny hair and sweet smile and your father holding Mabel by the hand, following". At the time Lewin met her she was thirty-two years old, a rich widow with three young daughters, living at 50 Eaton Square in a fashionable quarter of London.

She was the fourth of the five children of an eminent Scottish civil engineer, John Robinson McClean and his wife Anna, both of whom were born in northern Ireland. McClean had been associated with the construction of harbours, docks and railways and other major projects, and as a member of parliament had introduced an unsuccessful bill for supplying London with water from

Henley-on-Thames. He had reported on the feasibility of repeating in Paris the English system of public baths and workhouses, and was concerned with de Lesseps' proposal to cut a canal across the isthmus of Suez. In later life he became chairman of the Anglo-American Telegraph Company, president of the Institution of Chartered Engineers, and a fellow of the Royal, Geological, Astrological and other learned societies. He also travelled extensively, and it was on a visit to India that he received a sunstroke from which he never fully recovered, dying at Stonehouse in Thanet in July 1873, three years before his daughter Margaret met Lewin.

In August 1863 when she was barely out of her teens Margaret had been prevailed on to enter into a marriage of convenience with Ralph Elliot, the twenty-three year old elder son of George Elliot, a man of wealth who entered parliament as MP for North Durham in 1868 and six years later was given a baronetcy, a few months after Ralph's death. Although three daughters were born to them — Anna, Margaret (known as Daisy) and Mabel — the marriage which had never been a love match was not a happy one, perhaps because Ralph was too fond of the bottle, and at the age of thirty Margaret was left a widow with three little girls to bring up.

Replying from Suez to Harriet's disturbing letter Lewin asked her to obtain Margaret's permission for him to write to her occasionally, to keep her remembrance of him fresh and green until he returned. He also asked her to let him have back Margaret's photograph which he now regretted having given back to Harriet. Although he did not know it at the time, his sister had taken it upon herself to give Margaret a photograph of him with a message purporting to have come from him, which must have given her a fair idea of the state of his heart.

When his ship docked at Calcutta Lewin found that his path, due to aunt Grote's intervention, had been made smooth for him, and once more he basked in the favour of his superiors. The lieutenant-governor positively crawled.

> It was a great pleasure to me to serve Captain Lewin [he wrote to Mrs Grote]. He is an officer of superior zeal, intelligence, and self-devotion [sic], and is in every way deserving of your regard and interest.

The service Sir Richard rendered him was to appoint him superintendent of Cooch Behar State, a sinecure in which his functions fully met the specifications once desiderated by the Kalindi rani, being mainly decorative. Cooch Behar was an unimportant princely state bordering on the kingdom of Bhutan and lay under the foothills of the Himalayas which to the north raised their snowy summits to the sky. A sort of Sleepy Hollow Lewin called it where, though he was his own master, he had little real work to do. The climate was healthy, the pay generous, and he was provided with a rent-free house which even boasted a billiard-room. His principal duty, he found, was to look after the young rajah, a boy of fourteen, and to try and keep order among the one hundred and fifty wives and concubines the late rajah had left behind.

13. Sir Alexander Mackenzie, KCSI

14. Margaret Elliot in 1876

15. Parkhurst
16. Family Music

17. William Terriss as Henry VIII

18. Dr. Friend Lewin

19. Everset Macdonald with Ursula and Diana

20. T.H. Lewin and Margaret in 1900

21. T.H. Lewin in 1910

There were only two other European officials in the place, the doctor whose vulgar wife Lewin called a sort of breeding machine which had already brought forth nine young ones, and Mr Beckett a young man with a sixty-year-old wife whom he had married (it was said) because her daughter had.refused him.

Cooch Behar state with a population of about five million comprised some thirteen thousand square miles of flat paddyland situated under the western Duars, the tract of Himalayan *terai* acquired as a result of the forgotten Bhutan War (1864, 1866) when the British initially suffered a military disaster at Dewangiri. The state was watered by six principal rivers, four of them flowing from north-east to south-west and eventually discharging into the great Brahmaputra. In Lewin's time there were no villages as such in the state, the whole country being dotted with farmsteads, each surrounded by a circle of cultivation, and the only aggregation of buildings deserving the name of a town was the administrative centre, also known as Cooch Behar, with a population of upwards of seven thousand. It comprised a brick mansion which did service as the rajah's palace surrounded by a congeries of mud huts, a small bazaar and a few public buildings including the dispensary, public library, record rooms and printing office. It was in contemplation to build a more suitable residence for the rajah as well as improved law courts and schools. The rajahship had been held by the Narain family since the early sixteenth century, and on the death through intemperance in 1863 of the then incumbent, his son Nripendro Narain being at the time an infant, the administration of the state had been placed for the period of his minority in the hands of a British officer with the title of Superintendent of the Native State of Koch Bihar, subject to the supervision and control of the commissioner of the Rajshaye division of the province of Bengal. All the other state officials were natives.

In June Lewin was put to his first test as master of ceremonies when he had to organize a grand reception for Sir Richard who was paying a visit of inspection to the state. It took thirty horses, fifteen elephants, two carriages and two *palkis* to transport him and his party with all their impedimenta from the eastern boundary to the capital. With the lieutenant-governor came his aide-de-camp, his private secretary and thirty servants, and also the bishop of Calcutta with his chaplain and their servants. They made their progress with an escort of cavalry, Lewin riding beside the lieutenant-governor's carriage, and at the entrance of the town a triumphal arch had been constructed on which hung a scarlet and white cloth inscribed with suitable words of welcome. Beyond the arch were congregated all the state officials gleaming in cloth of gold and silver, scarlet-clad sepoys presented arms, and elephants salaamed as they went slowly by. Schoolchildren sang and scattered flowers in the roadway; the women of the place expressed their welcome by a curious ululation caused by rapidly agitating the tongue; cannons boomed a seventeen-gun salute. Due respect having been paid, the party proceeded to Lewin's house where they relaxed over drinks. Next day the lieutenant-governor received all the state's officials, European and native, at a durbar while Lewin stood by, sweating in full uniform. Afterwards he took them on a tour of inspection of schools, treasury, printing press, jail, barracks, high court, temples and other places of interest. Though he hated pomp and ceremony, everything had gone well, and when it was all over he escorted the party to the state's western boundary where the lieutenant-governor's yacht lay at anchor in the Teesta, and Sir Richard, thinking the change would do him good, took him for a trip on the river.

Among the positive results of the descent of the lieutenant-governor on Cooch Behar was the sanction of the building of a new palace for the rajah and new public buildings, an increase in the state's military strength, and the purchase of a steam yacht for the superintendent's use. He was also given permission — such was aunt Grote's continued influence — to stay at Buksa on Bhutan's border with Cooch Behar thirty miles from the capital at an elevation of 2000 feet, if he was not well or he found the weather had become too hot. Buksa reminded Lewin of his old solitudes on Sirte Tlang, though he found the Bhutias less likeable than his Lushai hill folk, being rude in manner and dirty in person, with an ill look and a sour smell. He took the opportunity to begin to study the Tibetan language under the tutelage of a lama, for Bhutan was no more than a detached district of Tibet, its language, people, customs and religion all being Tibetan.

Meanwhile he had made no progress with Margaret. Harriet had complied with his request to send him her photograph, but at the same time had indicated ambiguously that Margaret had not given him permission to write to her, a check which had the, perhaps intended, effect of inducing Lewin to get off a twelve-page letter to her without further delay. "My dear Mrs Elliot," it began, "I have been forbidden to write to you — that alone is an incentive, for what is forbidden cannot but be dear to the sons and daughters of Eve ...", marking the overture to the burgeoning correspondence that now began to develop between two exceptionally intelligent, self-willed, high-spirited people. Like any other suitor at the commencement of his suit Lewin began by laying out his wares like an oriental carpet-seller, trying to light upon the colour or pattern that would most appeal to his lady. He described his present surroundings in primary colours, suggested his own versatility by reference to his 'cello and harmonium, Wagner and Beethoven, and mentioned as his current reading Tennyson's play *Queen Mary*, which he had the good taste to think little of. He managed to glamorize whilst appearing to depreciate his manifold duties in Cooch Behar, where he served as *locum tenens* for the young rajah, dispensing justice, supervising education and multifariously acting as minister for war (with an army of two hundred men), commissioner-general (having charge of twelve elephants), master of the horse (his cavalry consisting of ten horses with carriages), foreign secretary (dealing only with neighbouring Tibet) and chancellor of the exchequer (with an annual revenue of £10,000 a year and a national debt).

Margaret's reply has not survived for Lewin later tore it up "because it hurt", but Harriet must have jokingly suggested to her that her brother had had a shipboard romance with Miss Hatch, about whom she had gently teased him. For a while the correspondence lapsed while Lewin thought things over; besides he had become involved in organizing a state visit of even greater importance than the previous one.

On this occasion the lieutenant-governor was to meet the Deb Rajah, the ruling monarch of Bhutan, at Buksa, for which elaborate preparations had to be made. Sir Richard with his retinue including the deputy commissioner of nearby Jalpaiguri and his private secretary arrived there on the evening of 21 October, to be joined next day by the Cooch Behar contingent. A large durbar tent complete with carpets and dais, gold throne cloths and gold and silver *golabdans* and *pandans*, was made ready, and at noon next day there took place a picturesque meeting of the middle ages with the modern world, graphically described by Lewin in his official report.

There followed a formal reception when courteous greetings were offered to the rajah and in the evening a display of fireworks which much delighted the Bhutias. The formal durbar took place next day at which official gifts were exchanged, and afterwards the 38th Bengal

Infantry which was stationed in Cooch Behar gave an exhibition of foot drill and musketry before the two embassies went their separate ways. Aunt Grote who had been responsible for his appointment was delighted by his account of the pageant, imagining him as some lordly diplomatist "cajoling semi-barbarous princes of the Tartar Steppes". For Lewin the most promising aspect of a tiring affair was the letter he received from the Deb Rajah in the following terms:

> Now hear on account of the Deb Rajah's friendship for Captain Lewin, Deputy Commissioner of Cooch Behar, that officer is requested and invited to come for two or three months to visit me in my house at Punakha to learn religious wisdom. On the road both small and great shall assist him in his journey.
>
> *Dated the 18th day of the 9th month of the Year Shinphak (Wood Hog). [Seal of Deb Rajah].*

It cannot be doubted that Lewin himself, with the help of the lama under whom he had been learning Tibetan, had engineered the invitation, but such high matters of state were beyond the authority of his protector Sir Richard and required the sanction of the viceroy himself, and Lewin had no great hope that permission would be forthcoming.

In a mood of dejection Lewin spent Christmas staying at the United Service Club in Calcutta, where he had to take part in various functions in honour of the visit of the Prince of Wales, the future King Edward VII, which gave him no peace day or night. There was a polo match played by Manipuris, whose state had been the cradle of the game, and an exhibition by torchlight of national dances performed by Naga and Lushai men and women, the men tattooed and adorned with plumes of hornbill feathers, the women decked out in bright beads and bracelets of coral, silver and brass. He had to attend one or two balls but declined to waltz, only taking part in conventional quadrilles. A gathering of the Star of India he avoided, still smarting under the disappointment that he had not been made a companion of the order. Dissatisfied with his sinecure in Cooch Behar, he applied for a transfer to another appointment, which being refused he considered asking to be placed on special duty travelling in Bhutan and Tibet in order to complete his Tibetan studies, after which he would take retirement at the end of 1876 and live in Darjeeling, which was said to be the healthiest place in Bengal. He might even be allowed to return to his old Chittagong appointment where at least he had the excitement of danger and the pleasure of rule, for he had heard that in the two years since he had ruled over the tribes things had gone from bad to worse. A report in a local newspaper had stated that the hill tracts were already feeling his loss: "It is not given to every man," it ran, "to fiddle his way through the jooms from the Sangoo to Arracan, and to make the rudest savage know his master in hill travel". In such ways are legends born. But by now Lewin had come to reflect on the defects of a system of government dependent on one man, on whose departure or death temporary or permanent chaos was bound to supervene. Besides, he felt that his work there was done. In such a frame of mind he took up his pen on 31 December to write a second letter to Margaret.

He first tried to explain, not entirely truthfully, why he had not answered her letter sooner. He had not been well, he wrote; his district was unhealthy; and his lonely life and heavy responsibility had told upon him. He had now become so altered, so grey, so despondent, that she would hardly recognize him. He had also been deterred from writing to her by what she had written about Miss Hatch. Whatever the source of her information — which must surely have been Harriet — he assured her that, as far as he was concerned, his feelings towards the young lady were not such as seemed to have been attributed to him. With the words "I think sometimes I shall never marry at all" he entered upon an un-characteristic passage of self-pity, bemoaning his fate to be deprived of love, "to see children like flowers, to love their voices and the patter of little feet, and then go back into the wilderness where is nought". There was more in similar vein before he managed to pull himself together and write of such prosaic things as the durbar at Buksa and the prince's visit to Calcutta, ending with a wish that one could get through life without monetary considerations, which must have revealed to Margaret which way his thoughts were tending.

As compared with earlier times Lewin's cor-respondence with his mother had diminished at this time to brief, occasional notes, and he took less interest in the affairs of his immediate family than he had previously done. Bob was off on his voyages as ship's surgeon in P&O vessels, and he had heard that Will was having success as an actor; but his attention was now almost exclusively engaged in this new, delightful obsession.

No second letter came from Margaret to lift his spirits, but at this critical moment Harriet who had been staying with her provided the necessary incentive for him to continue the correspondence, writing to say that he was wrong, Margaret did not dislike his letters, and so gave him all the encouragement he needed. On 2 February he wrote eight pages to her, a blend of flattery, news of his doings and hints of his real feelings towards her. He could take pension in 1877 with the rank of lieutenant-colonel: should he retire, for the sake of his mother? Less than a fortnight later he wrote again ("You will perhaps be surprised to receive another letter from me so soon upon the heels of the previous one ...") with the startling news that, after much self-communing, he was coming home and would probably be in England by the end of April. Aunt Charlotte had died leaving him a legacy, giving him a pretext for applying for six months' leave to attend to private affairs. She had looked forward to death as a release and died imperceptibly in the early hours of a morning in August in her bed at Barn House, Eltham, where she had been looked after by Jeannie, who as ever was ready with a gracious word. "And so," she wrote to Lewin, "her kind heart and bright presence are gone from among us, and we shall not look upon her like again."

Lewin had bought in the bazaar an Italian 'cello and two violins, one by Guanerius, the other a Stradivarius — relics of a previous rajah's enthusiasm for western music — which he would bring home with him; "bringing my sheaves with me, you see", referring to a passage in Thackeray's *Henry Esmond* he knew she would recognize. It illustrates how he had come to view their relationship that he saw himself in the rôle of Esmond laying his heart at the feet of Lady Castlewood. Abruptly he moved on to describe an encounter with a rogue elephant which was still at large. A fortnight later he wrote her yet another eight pages ("You will perhaps open big eyes at me in astonishment at my venturing to write again so soon ..."), for he was by now beyond restraint of propriety, and words poured from his pen. He would not write about the people in his hills at Chittagong, "for you see that was the work of my life", being afraid of boring her, but nevertheless embarked on a lush description of the beautiful woods and breezy hills among which he used to wander, the silvery brattle of the silver-voiced streams, the musical cry of the hoolock gibbons, and the *jödel* of the hill folk echoing from one slope to another. By an easy transition he moved on to praising her singing, nothing being so sweet to him as the pure passionate notes of a woman's contralto, and to her promise that, when he did come home, she would play the piano at quartets, for which he was working away at his 'cello.

Due to what he described as the innate perverseness of officialdom there was a delay in his leave being sanctioned, so that before he left for Calcutta to embark for England Margaret's second letter arrived at Cooch Behar, written on 10 February before she had news of his imminent return and at a time when she still believed he would not be home to trouble her for at least two years. Written in reply to his despondent letter from Calcutta, she tried to allay his depression, referring to her own far greater cause for despondency. For so many years, she wrote, had she looked upon death as her best friend that life seemed almost strange to her, and she had forgotten how to look forward. She shared his loneliness of spirit, and sometimes on entering a room the very air seemed antipathetic, and turning over whole books of songs she could not find one she had the heart to sing. As to his wishing for her friendship and esteem, she sent him the equivalent in writing of her best curtsy.

A strange, sad, sweet letter, he called it, which nevertheless set his spirits soaring, and looking forward to the pleasure of dancing with her he speculated on the propriety of his rushing off to some dancing school to attain the intricacies of the latest capers.

2

The time-lag of six weeks or more between the writing and the receiving of letters between India and England meant that events might have overtaken them before they arrived. Lewin's letter of 2 February reached Margaret unusually quickly on 6 March, and ten days later in her sitting-room in Eaton Square, while her children were asleep and the house still, she wrote to him in reply a calm, thoughtful, newsy letter spiced with coquetry — "I wonder what that bad Harriet said to you to make you think that I did not dislike your letters, particularly as when she was with me you had written only *one*" — but for some reason delayed posting it. Then she received his letter with the news that he was on his way home, which put her in a state of agitation that reached fever pitch when Harriet told her plainly, what she should have known from his letters, that her brother was in love with her.

In her perplexity she reached for a pen and poured out her thoughts in the form of a letter to him, but one she never intended to let him see. She was sure he had some absurd idea about her and would be disappointed when he saw her again, but even if he did love her with all his strength — what then? She only knew that he moved her as nothing had ever done before, sometimes she found strange dreams stealing over her, of true happiness, of perfect trust, of absolute rest, but if she went back to India with him, it would mean parting with her two older girls, though the youngest might go with them. What should she do? She had freedom and independence, should she give them up for love?

She broke off and two weeks later resumed her self-communings, having a presentiment that he would arrive any day. He disturbed her peace but was nothing to her, absolutely nothing, and yet she could not forget him, try as she would. He was a stranger to her, she didn't know him, didn't want to know him; didn't care for him, didn't want to care for him. Idiot that she had been to have written that letter — what garrulous spirit or demon had possessed her? Never had she felt so nervous in her life.... He could not really care for her but had imagined some impossible ideal and when they met would wonder at his own absurdity in coming so far after a phantom. It was not in her to love anyone as much as her children. Foolish man, he should love some young girl with fresh young life all before her, some bright girl who had no past, though she had already persuaded herself that her own past was a bad dream, buried (thank God) and well-nigh forgotten. But could he forget it? Could he love her little girls? I wonder, I wonder. If not, let him pass on and leave me in peace.

When Lewin arrived in England a few days later his euphoria had somewhat abated. "Do you know," he wrote in a postscript to the polite note he wrote to her on the night of Sunday 14 May, "it is not so easy to write letters in England as it was in India." He enlisted the support of both his sisters so that one or other of them would be available to act as chaperone when, as he hoped, Margaret accepted his invitation to a performance of *Tannhauser*; but no, she was unfortunately engaged for the evening he suggested, and if he found it less easy to write letters to her in England, that showed that imagination was stronger than reality. At once he replied, "I cannot possibly go to bed tonight without offering an emphatic denial of your thesis in regard to letter writing...", and so the age-old ritual of courtship got under way. For him it was like a dream in which the streets and the people of London became unreal to him as they rehearsed the familiar steps. He reproached her for having, as he had been credibly informed, destroyed a letter she had written to him. "When you inform me," she retorted, "what you allude to as 'the letter that should have come to you', I will tell you why I did (or did not) deliberately destroy it." She in her turn had not liked his calling her second letter to him "strange", because it sounded like an adverse criticism "as though I had written something I should not". So they lightly provoked each other in between playing trios with a certain Mademoiselle Vaillant combining the functions of violinist and duenna. They saw *Tannhauser* together and as a change from Wagner — and surely at Harriet's suggestion as a spur to their romance — Shakespeare's *Much Ado About Nothing* at the Haymarket Theatre; and it would be strange if they were unable to view their own situation more lightheartedly after listening to the exchanges between Benedick and Beatrice. Soon he began to pay her open compliments, fearing her, he said, because she was so pure and true; never had he seen anyone like her in his life, was never in her society for five minutes but his heart spoke — but no, she protested, she was neither as clever nor as learned as he thought, and he was so earnest that he took her tinsel for gold.

It is not difficult to identify the qualities, besides his obvious devotion to her and the aura of romance that clung to him because he had lived an adventurous life in wild places, that made Lewin so attractive to Margaret. Not only a man of action, he also had rare intellectual and artistic accomplishments being a linguist, an anthropologist, a writer in several modes, a musician and a talented draftsman. In person he was an inch or so below six foot, spare in his figure from moderate eating and drinking, and something of a dandy in his dress. He had masculine good looks with a determined mouth and fearless eyes. The good health he enjoyed gave him vitality, and above everything he was gifted with an animal gracefulness of movement which must have contributed to the "animal magnetism" General Brownlow had noticed he possessed. And along with his strong personality went an unusual tact in his personal relations, a fineness of perception like the antennae of insects, which Margaret found particularly appealing.

They met on Tuesday 22 May for a heart-to-heart talk, speaking to one another seriously and at length, she of her first marriage, he (it would seem) of equally personal matters, for that evening he wrote to assure her that he had hidden nothing from her. He would visit her again next day, and because he hated to take her by surprise, or so he thought, he proceeded to make his proposal in form, simply, directly and urgently. She replied next day, briefly but kindly, saying she had known in a way that he loved her and confessing that she felt she was drifting into loving him so fast that she grasped vainly at her old moods of defiance and mistrust and felt they were slipping away. Withholding her answer, she asked him to come and see her.

He received her letter after spending a quiet evening with aunt Grote in preference to accompanying Harriet and Bella to the Goldsmiths' ball, and at midnight in an agony of uncertainty dashed off another letter to Margaret to say that he loved her so much that it hurt him and begging her not to keep him long in suspense. On Thursday he called at her house in Eaton Square, and they quickly concluded the matter. Their engagement with the endless vistas it opened for them affected each of them in a different way. Harriet, meeting Margaret at a dinner party that evening, reported that she was very nervous, her hands quite cold, while Lewin went home and at 11.30 sat down and wrote her a letter, a little white-winged messenger to greet her in the morning with loving words and to say how very happy he was. Regardless of the pouring rain he rushed out to post it and performed a species of Red Indian dance around the letter box.

Both families were delighted though perhaps not surprised when they learnt of the engagement and many happy meetings were exchanged. Any anxiety Margaret may have had about how her children would react to the news was soon dispelled.

"Do you like Captain Lewin as well as uncle George?"

"Oh yes!"

"Would you like to have a papa as your cousins have?"

"Oh yes!"

"Would you like Captain Lewin for a papa, my little girls?"

"Oh yes yes!" Then, after a pause: "You will have to marry him, Mama."

And there was much to be done. Lewin had been looking ill and weary and needed another spell at the German spa, and since he refused to go without Margaret they decided to be married in July, choosing the 24th because it was her birthday. Arrangements had to be made for renting a house in Surrey called Moorhurst, where they proposed to live temporarily, and thither was sent a locked box containing Lewin's writings and Indian diaries. She longed for a fuller knowledge of his life and doings, but wisely only cared to see such papers as he wished her to see. There were relations to be visited, among them aunt Grote with whom Lewin stayed at her house The Ridgeway at Shere, and letters to be written, for wedding presents were beginning to arrive. Bankes Tomlin gave them a silver claret jug, but seemed keener to show his brother-in-law his new horse, which he claimed to be the finest cob in London. Lawyers had to be instructed to draw up a marriage settlement, in which Margaret insisted on putting up the lion's share, brushing aside Lewin's worries about her being rich and he without fortune with the unanswerable pronouncement that, like the early Christians, they would have all things in common. She may not have told him then that, under her former husband's will, on her remarriage the capital in which she had enjoyed a life interest passed to the three children, though she was advised that she could claim a third of it for herself. Since she had inherited a substantial fortune from her father, she declined to insist on her strict legal rights.

On the evenings when they did not meet Lewin consoled himself with practice on his 'cello, though once he took his mother to the Adelphi to see brother Will perform in a curtain-raiser *Struck Oil* followed by Boucicault's play *The Colleen Bawn,* or *The Brides of Garrygowen.* Mrs Lewin was mighty pleased with the show, but Tom disliked it, feeling humiliated to see his brother, not merely as an actor, but a second-rate one at that. Another evening he took Margaret to *Lohengrin* and outraged his mother by the impropriety of his taking his fiancée home in a hansom cab. He also found time to write love poems addressed to her, one of which 'Love-greeting' he set to music of his own composition. Her favourite, though, was 'Affinity':

> If you my dear at church should be
> And I should be there too
> Turn round your face and look at me
> And I will look at you.
>
> Or on some starry summer night
> When 'twixt us lies the sea
> Let me be present in thy dreams
> And I will dream of thee.

MARGARET

Or if upon my bier I lie
Bend down thy tender eyes
Lay but one kiss upon my lips
And I will straight arise.

Early in July Mrs McClean took her daughter to
Sandgate on the south coast of Kent for a short holiday
before the wedding, and Margaret became so brown
from sunbathing after swimming in the sea from a bathing machine that her mother grew uneasy about her
appearance on the 24th. After a late breakfast she would
walk or bathe or laze in the garden with her mother until
lunch, after which they sat in the drawing-room making
small talk with the other guests in the hotel until four and
then went for a drive. When the lamps had been lit after
dinner Margaret sang or played whist with her mother
before they retired early to bed. Lewin remained in
London allaying his impatience as best he could. Will
used to come over before the evening performance to
play chess with him and, to his chagrin, unaccountably
beat him, and later Harriet would call in to play duets with
him. On 11 July he escorted Bella on a train journey to
Liverpool and saw her safely aboard the *Caspian* bound
for Ireland to rejoin her husband who was stationed
there, and that evening in the North Western Hotel wrote
to Margaret giving her an amusing description of the
Liverpudlians, men and women of preternatural ugliness
stumping about in clogs and addressing one another in
stage dialect.

Both of them were shy of the coming wedding

ceremony, thinking it barbarous having to make a parade of themselves, but took comfort in the reflection that it would be over in a few minutes that would magically transform their lives. She would not be dressed as the conventional bride, and he declined to wear the frock-coat his friends advised him was *de rigueur*, preferring the comparative informality of blue morning coat, white waistcoat and grey trousers. The marriage duly took place at Sandgate Church in the Parish of Folkestone, the bride's brother Frank McClean, Bob luckily home between voyages, and Harriet who had stage-managed the whole affair, signing the register as witnesses. After spending the night at the Lord Warden Hotel in Dover the couple went off for their German honeymoon having made plans to spend August visiting relations, then to have two months settling in at Moorhurst before taking the children for the winter to Italy where, instead of travelling about, they would rent a villa.

It was less than three months since Lewin had arrived back in England. "It seems absolutely impossible to believe," Margaret marvelled. "Woo'd an' married an' a' in such a short space as that. Gracious heavens, my head feels positively giddy."

Chapter Sixteen
A Year in Darjeeling

The P&O vessel *Pekin* in which the Lewins travelled to Calcutta was overcrowded with colonial passengers and their screaming children. On 24 November 1877 after a tiresome and often uncomfortably hot voyage, during which Lewin never once wrote to his mother, they reached the Hooghly where they anchored some miles below the port. Taken off by steam launch they transferred further down to a dinghy in which they were paddled ashore at Garden Reach, there to be met by a carriage sent by a friend in whose house in Russell Street they had been invited to stay. Lewin's six months' home leave to attend to private affairs had prolonged itself to a year and a half, during which period he had risen in rank from captain to major. Margaret's three little girls had been left behind in the care of her sister Mrs Annie Bidder, their lives to be divided between their foster home in Clapham, later in Mitcham, and a boarding school at Little Highfield.

Margaret, who had given birth to a stillborn child in June, was again pregnant and, due to an accident she suffered while getting ashore in Calcutta, was feeling far from well during her first week in India. So much so that she was unable to appreciate the service, very "high church", she was taken to in the cathedral attended by overdressed women and swarms of mosquitoes, nor her first sight of the *Maidan*, the Mall with its backcloth of cluttered shipping, the band playing in the Eden Gardens, or even a performance of Marchetti's opera based on Victor Hugo's dramatic romance *Ruy Blas* at the opera-house. The reason for her discomfort became apparent when at 10 p.m. on 30 November she grew much worse and, having failed to secure the attendance of Dr Charles who was already in bed and not to be disturbed, she suffered a miscarriage of a four-month son with only her husband to assist her. Ten days later they moved to rooms in Middleton Street, and it was another ten days before she was up and about again. While she was recuperating from her mishap she received news that her mother had died.

As soon as Margaret was well enough the Lewins were caught up in the winter whirl of Calcutta society that left them little time to themselves. They dined at Belvedere with Mr Ashley Eden, successor as lieutenant-governor of Bengal to Sir Richard Temple now the governor of Bombay, whom they also met and whom Margaret thought the most grotesquely ugly man she had ever seen; and the next evening were the guests of Alexander Mackenzie, secretary to the government of Bengal: a clever man, she noted in her diary, with a stupid wife. They spent Christmas night on their own, thinking of absent loved ones at home, and then resumed the weary round of dinners, balls, garden parties, operas, *soirées* and musical gatherings, and from time to time themselves invited

friends to dinner. Among their guests were Lord Ulrick
Browne, now commissioner of Assam, who had been a
good friend to Lewin as commissioner of Chittagong;
John Edgar his "rival" political officer during the Lushai
campaign, now district commissioner of Darjeeling; Sir
John Strachey the finance member on the viceroy's
council (and uncle of the biographer-to-be Lytton
Strachey) and his wife; and his old friend of Mutiny days
Dr Busteed, the superintendent of the Calcutta mint.
They attended at Government House the installation of
Scindia as maharajah of Gwalior, a glittering spectacle
though the viceroy Lord Lytton cut a poor figure, Lewin
thought; "a queer little man," he told his mother,
"something like a French cook" with a tall, handsome
wife with a remarkable appetite. At the ceremony he had
the chagrin to see the portly figure of Edgar walking in
the procession resplendent with the star and robes of a
Companion of the Star of India. They hired a piano and
managed to snatch a few musical evenings at home.

The beneficent influence of aunt Grote was still
operating in Lewin's favour, for on his arrival the
lieutenant-governor sent for him to inform him that he
had been appointed to succeed Edgar as the deputy
commissioner of Darjeeling. This was a plum job in one
of the most beautiful and healthy stations in India,
Darjeeling — Dorje-ling meaning in Tibetan the land of
the thunderbolt, the ritual sceptre of the lamas — being
a sanatorium built at an elevation of some 7000 feet in a
tract of the eastern Himalayas that had been ceded to the

British by the rajah of Sikkim in 1835. Once a Gurkha military station, it was intended to provide for the European population of Bengal a hill station and place of convalescence such as Simla, Poona and Ootacamund already provided for those of Delhi, Bombay and Madras respectively. It had ousted in this function the earlier sanatorium at Cherrapunji — where Jeannie had been born and uncle William had died — which had been found to be unsuitable owing to its spectacular rainfall.

The journey thither from Calcutta was a complicated one. Leaving on 20 January 1878 from Howrah station the train took them overnight to Sahibganj where they transferred to a steamer in which they sailed for four hours up the Ganges. Disembarking they proceeded overland, Margaret being carried in a *palki*, Tom walking along beside her, the servants — including her Indian Christian *ayah* Lucy — following behind with the baggage in a bullock-cart. At a *dâk* bungalow they changed to gharries in which they set off at a good pace for Purnea where they dined, then galloped on through the night. Once more they changed their mode of transport and in a creaking bullock-cart crossed a river by a ferry and then ambled on to Siliguri. From there a covered cart called a *tonga*, in which Lucy sat in front with the driver while Tom and Margaret sat behind with a *syce* crouching at their feet, took them clattering over a wooden bridge at the boundary between the plains and Tom's new district, from which point passing through the marshy jungle known as the *terai* the road began to ascend into the hills.

At 6 p.m. they reached a bungalow where they dined and slept and next day continued on their way, riding ponies along a road that zigzagged up the mountainside amid glorious scenery through forest and occasional tea gardens, halting for breakfast at a hotel twenty miles short of Darjeeling. Here no driver could be found for the *tonga* that was to take them on the next stage of their journey, so Tom — with more success than he had managed a bullock-cart all those years ago on the way to join his regiment at Cawnpore — took over the reins and steered the vehicle along a road that climbed between a cliff rising sheer on one side and a precipice falling away on the other, to the next staging post where the ponies were changed. Now the mist descended, and since here, too, there was no driver and the new ponies proved unruly, Tom and Margaret left the servants to follow on with the baggage and covered the last few miles on foot, reaching their destination at dusk on the third day, to find Edgar awaiting them in his bungalow.

Margaret's first sight of the surrounding scenery was breathtaking. "Oh such a lovely place is this Darjeeling," she wrote in her diary, "no words can describe it. Valleys over 6000 feet deep, the lovely woods, the paths winding in all directions; but as yet no snows visible, only the great white cloud that Kinchinjunga has wrapped round his mighty shoulders." She was at first less impressed by the house called Beechwood that had been allotted to them as their residence, which in its deserted state looked a hopeless sort of place. But once Edgar had left to take up his new appointment she set about arranging their furniture and belongings as she wanted them, and with their piano, the 'cellos, books and pictures around them it began to take on the appearance of home. She had the interior of the house done up with papers and cretonnes from Whiteley's, the drawing-room being papered light blue with a dark dado of gold and green, the chairs covered in light blue and black cretonne. Quaint tables and cabinets in black and gold contributed to the general effect. And soon she became familiar with the local landmarks: the barracks, hospital and officers' quarters on Jella Pahar; further on the convalescent depot, the Roman Catholic chapel, the bazaars, and the larger houses such as the lieutenant-governor's summer residence called The Shrubbery built on the spur of a hill overlooking a fearsome void filled with rolling, tumbling white clouds; the Anglican church, the schools of various denomination, the Mall, the Town Hall and the Club; the botanical gardens, and the Buddhist monastery reeking of incense and resonant with gong and conch.

She tried not to let Tom see how much she missed her children, but it was painful to her to be separated from them, and she eagerly awaited each mail hoping for news of them from her sister: how Anna had been top of the school and would move on to the big school next term; how Daisy had been thought too delicate to be sent away to school; and how Mabel the youngest had taken to school life, going through her lessons with edifying gravity. Amid the many distractions of Darjeeling the gnawing anxiety about her children never for a moment left her. It was fortunate that they were able to live on Tom's salary without recourse to Margaret's income, for this had been drastically reduced when her father-in-law Sir George Elliot, who had been making irregular voluntary payments towards the maintenance and school fees of his grandchildren, having had an audit of his accounts informed her that she had received several thousand pounds more than he had intended. He had therefore stopped paying the allowance until the overpayment had been worked off.

As the deputy commissioner's wife Margaret's social duties were formidable. Her first important house-guests were the commander-in-chief His Excellency Sir Frederick Harris KCB, CSI, a big man, slightly lame and blind in one eye, his dull and loutish son who was lame in one leg, and the quartermaster-general Major-General Frederick Roberts, VC, very bright and pleasant, who in an already distinguished career had been the senior staff officer with the Cachar Column during the Lushai campaign. Besides frequent dinner parties she was expected to help organize and preside over badminton parties, a children's party with magic-lantern slides, a flower show in the grounds of Beechwood, and weekly gatherings of the Glee Club comprising twenty singers at which she played the piano while Tom conducted. She was made secretary of the Diocesan Girls' School, one of the most popular schools in Bengal, and when the chaplain was away virtually became its manager. Later she gave a grand dinner party in honour of the commissioner of the district Mr Wells, an old friend of Lewin.

His duties as deputy commissioner, 2nd grade, were not dissimilar from hers, being for the most part of the decorative kind; for example in a single week he had the management and organization of two official balls, the flower show, and a race meeting. He presided in the *cutchery*, sat on the municipal council, had charge of the police, the gaol and the botanical gardens, was an examiner in Hindustani and commandant of the local volunteer rifle corps, all of which involved a great deal of paperwork. An important function of his was to dance attendance on the lieutenant-governor Mr., soon to become Sir, Ashley Eden, to whom he owed his appointment, who paid frequent visits both private and official to Darjeeling, requiring Lewin on each occasion to ride forty miles to the boundary of his district on his arrival and again on his departure. In his spare moments with the help of Yapa Ugyen Gyatsho, a learned lama of Pemiongehi monastery, he worked on the *Manual of Tibetan* he had begun in Cooch Behar. At first Margaret used to come in to inspect Tom's musty old lama until, in honour of her visits, he took to scenting himself with musk, which proved too much for her. The completed manual with a dedication to Sir Ashley was published in Calcutta at government expense in 1879. Another reminder of Cooch Behar was when he received a letter from the rajah of Bhutan requesting him to apprehend and deliver up to him certain of his rebellious magnates who on being defeated had fled and sought refuge in Darjeeling; a request Lewin felt unable to comply with.

That was in April, but the rainy season brought its own problems with frequent landslips that sent whole sections of garden or road sliding down the hillsides. Then Margaret had to be carried about in a *dandi* on men's shoulders while Lewin tramped beside her through the mud, and fires were kept alight in all their rooms against the damp. Their busiest time was the Durga Puja vacation in September when the Darjeeling Season was at its height and holiday-makers flocked in and inundated them with their cards and with letters asking for assistance in carrying out their various plans of pleasure. "How pleasant," Lewin wrote to his mother, "life would be were it not for its pleasures."

Not that they lacked pleasures of their own. For Margaret there was the garden to attend to, especially the fernery she had created by a small spring. She and Tom went walking or riding in the neighbourhood and sometimes made more extensive excursions, such as one he noted in his diary:

> M rode & so did I — beautiful mountain path — up up up along the ridge — Tongloo alt. 12,000 ft., a rather breathless place — forest of rhododendrons as big as oaks brilliant with blossom — the whole place on fire with crimson bloom, the ground studded thick with white and mauve primulas, wild of course — such beautiful ferns: the gold fern, the silver fern & another sort transparent like green tissue paper.

Both of them were talented amateur artists and made many sketches of the surrounding scenery, and when they had a free evening they played music, or chess. Margaret could not take part in Tom's more strenuous enjoyments of tennis or badminton, because she soon found herself pregnant again.

On Tuesday 1 October at five minutes to midnight after a difficult labour a daughter was born, and both mother and baby flourished. The baby was given three Christian names, Everest because she was born within sight (on a clear day) of the highest mountain in the world, Harriet Grote after her great-aunt and her father's benefactor who, though they did not know it at the time, lay seriously ill in her house at Shere. Lewin watched over his daughter fondly, marvelling how fast she grew, "a-swellin' wisibly before my eyes", he reported to his mother, quoting Mr Weller on the old lady who drank eighteen cups of tea. She had a fair white complexion, no hair to speak of, and eyes as big as saucers and as blue as the ocean; only her nose seemed less than perfection.

> Tell me then [he asked] where do we get the nose from? The Friends have not got it. The Lewins do not possess a celestial beak. The McCleans are rather hookey than otherwise. I am at a loss therefore to know where first I and now my innocent offspring get our turn-ups.

The baby caused them little trouble, taking no ill effects from her vaccination and suffering from nothing more serious than coughs and colds, though at two months she used to wake at night and weep bitterly between three and six. When scarcely a month old she went on her first extended outing when her parents took her with them to Kalimpong where the rajah of Sikkim was to be received in durbar by the lieutenant-governor.

It was a shabby affair, Lewin thought, rather "second chop" after the Deb Rajah's reception at Buksa in 1875, for there was no public durbar, just a formal exchange of courtesies and presents between the two potentates; but doubtless picturesque to any fresh observer, with the rajah and his ministers dressed in Chinese-style costume surrounded by shaven-crowned, yellow-robed priests twirling prayer-wheels. During their stay the Lewins like the rest of the British entourage lived in tents and dined every night with Sir Ashley. The occasion was most memorable for Margaret's feat of rope-dancing when she crossed the Teesta river some 300-feet across by a swaying cane suspension-bridge with her baby buttoned up in her cloak. Everest, too, had her part to play, receiving visits from the lieutenant-governor and the rajah's sister with decorum and dignity, and when taken out for an airing attracting a following of the populace who begged to be allowed to look at the face of the first white child ever seen in Kalimpong.

With the coming of winter they woke every morning to find their world white with hoar frost, and when in December they took the baby on a trip to the Nepal frontier at an altitude of 14,000 feet they were unable to sketch because their fingers were too cold to hold a pencil. Later in the month Lewin went to Siligiri in the *terai* — his first separation from Margaret since they were married — to preside over the volunteers' camp of exercise, at which he presented "Major Lewin's Challenge Cup" for rifle shooting. He dined every evening with the volunteers, between forty and fifty in number, in the large mess tent which with the long lines of plates and glasses on each side of the table looked quite military and reminded him of Mutiny times.

As always he was keeping in close touch with family matters at home. He wrote to Jeannie who was staying with the von Kochs in Sweden. Bella had returned to England with her husband Nathaniel and Lewin's god-daughter Harrie (short for Harriet) and soon afterwards gave birth prematurely to twin boys, both of whom died. Saddened by the news he remembered her many years before as a fancy, winning little lass flirting in Talbot Road. His sister Harriet and her husband Bankes were now getting on well together, and both were so true-hearted that it was a mystery to Lewin why they had ever disagreed. They were still living at Dumpton Park in East Anglia, worried about the health of Gore their first-born, but managing to get away to London for the season. Hearing she had had a triumph singing at some function, Lewin adopted, as he sometimes did, the stance of stern elder brother, expressing the hope that she would not be dazzled by her success, for by her position and talent she was above singing in public. When their mother went to stay at Dumpton shortly afterwards she found Harriet unwell after the feverish gaiety of London, and no more was heard of her taking to a singing career. In May Bob had gone off on another voyage, this time to Valparaiso on the unhealthy South American run, and on his return in September safe and well had thrown up the seafaring life for good, though he had no particular plans for the future. Again Lewin took up a high-handed attitude, criticizing his brother for throwing away his talents when he could earn between two and three thousand pounds a year practising as a doctor in India. Remembering Harriet's recent public exhibition of herself, he shuddered to think of Bob singing for a living, though he had a beautiful voice; but he was sure he had too much self-respect to descend to such a thing.

Will's theatrical career was meanwhile going from strength to strength. After leaving Drury Lane he had played in comedy for some years at the Strand Theatre before returning to Drury Lane in the spring of 1878 where he made a considerable hit playing the villain Squire Thornhill in *Olivia*, W.G. Wills' adaptation of Goldsmith's *The Vicar of Wakefield*. He had also become a real-life hero. On holiday by the sea at Deal with his family he had taken his six-year-old son Tom out in a rowing boat and, seeing two boys had got into difficulty, dived in and rescued them, an act of bravery for which he received the medal of the Royal Humane Society.

At this time Harry Graves brought himself back to Lewin's attention by repaying him £10 out of the considerable amount he had received from him over the years, but Lewin declined to accept the olive branch. He was glad for old friendship's sake that Harry now appeared to be doing well, but felt he had been treated badly and preferred to let bygones be bygones. If Harry's gesture left him unmoved, he was saddened to learn not long afterwards that Annie Graves had suffered a mental breakdown, which effectively brought to a close Harry's brief interval of prosperity.

For Lewin, despite the happiness of his marriage and his delight in Everest, his year as deputy commissioner of Darjeeling marked the lowest point of his Indian career. He found the public and popular position it required him to sustain not at all to his mind, his life having hitherto been passed in less populous places; besides, Margaret though she put a brave face on it was unhappy to be separated so long from her children; so he decided to bring his career to an end and sent in his resignation, to have effect on his fortieth birthday, 1 April 1879. After more than twenty years' service he was entitled to retire as a lieutenant-colonel on a paltry pension of £171.17s.0d. a year. But their year abroad had at least enabled Margaret to work off part of the amount her Elliot father-in-law claimed he had overpaid her, and even though the holding of colliery shares she had inherited from her father seemed for the moment precarious, Lewin was not unduly worried.

> If it pleases God that we should be poor, I shall not mind, for I have a great treasure in my dear wife, and with her by my side I do not fear the future but am content with whatever God may send us.

The closing weeks of his time in India were over-shadowed by a quarrel with his brothers, brought about by their mother's unfortunate habit of letting them read the letters he wrote to her. The rift with Will seems to have arisen from his retort to his mother's suggestion that when Will's little daughter Ellaline grew up her choice of career would be between becoming a governess or an actress. Lewin disagreed, pointing out that many other occupations such as medicine and the law were opening out for women, and adding:

> To be an actress is in *most* cases synonymous with prostitution of some degree or other, and I never willingly would allow anyone connected with me to enter that profession. You know how hard I have tried to prevent Will remaining in it.

No doubt by underlining the word "most" he had sought, belatedly, to exclude from his strictures Will's wife Izzy, who had herself been briefly on the stage; but the damage was done. He was no less offensive in what he wrote of Bob, still blaming him for wasting his great qualities and abilities between ship's doctoring and punting for eels. If, as he ought, he now stayed at home, was there no means of getting him a job in London as a sanitary inspector or a hospital surgeon or something, instead of hiding his great talents up in a napkin?

The letter Bob wrote to him has not survived among Lewin's papers, but its tenor may be gathered from Lewin's next letter to their mother:

> It was with pain that I received Bob's letter last week. I shall not reply to it — I loved him and my brother Will very dearly, but if they chose to sever their lives from mine, I do not dispute their right to do so.

The note of injured dignity gave place at the end of the letter to conciliatory words, and he asked his mother to tell Bob that he would for the future try to avoid giving him offence. Neither of his brothers were men to harbour malice, and the offending words were soon forgotten or at least forgiven.

The close of Lewin's Indian career coincided with the ending of another chapter, for he received news that aunt Grote had died at The Ridgeway, and with her seemed to go an entire epoch. She had remained in robust health well into old age and, still a tomboy when over seventy, would set off for a tramp over the heath with her little dog Pixie frolicking around her, and on another occasion boasted that she had "got into the saddle yesterday on a fine young mare 17.1 high, and rode three miles". She did not need spectacles, and at eighty, her fingers being fortunately free from rheumatics, could be heard playing pieces by Beethoven, Mozart and Correlli on her piano in the drawing-room. And the flow of her letters to Babbie continued until the very end, the last of them having been written from The Ridgeway only a few weeks before her death. "Here is my paper at an end," were its concluding words, "so I send you my aged blessing and sweet words of affection undiminished by long years." Lewin genuinely mourned her as a notable figure on their little family stage whom no one could replace unless perhaps it was his sister Harriet. His aunt had been consistently kind to him from his earliest years when she had given him his first boy's suit to the end, for he learnt that under her will she had bequeathed him a substantial legacy, and even more generous ones to Bella and Bob. He was sorry, he wrote to his mother, that the family which had benefited so largely from the old lady's death had not been represented at her funeral. Of his two last surviving uncles, the fox-hunting Frederick had died at The Hollies two years before, to be followed next year by Edward who by now had become senile and cranky, having lost all relish for life. So of Thomas Lewin senior's large family only aunt Babbie remained, much cherished by her family in faraway Sweden. A little later Lewin heard from his cousin Jessie Lewin who had been aunt Grote's companion during her last years, asking him if he would like to buy The Ridgeway, and he had replied that it was not the kind of place to tempt Margaret or himself.

Meanwhile they were putting their affairs in order and packing up at Beechwood. They sold such of the furniture, goods and stores as they could not take away with them, much of it being purchased by Lord Ulrick Browne and Sir Ashley Eden, and realized a good sum, even for the items they had bought from Edgar at what Lewin had thought an exorbitant price. He also sent off to the Baptist Mission Press in Calcutta the manuscript of his *Manual of Tibetan / being / A Guide to the Colloquial Speech of Tibet / in a series of progressive exercises / prepared with the assistance of / Yapa Ugyen Gyatsho / a learned lama of the / monastery of Pemiongehi,* which with a dedication to Sir Ashley Eden, KCSI, was published under the orders of the Bengal Government the following year. As with the *Colloquial Exercises* in Lushai he acknowledged in the preface that the work was neither exhaustive nor complete, but there was then no existing text-book of the language. He had lived, he wrote, on the borders of Tibet for nearly three years, studying with Tibetan lamas in the hope, which now seemed unlikely to be fulfilled, of one day entering the land. The book contains ninety-seven exercises set out in three columns: English, Tibetan in Roman script, Tibetan in Tibetan script, followed by three specimens of the Tibetan language — 'Attributes of a Virtuous Woman'; 'Verses against Wearing the Veil'; and 'Ratnavali's Letter to Shakya' — and a vocabulary. Like the Lushai book it has since been superseded by later scholarship, and a factor limiting its usefulness was that Lewin had inevitably been influenced by Bhutia provincialisms in the use of words and in orthography.

On 24 January 1879 the three of them started on their long and slow journey home. At Serail they ran into Lieutenant-General Sir Richard Strachey and his wife (parents-to-be of the biographer born the following year), old Calcutta acquaintances who were staying at the same hotel; and at Chumbatta had to say goodbye to their servants, some of whom had been with Lewin for many years. Their Magh cook Tobe-dhun who had followed his fortunes since Chittagong days was convulsed with sobs; unwilling to serve any other master, he was returning to his home in the hills. In Calcutta they stayed as the lieutenant-governor's guests at Belvedere, where they were visited by the young rajah of Cooch Behar who had been under Lewin's care. At Arrah they stayed with Edgar who was remaining in India until he qualified for his full pension, then proceeded to Benares and on to Agra so that Margaret could see the Taj Mahal; and thence to Bombay where they boarded the P&O vessel *Mirzapore* bound for Southampton.

In moments of discouragement Lewin had often consoled himself with the words Jesus had enjoined on His disciples as recorded in St Luke, XVII.10, and now he repeated them as a fitting epitaph to his entire Indian career: "I am an unprofitable servant: I have done that which it was my duty to do". He left India without reluctance and with grave forebodings as to the future of the British connection, views he had already expressed to Margaret in one of his early letters to her from Cooch Behar:

> ... it seems to me that our real danger in India lies not in the direction of Russia but in the hearts of the people, with whom another Mutiny is always possible & I think a probable contingency. You see that with all our justice and thorough uprightness of intention our national character is so unsympathetic that we are if anything greater aliens to the people of India than we were 50 years ago.

Chapter Seventeen
Parkhurst

1

The three Lewins — Tom, Margaret and their baby daughter Everest — landed in England in the summer of 1879 and went straight from the ship to stay with Margaret's married sister at Mitcham, where the younger children Mabel and Daisy were to join them. Next day Lewin hurried off to see his mother in Clapham. For some months there is a gap in the record, then the curtain lifts on Lewin and his younger sister Bella travelling by train, 2nd class, from London to Brighton to visit their mother who with Harriet and her husband Bankes were on holiday at an address in King's Road, enjoying the fine March weather and the sea breezes. On 21 August he went to Sheffield where the 49th meeting of the British Association for the Advancement of Science was being held, to read his paper on 'The Trade Routes from Bengal to Tibet', in which he advocated the establishment of permanent trade agents at Shigatze and Lhasa. In September Margaret sent him off to Birmingham to investigate the possibility of his standing for parliament in the Liberal interest, a prospect he viewed with little enthusiasm, claiming to have scant political proclivities and only one strong inclination, which was to return as soon as he could to Margaret's staylaces; for by now the whole weight of his emotional nature had shifted from his mother, who had borne the burden for so long, to his wife. His suitability as a candidate may also be doubted for, apart from holding, as he later claimed, advanced liberal views, he was of independent judgment in matters social, religious and political, but strongly opposed the extension of the franchise to women. In any case he was advised that the prime minister Lord Beaconsfield was unlikely to call an election until the following spring, not wishing to annoy the farmers at harvest time. Going on to Walsall, he heard there was no question of his contesting the seat in that constituency, though Lichfield might be a possibility, and concluded that nothing could be done without the backing of the wire-pullers of the Liberal party in London. He took the opportunity of making enquiries about the ailing Cannock Chase Colliery Company, in which Margaret had inherited a substantial investment, and heard incidentally of a house to be let furnished at Lyme Regis on the Dorset coast, which he thought might suit them. With that news he returned thankfully to his family in the house they were then renting near Holmwood in Surrey.

By the time they took possession of Marly Cottage in Lyme Regis in June 1881 there had been an addition to the family, Charles being only a few months old, but somehow they all managed to squeeze in. Anna and Daisy were away at the girls' college at Cheltenham run by a Mrs Beale, where they were much happier than they had been at Miss Metcalfe's aristocratic institution at

Hendon. Now Lewin was able to relax and do as he pleased, dividing his time between wood carving, sketching, reading vigorously, writing somewhat and, when the weather was fine, taking long walks with Margaret. Once a week a violinist came in and played trios with them. "We are all," he wrote to Jeannie in September, "thank the Good God very well & very happy & my heart is at rest & desires nothing. It is a quiet haven after all the past storms of my life for wh. I am devoutly thankful." A page of the letter now missing may have referred to the fact that earlier in the year Margaret had had another miscarriage.

Lewin's life at Lyme Regis was not as purposeless as the account he gave Jeannie suggests, for he had put his hand to writing an autobiography in which he recalled the past storms of his life in graphic, sometimes inventive detail. He saw few people besides his immediate family. His mother having gone down with influenza had been taken by Bella to Ireland to recuperate. Nothing is known of Bob's movements at this time, but Will's transformation from black sheep to popular London stage actor is a matter of public record. His chance had come when he had been cast as Squire Thornhill in *Olivia*, which had a successful run at Drury Lane. Ellen Terry who played the name part had been greatly taken with his charm and impudence —

> Sometimes he reminded me of a butcher-boy flashing past whistling on the high seat of his cart, or of Phaet[h]on driving the chariot of the sun — pretty much the same thing, I imagine —

and considered that he played the part absolutely to the life. He made such an impression on her that, after she had begun her historic association with Henry Irving, Terriss was invited to join the Lyceum company, with which he was to be associated for the next fifteen years. His naturalistic style of acting was the perfect foil to Irving's sardonic elaborations, besides which "the Guv'nor" found his effrontery off-stage irresistible. While Tom was busy drafting his autobiography in the cottage at Lyme Regis, Will was appearing in London in a succession of plays, which at the end of the season were taken on a tour of the provinces.

In September 1883, his autobiography finished and left with Margaret to read in manuscript, Lewin went to stay with the Tomlins at Snare Hill Park in East Anglia, a desolate, dreary county, he wrote to her, filled with dull, ugly people. His mother who was staying there too was full of joy at having him with her, and on fine days he rowed her and Harriet on the river that surrounded the park, talking of family matters. His third child Audrey had been born a few months before (Jeannie was one of her two godmothers), Will was about to leave for an American tour with the Lyceum company, and Bella was due to come over to fetch their mother for another visit to Ireland in November. Harriet he considered a restless creature; she had a good heart but would never be happy, and by her conduct now seemed to have uprooted any love Bankes may have felt for her. Bankes with his younger brother who was also staying there — a burly six-footer who had served in the Bays — were entirely preoccupied with shooting pheasants; in fact, Lewin reported, "they shoot for their living and live for their shooting". Bankes at sixty had become something of an eccentric, given of a sudden to turning his back on the view and admiring it from between his legs, and recommending to all and sundry Dixon's Antholeon for Burns, Bruises, Sprains, Rheumatism and Piles, which was to be had from the local chemist. Lewin's mood during his stay was reflected in the landscape seen through the drawing-room window:

> The rain is pouring in torrents over the shut-in sylvanry of Snare Hill Park, even the pheasants have sought shelter, and nothing is to be seen save cohorts of great trees gloomily waving their arms and a few fat sheep who feed regardless of rain in their warm overcoats.

While he was away Margaret had been reading the manuscript of his autobiography, and her verdict was that it was well worth publishing. The publishers he approached were W.H. Allen & Co. of Waterloo Place, Pall Mall, who had brought out an English edition of his *Chittagong Hill Tracts and the Dwellers Therein* under the title *Wild Races of South-Eastern India* in 1870, and they had their own ideas about the sort of book that was marketable. Though his correspondence with them has disappeared, the changes they required to be made to his draft can be inferred from a letter he received from John Ruskin who, having read the published version with glowing interest, regretted that they had made it "too much of a hunting story book". Lewin's explanation caused Ruskin to explode:

> Again, those cursed publishers are the pestilence of literature. They have made you destroy the dignity and simplicity of your book, and robbed it of half its historical value. It is one of the most wonderful and beautiful stories I have ever read. Surely an edition might be brought out in reduced form, with not a word in it that was not your own, and yours deliberately.

From this it is clear that the published book incorporates matter, supplied either by Lewin himself at his publishers' insistence or by one of their editors, designed to convert his soberly factual narrative into an adventure story that would appeal to a wider readership. In its more lurid passages can be detected the influence of Fennimore Cooper's novels of life on the American frontier which had fascinated Lewin as a boy. Fortunately the book's historical value, though diminished, was not completely destroyed by the process, because it is not difficult to guess which scenes were invented or touched up to please the publishers; and it was well received when it was published in 1884, not only by the author's relations, friends and former colleagues, but by the reviewers as well.

The book's title, *A Fly on the Wheel, or How I Helped to Govern India*, was taken from the opening of Francis Bacon's essay 'Of Vain-Glory':

> It was prettily devised of Aesop; 'the fly sat upon the axle tree of the chariot wheel, and said, What a dust do I

raise!' So are there some vain persons, that whatsoever goeth alone or moveth upon greater means, if they have never so little hand in it, they think it is they that carry it.

Of the twenty-five black-and-white illustrations Lewin drew for his book, only nine were used. Based on the letters he had written to his mother and on the diaries he had kept during his years in India, the book opens with a description of his experiences as a young ensign during the Mutiny and closes with his departure from the Lushai Hills, "somewhat weary and broken", his pioneer work as a frontier administrator having received little official recognition. In between are chapters on his days in the Indian police at Hazaribagh, Noakhali and Chittagong, leading to the climax of his career among the hill tribes on the north-east frontier.

The book was a revelation to most of his relations, who had previously had no clear idea how he had spent his service in India. Aunt Babbie felt it was intolerably cruel and wrong that, at an early age and with such scanty opportunity for moral and intellectual development, his youth had been exposed to such trials; but saw in his deliverance from all his perils evidence of God's hand, "an uplifting message from the Supreme One which overjoyed and sanctified my heart". Of the many other congratulatory letters he received, including ones from Jeannie, Arthur Grote, Sir George Campbell and General Brownlow (who was Charlie's godfather), one that gave him particular pleasure was from Henry Yule, recently knighted, who had been secretary to Sir Arthur Phayre's embassy to Burma in 1855, of which he had written an account in his *Narrative of a Mission to Ava* published three years later. He was at the time of his letter putting the finishing touches to his glossary of Anglo-Indian colloquial words and phrases which was published in 1886 under the title *Hobson-Jobson*. Of *A Fly on the Wheel* he wrote:

> I did enjoy it thoroughly; and if I wished to give a foreigner of intelligence an idea of the sort of life and work that was led by our good officers in India, I would say, 'Read this'. But I had also a special attraction in your dealings with those eastern frontier folk; for although I never met with such adventures as yours, I always felt drawn to them from my earliest days in India, when I used to wander among the Khassia jungles and villages, and in after years when I spent several months in wandering on the Arracan Yoma to report on that frontier and its defence, associating with Khyens [Chins].

The publication of his autobiography forms a watershed in Lewin's life, on one side of which lay his adventurous career in India, on the other his thirty years as a country gentleman; for he and Margaret had now found a small estate in Surrey where they felt they could put down roots.

2

Parkhurst was originally built in the late seventeenth century as a farmhouse for the Guildford-based family of that name who farmed the surrounding land. It came into the ownership of John Spence a dyer of Wandsworth, who for a month in 1766 had for his guest there Jean-Jacques Rousseau the Swiss philosopher of noble savage fame. During the second half of the eighteenth century it was owned in succession by various tradesmen of the City of London before its purchase in 1787 by Lord, later Earl, Macartney, the diplomatist whose career had included his being sent as envoy extraordinary to St. Petersburg, his governorship of the Carabee Islands and a spell as president of Fort St. George at Madras. He knew James Boswell, since both were members of the Literary Club that met in London, but was altogether too exalted a personage to have been invited to the supper at The London tavern where he would have met in the old Sea Captain, the great-grandfather of the Lewin who was to purchase Parkhurst a hundred years later. While the estate was in his ownership he was sent as ambassador extraordinary to Pekin — Boswell for a while toyed with the notion of accompanying him to China as a member of his entourage — and later became governor of the Cape of Good Hope. During the interval at home between these two appointments he planted the cedars on the lawn to the south of the house from seedlings brought back from China, some Chinese acacias, the larch trees grown from seedlings sent to him by the Duke of Atholl and a large Norway spruce which became a landmark for miles around, all of which were flourishing in Lewin's day. A walk bordered with laurels was then still known as Lord Macartney's Walk.

In 1799 Parkhurst was bought for £10,000 by William

Perrin who partly rebuilt and extended the house, the work being unfinished when he died leaving the property to his nephew Sir Henry Fitzherbert, bart., who never resided there. Its next owner Edward Lomax made further alterations and also planted the line of spruce trees marking the old boundary. From him it descended through the female line to the Colonel Leopold Scarlett from whom the Lewins bought the place in 1884.

Such a substantial property required a large staff, and perhaps on account of an unfortunate lapse on the part of one of the maids (to whom and to whose offspring Margaret showed great kindness) the Lewins sought to impose on their servants a somewhat restrictive regime. According to a little printed booklet with the title *General Rules for Parkhurst Household* they were not allowed to go out for more than one hour without leave, the menservants never during visiting hours, the maidservants never during dressing hours; nor was any girl under twenty to be out after dark without leave. There were strict rules about servants' visitors, which were slightly relaxed in the case of an acknowledged engagement of one of them to be married (not simply keeping company), provided the respectability of the proposed visitor was first ascertained. It was Colonel and Mrs Lewin's wish that their servants should treat their house (as far as possible) as a home, but they discouraged going out or having visitors as likely to disturb the general comfort of the household. They would willingly supply books and games or anything else in reason to make the evenings more homelike for them.

Although living in retirement after a strenuously active career in India Lewin was not the kind of person to vegetate and pursued his various interests with characteristic vigour. For relaxation there was tennis on the court he had caused to be laid out in the garden of Parkhurst; billiards in the billiard-room, often with Margaret or, as they grew older, one of his children or step-children for opponent; and chess which he used to play with like-minded friends by correspondence. He no longer kept dogs because Margaret would have disapproved of their being allowed inside the house; besides, he no longer needed their companionship, for she had become the centre and pivot of his life, and he cherished her with a devotion that retained its ardency to the end of his life. Next to her came the children, all six of them, for he lavished as much love and care on his three stepdaughters as on his own children, and all of them returned his affection in equal measure. He remained close to his mother, brothers and sisters, although each was now leading his or her own life, for he was now in effect the head of the Lewin family. He kept in touch with old friends, being an assiduous letter-writer, and soon began to make new ones in the neighbourhood of Parkhurst.

Among them was the novelist George Meredith, who lived at Flint Cottage near Box Hill some ten miles away. He was by then a revered man of letters whose most successful novel *Diana of the Crossways* was published soon after the Lewins moved into Parkhurst. His second wife had died of cancer not long before, leaving in his care a son William aged eighteen, whom he summed up as, though not brilliant, a kindly fellow with wits of a slow sort, and a younger daughter Marie — his "Dearie" — a good, humane, intelligent girl whose upbringing he was anxiously supervising. Something of the florid, ornate prose style of his novels overflowed into the letters he wrote from time to time to the Lewins, but though heavily facetious and crammed with convoluted metaphors a genuine affection for them can be detected struggling for expression from beneath the persiflage. He was fulsome in his compliments to Margaret, professing himself to be the colonel's rival for her heart, of which however he was content to take a merest portion. For him, he declared, Parkhurst had this resemblance to Paradise that one could not conceive the possibility of declining an invitation to enter its open gates. The association of the two families was cemented when William Meredith and Daisy Elliot became engaged to be married, and in his letter to Lewin giving his blessing to the union Meredith betrayed something of a parvenu's uneasiness (he being the son of an improvident Portsmouth tailor) when he described his son as "a gentleman with whom the best bred girl may live and feel at home". He also regretted William "not being yet established on a footing to command the position she deserves", leaving it to the Lewins to put up the capital to advance him in his publishing career.

Another friend of these years, Edward Burne-Jones

the painter, was altogether a warmer, more spontaneous character who had once been described as a cross between a monk and Puck. Already successful, famous and rich, he lived at his house in Fulham called The Grange, getting away whenever he could to his cottage at Rottingdean near Brighton. Like Meredith he came from a lower-middle-class family (he added the hyphen to his name to disguise the fact), his father having been a picture-framer who nevertheless managed to send him to Oxford where he entered on his lifelong friendship with William Morris. Both came to admire Ruskin's art criticism and, in reaction against the ugliness of Victorian England, developed a cult of the middle ages as romanticized in such works as Tennyson's *Morte d'Arthur*. In London Burne-Jones came under the influence of Dante Gabriel Rossetti who remained a friend for many years. In 1860 he had married Georgiana Mcdonald by whom he had two children and, like Lewin, derived great satisfaction from the company of his family. One would not have expected Lewin to care much for Burne-Jones' paintings, in which he created a dream-world full of maidens loth and androgynous knights, all of them steeped in a wistful melancholy, but he did once try, unsuccessfully, to purchase one. When he asked what the price would be Burne-Jones had replied: "Tell him that some of my pictures are worth £40,000 & some are worth 4d. Below 4d. I have never gone".

The fact was that each enjoyed the other's company. Who else ever addressed Lewin as "Much the dearest of all colonels" or "My dear old fellow! Chum of chums! Boon Companion!"? They took a close interest in each other's families, Georgiana writing with felicitations on Daisy's marriage to William Meredith, Burne-Jones beguiling Lewin with news of the birth of his second grandchild, a brother for Angela who had been banished for the occasion to Uxbridge, "and there, as it were by the Waters of Babylon, she sits down and weeps for the time when she reigned alone". "But send me a word," he wrote later, "there's a dear, and let it be a comfortable word and above all let it be a true word."

Through Meredith and Burne-Jones Lewin had access to the worlds of literature and painting, but music was his first and greatest love and even prompted him in October 1891 to write a fan letter to Johannes Brahms at Vienna, thanking him for the pleasure his compositions had given him and inviting him, should he ever come to England, to visit him at Parkhurst; a letter which brought him a courteous acknowledgement from the composer enclosing a signed photograph of himself. All Lewin's children were taught to play some stringed instrument, and he himself assiduously practised on his 'cello for an hour every morning. More than anything else music became the factor that bound all the members of the family together. The truth of this has been uniquely preserved in a photograph taken in the billiard-room at Parkhurst on a summer afternoon when the sunlight came pouring in through the windows. Margaret sits at the piano with Lewin standing beside her holding his 'cello. Of the Elliot girls, Anna is not present, but Mabel sits looking haughtily at the camera while Daisy stands behind her gazing dreamily into the garden, both holding violins. Everest on the left preparing to play her violin looks across at her mother. Charlie in profile wearing an Eton collar sits with his smaller 'cello between his knees. Audrey the youngest of all stands with her back to the light peering over a music stand. The photographer has managed to capture a single instant of those golden early years at Parkhurst before the children began one by one to leave home to make their own lives.

A few years after acquiring Parkhurst Lewin came into collision with some of his neighbours over his proposal to divert the public road passing through the property close to the house so as to follow a route further to the north. The mischief began when the rector of Felday, a village to the west, sold his glebe land for housing development, thus causing a great increase in the wheeled traffic along a road which had previously been little used. In an endeavour to achieve his object amicably Lewin canvassed the people living in the neighbourhood, but although the new route, besides benefiting Parkhurst, would be for the greater convenience of the public, a hard core of the local inhabitants chose to oppose the scheme. All seemed set fair when the two magistrates at Dorking Petty Sessions — one of them, Sir Thomas Farrer of Abinger Hall, a friend of Lewin — issued a certificate under the Highway Act 1835 sanctioning the diversion; but the objectors then appealed to the justices at Newington Quarter

Sessions, who quashed the magistrates' order on the technical ground that the statutory notices had not been posted up precisely where the Act required. Lewin thereupon applied to the Queen's Bench Division of the High Court of Justice at Westminster for a write of *mandamus* to be issued directing the justices to endorse the certificate authorizing the diversion. The two judges issued the required rule *nisi* which, after hearing arguments from counsel for both sides, they duly made absolute. Still the objectors persisted and gave notice of their intention to lodge an appeal to the Court of Appeal, this despite the fact that Lewin as an additional inducement had volunteered to make a new footpath over his property, running parallel to the old road, which he would dedicate to the public in perpetuity. On second thoughts, no doubt deterred by the heavy legal costs they would incur if they proceeded with their appeal, the objectors withdrew from the field, leaving Lewin free to effect the diversion and open up the new footpath; and all was tranquillity at Parkhurst once more.

About this time Lewin began to keep a record of the health and development of his three children in a *Life History Album*, a publication prepared by direction of the British Medical Association. In it he also permitted himself more general comments than were required by the printed questionnaires, such as his convictions (not shared by Margaret) that Everest was a true Lewin, while Charlie seemed more of a McClean. Audrey he thought perhaps the cleverest and most original of the three. Audrey with her grey eyes and dark brown hair reminded him of both his grandmother Mary (Hale) Lewin and his sister Bella, whereas Everest with her light grey eyes and light brown hair resembled her great-aunts Grote and Charlotte. All three of the Lewin children showed early signs of having artistic and musical talent as well as enjoying outdoor pursuits like riding, tennis and skating. The last entry in the album is headed 'Counsel' and was clearly intended for Charlie's guidance:

> Walk two hours a day: sleep seven hours: go to bed when you feel sleepy and get up when you awake: set to work as soon as you are up.
>
> Eat only when hungry and do not drink except to quench thirst — do both slowly and in measure.
>
> Speak only when necessary and never say more than half of what you think; write only what you can put your name to, and do only what will bear speaking of.
>
> Remember that although others may & should rely upon you — yet you should rely on no-one but yourself.
>
> Do not value money for more than it is worth. Like fire, it is a good servant but a very bad master.
>
> Beware of women until you are twenty: and steer clear of them after you are forty.
>
> Do not despise your fellow men, nor hate them much, nor laugh at anyone excessively.
>
> Be pitiful & compassionate. Think of God, each morning when His light returns; and each night, before sleep (Death's brother) overshadows you.

The first of the children to leave home was Anna. In 1887 she married John Young, a barrister and the eldest son of William Young of Charlwood who came of a family of Glasgow-merchants, and went to live at Lexham Gardens in London. Daisy went next, her life with William Meredith alternating between London, where he worked for the publishing firm of Constable & Co. while she pursued a musical career of her own, and Fleet in Hampshire where they bought a house. That same autumn of 1892 Charlie was taken down to Eton by his parents to begin his first half there. A quiet, good-looking boy, he soon settled down, his cheerful letters home placing equal emphasis on his Latin, Greek, and English history studies and anchovy paste, Marie biscuits and blackberry jam. Everest — variously called Speff or Peffkin or Effie by the family — being five years the elder was leaving school about the time that Audrey was starting at Rathgowrie in Eastbourne in the autumn of 1895. She, too, settled down well, soon making friends among the sixty-five girls in the school and enjoying almost everything:

> but there is one awful thing that makes me hate the place [she wrote home] and Father would hate it too — It is infested with black beetles! The other morning one of the girls found one in her porridge! and the day before yesterday I found one crawling on the bedroom wall. It really is awful. They do not emerge in the shadow of night but walk about shamelessly in the daytime. I don't know how to endure it.

Mabel was the next to get married. Among Lewin's friends of old days in India was Alexander Mackenzie who had been the secretary to the government of Bengal. An expert on the north-east frontier, he had been well placed to follow Lewin's career, having been in charge of the government's political correspondence between 1866 and 1873. His crowning achievement in this field had been the publication in 1884 by the Home Department Press in Calcutta of his monumental *History of the Relations of the Government with the Hill Tribes of the North-East Frontier of Bengal*, in which incidentally Lewin's work among the Lushais was given its only official recognition. Ascending the hierarchy of the Indian Civil Service he had received a knighthood. After the death of his first wife he had come home on leave and, visiting Lewin at Parkhurst, had fallen in love with Mabel and married her before going out again to take up his new appointment as chief commissioner of Burma. He wrote to Lewin in December 1884 from the government yacht *Shwelaung* which was making slow progress up the Irrawaddy towards the utmost limits of his domain, having left Mabel and their small baby at Mandalay. At that time he anticipated that the New Year would bring his work in the east to an end, since he had no hope of "getting Bengal", being sure that the viceroy Lord Lansdowne would promote his own favourite to the job. In this he was wrong, and in 1896 Mackenzie was appointed lieutenant-governor of Bengal.

By that time the government of Bengal had ceased to have any responsibility for the Lushai Hills. For thirteen years after Lewin's departure peace had reigned there, only occasionally disturbed by dissentions among the clans. Rothangpuia had died in 1876, Benkhuaia in 1879, Suakpuilala a year later. The flowering of the bamboos the following year had caused a plague of rats which, by devouring the stocks of grain in the granaries, led to a serious famine. Things had returned to normal when the first of several outrages occurred which put an end to the period of tranquillity. It was the work of Lakhers under a chief called Hausata whose father-in-law had demanded Lushai heads as his price for effecting a reconciliation between his daughter and son-in-law, who were estranged. In January 1888 word was received at Rangamati from Lewin's old friend the Haolong chief Seipuia, who had remained loyal to his oath of friendship with the British, that a raiding party more than two hundred strong led by Hausata and his two brothers Vantura and Dakola was heading for British territory. Unfortunately his warning was discounted.

Coming by chance on Lieutenant Stewart who was out surveying with only a small escort, the Lakhers set upon them, killing several and carrying off their heads including Stewart's. Not long afterwards another raiding party led by three chiefs from the northern part of the hills, Nikama, Kairuma and Lungliena, attacked a village only four miles from Demagri, killing its chieftainess and more than twenty of her people and seizing fifteen captives. While a punitive force under Brigadier-General Tregear was assembling at Rangamati news came in of widespread raiding in the Chengri valley some forty miles to the north-east instigated by the Sailo chief Lianphunga, a kinsman of the Savunga who had so bitterly opposed the Lushai expedition sixteen years before. In the ensuing massacre twenty-three villages were destroyed, more than a hundred people killed and ninety-one carried off. The bad old days had returned with a vengeance. One of the villages destroyed was that of Rothangpuia's son Lalchheuva in punishment for his refusal to repay the elephant's tusk his father had borrowed long ago to enable him to pay a fine. Among the possessions he lost in the flames was the certificate that had been presented to his father by a grateful government for the part he had played in the expedition.

This tribal unrest happened to coincide with even greater disturbances in the Chin Hills to the east where, consequent upon the annexation of Upper Burma in 1885-86, the British had for the first time come into conflict with the turbulent Chins, the Lushai's more savage cousins over the Burma border. There followed the Chin-Lushai Expedition of 1889-90 when, after engaging in sporadic fighting as the columns marched on the guilty villages (eventually recovering Stewart's head, which was given a decent burial), a force advancing westwards from Haka joined hands at the halfway point of Tao with a force advancing eastwards from Lungleh, establishing for the first time an overland link between

Bengal and Burma.

To maintain the peace, posts were established at Lungleh not far from Seipuia's village, and at Darzo and Fort Tregear, under the command of Captain John Shakespear of the Leinsters who already had some experience of dealing with the Lushais; and at Fort Aijal some miles to the north under Captain Browne. The latter, ordered to apprehend chief Lianphunga, ill-advisedly sought the co-operation of the northern Lushai chiefs who, interpreting his approach to them as a sign of weakness, had him ambushed and killed. To exact punishment for his murder R.B. McCabe, ICS, who had made his name as a tough administrator in the Naga Hills, was appointed political officer at Aijal under the government of Assam; and so heavy-handedly did he carry out his instructions until he had laid hands on Lianphunga and his fellow chiefs (who were deported) that he became known throughout the hills as Lalmantu, meaning betrayer of chiefs. Shakespear, now the superintendent for the South Lushai Hills under the government of Bengal, earned the more affectionate nickname of Tarmita meaning old man's eyes, for he was the first Englishman the Lushais had seen who wore spectacles. Before long these two officers had to cope with a full-scale rebellion which stretched their meagre military resources to the fullest extent during the early months of 1892, and only the support of a loyal chief Lalluova and the timely arrival of a flying column from the Chin Hills under Captain Rose to take the rebels in the rear averted a major disaster. Operations continued for several years while the guilty chiefs were rounded up one by one, and the process of pacification was not completed until 1898 when the sensible step was taken of placing the whole Lushai tract, with its administrative centre at Aijal, under the government of Assam, relieving Mackenzie as lieutenant-governor of Bengal of further responsibility for them.

In the palatial Belvedere House at Alipur between the zoological and horticultural gardens Mabel saw what she could of her two young children Maggie and Jock amidst the manifold official duties her husband's position required of them. In January 1897 she gave her mother an account of a dinner party they had given in honour of the commander-in-chief Sir George White, VC, who was leaving India after a long and distinguished career, including service in the Chin Hills, to take up an appointment at the War Office in London. Lady White had put her at her ease by asking her about her babies, and they had music to entertain the guests afterwards. The following evening the Mackenzies were present at a state ball attended by the viceroy Lord Elgin and the vicereine, with whom Mabel had a nice chat while the dancing was in progress. Alex, she reported, had looked grand in his blue and gold uniform, white cloth breeches, silk stockings and buckled shoes, while she had worn last year's grey brocade, which her maid Sophie had trimmed with the lace fichu her mother had sent her the previous winter, and all her jewels including five diamond stars glittering in her hair. Next day she had to preside over committee meetings in the morning and in the afternoon to attend a garden party with Alex. That night he frightened her by having one of the minor heart-attacks to which he was subject, and it was clear that he could not stand the pace of such a hectic life for long.

The fact that Lewin, who had now been living in retirement in England for many years, was not only an old friend of his but also his stepfather-in-law did not seem to the lieutenant-governor to disqualify him from seeking to redress the wrong that had been done to Lewin after the Lushai Expedition, and accordingly in March 1897 he laid before Lord Elgin a lengthy minute on the subject. Lewin, he wrote, was one of the most distinguished officers on the north-east frontier, and his name still lived green all over the South Lushai Hills. His was an exceptionally strong personality, and few had ever wielded such magnetic (again that word) influence over savage races. He drew the viceroy's attention to what he had written about Lewin in his book on the north-east frontier and to Lewin's own fascinating story *A Fly on the Wheel*, even attaching as an appendix to his minute the entirely fanciful account Lewin had given in his autobiography of his confrontation with the Haolong chiefs at the Tuldung stream. Mackenzie had searched in the secretariat records to discover why Lewin had received no official reward for his services, but discovered nothing to the purpose, and surmised that the reason Edgar was given a CSI and Lewin was ignored lay in the fact that Edgar was a clever civilian then coming rapidly to the front who was personally known to the authorities in Calcutta, while Lewin had been a man of the woods with strong individual views which had not always been accepted by the Bengal government. He went over all the old ground in detail, drawing attention to the fact that the former viceroy Lord Northbrook in his order-in-council had expressed his approbation of Lewin's valuable services equally with Edgar's, and quoting the fulsome praise of Lewin which General Brownlow had included in his last despatch. The occasion of Her Majesty's Diamond Jubilee seemed to Mackenzie a fitting time for removing the substantial grievance of an old and faithful servant of the Crown, and he strongly recommended that even now justice should be done, and that as some compensation for past neglect Lewin be created a Knight Commander of the Indian Empire.

It was to no avail, and just as Lewin had been denied the CSI he had once so coveted, so now the viceroy declined to recommend him for a knighthood.

Chapter Eighteen
Murder at the Stage Door

1

Mary Lewin died in April 1890 aged seventy-nine at the London house in Earl's Court where Bankes and Harriet were staying. Her decline had been so gradual that her passing when it came affected her family less as a traumatic shock than as the sudden withdrawal of warmth from their lives. During her early widowhood, though disparaged behind her back by her sister-in-law as being incapable of disciplining her unruly brood, she had held her family together on a modest income by the power of her own loveableness. To her two daughters she had been like a favourite elder sister, and her sons had fought for her favour like rival suitors. She retained the love of them all throughout her long life, and they sincerely mourned her. Tom, who had been tied to her apron strings until middle life, had long since transferred the emotional burden to Margaret. Both her daughters were married with children of their own to preoccupy them, Harriet now having two sons, Gore and Julian, Bella two daughters, Harrie and Edna; and Will was a famous London stage actor. Of her five children Bob was, as always, the odd man out, a bachelor who though achieving little in the world's eyes yet rejoiced in a host of friends and, in his own eccentric way, was not unhappy.

Since he had resigned his appointment as ship's surgeon with the P&O his practice of medicine had been spasmodic; in fact, as his obituary notice in the *St. Mary's Hospital Gazette* was to record, he never did practise his profession very seriously, though his services were always at the disposal of the poorer classes.

> He was a typical Bohemian, who spent a great part of his life on the upper reaches of the Thames, where he occupied his time in fishing, in entertaining the natives, and in helping the poor and needy.

More detail for his portrait was provided by his cousin Mortimer Lewin, himself also (as he admitted) a "rum 'un", when recalling a month he had spent with him at Sandford Lock when after breakfast Bob would repair to the inn parlour to sing music-hall songs to his own accompaniment on the piano, then wander off to his punt on the river, ostensibly to fish though never catching anything, instead just lying for hours on his back, pipe in mouth, contemplating the sky. In the evening he would be found in the taproom singing songs with the locals. A wasted life, thought Mortimer, for someone with such great talents, having ten times the ability of his brother Will who was only a plodder; though of course Will could act.

Mortimer remembered Will at Windermere in a school production of *Henry VIII* playing the part of Elizabeth dressed in black velvet with a long train, head erect, every inch a queen. When the page addressed him, "Madam, you are called back", he had turned and given the well-known reply with great dignity and effect before sweeping off the stage. Since his return from his first American tour with the Lyceum company in 1885 Will had made a hit at the Adelphi as a dashing sailor in *Harbour Lights,* which had run for 513 nights and earned him the nickname "Breezy Bill". Three years later playing opposite Jessie Millward in *The Union Jack* their acting had transformed the piece into something better than the mere fustian that in fact it was. The pair were in marked contrast to one another, she dark, *embonpoint,* he fair and slight, keeping a trim figure through moderate eating and drinking. He toured America with her in a number of plays in the winter of 1889-90, returning to the Adelphi for a revival of *Harbour Lights.* Next year he was back at the Lyceum and shared with Henry Irving and Ellen Terry such triumphs as Much *Ado About Nothing, Henry VIII* (playing the king to Irving's Wolsey), *Lear,* Tennyson's *Beckett, The Merchant of Venice* and *The Bells.* He broke off his association with Irving in 1894 to make his headquarters the Adelphi where he staged many popular melodramas, always playing opposite Jessie Millward.

They had long since become lovers, and Jessie's flat in Prince's Street was now Will's West End base. Although their relationship put a strain on his marriage, Izzie, now grown comfortably stout, somehow managed to keep the family together. They had moved from their cottage in Barnes to a large red-brick house, though called The Cottage, in Bedford Park, Chiswick, on the western outskirts of London, for they now had a second son whom they had christened William after his father. Their other two children were both destined for the stage, Ellaline, who had grown into a beautiful girl, having made her début at the age of eighteen in 1888. Five years later, while her father was on tour in America, she had married by special licence the actor Seymour Hicks, her uncle Bob being one of the few people who was let in on the secret. It was at the flat in Prince's Street that Bernard Shaw called one afternoon, bringing with him his new play *The Devil's Disciple* which he had written with Terriss in mind for the part of Dick Dudgeon and Jessie as Judith Anderson. Unwisely Shaw insisted on reading the entire script aloud, which soon sent Terriss into a deep sleep, so enraging Shaw that he had stamped out. For the Christmas season of 1897 Terriss, then aged forty-nine, put on a revival of *Secret Service*, a play written by the American actor William Gillette (best known for his impersonation of Sherlock Holmes) set in Virginia during the last months of the Civil War. Terriss played a spy sent to infiltrate the secrets of the enemy's high command, Jessie the Southern belle who loved him.

On the afternoon of 16 December Will and Harry Graves, still an appendage of the Lewin family, after a game of poker at the Green Room Club with Fred Terry had walked over to the flat, where Jessie gave them a meal before going with her maid to the theatre to get ready for the evening performance, leaving them to come on later by cab after a game of chess. Having paid off the cabbie, Will paused at the stage door saying "Wait a minute,

Harry, till I get my key", and, just as he was about to enter the private door of the Adelphi which was in a narrow passage between Maiden Lane and the Strand, a figure wearing a slouch hat and a long cape like a stage villain rushed up and stabbed him three times in the back with a butcher's knife he carried in his pocket. In the commotion that ensued Harry grabbed the assailant, who made no attempt to escape, and hung on to him until a police constable arrived, when they escorted him to Bow Street police station. Jessie running downstairs found Will leaning against the wall just inside the private entrance and put her arms round him to support him. Together they fell on to the floorboards at the foot of the stairs, and a few moments later Will died in her arms.

The killer had been a disappointed actor Richard Archer, son of a Scots farm labourer, who had adopted the stage name of Prince. He had played walk-on parts in various Adelphi productions in which Terriss had appeared, but considered his talents fitted him for better things. "Fools often succeed," he would darkly declare, "where men of genius fail." He had shown signs of mental instability, which had caused managements to refuse to engage him, and had long fallen on evil days when, on the night of the murder, having failed to beg money from the secretary of the Actors' Benevolent Fund, to whom his shabby figure had become all too familiar, or from his half-sister, a prostitute who frequented the promenade at the Empire Theatre and whom he happened to encounter in the Strand arm in arm with a client, he had positioned himself near the stage door of the Adelphi, awaiting Will's arrival. On medical evidence he was declared insane and committed to Broadmoor for the rest of his life.

It is a measure of Will's popularity as an actor that when his funeral took place at Brompton Cemetery five days after his murder an estimated fifty thousand people thronged the pavements to see his cortège go by. This consisted of nearly a hundred mourning coaches being drawn slowly after the hearse. In the first sat Terriss's two sons Tom and William with their uncles Colonel Lewin and Dr Lewin. Gore Tomlin, General Stevenson and many actors followed behind in others. At the graveside awaiting the arrival of the coffin stood Jessie Millward, Sir Henry Irving, Seymour Hicks and Ellaline. Herbert Beerbohm Tree was among those who waited at the chapel entrance and followed the coffin to the grave in the Lewin family vault, which had been opened to disclose the coffins of Mary Lewin which had been laid there seven years before and that of Will's little grandchild, Ellaline's and Seymour's daughter. A simultaneous memorial service was held at the Chapel Royal, Savoy, for the benefit of those unable to be present at the interment.

Izzie who had been unwell before her husband's death only survived him by a few months. Harry, too, was grief-stricken and giving evidence at the inquest had burst out: "I would have given twenty lives to have saved him". For his eldest brother Tom the blow was as shattering as the one he had received on hearing the news of George Johnston's suicide, adding an even more sombre shade to the dark thoughts of mortality that had been obsessing him. His grief was ineradicable, and never again would he allow Will's name to be mentioned at Parkhurst, though he gave Everest a card in his memory on which were a poem about him that had appeared in *Punch* and a photograph, and himself kept among his papers a file containing newspaper cuttings about the murder and Archer's subsequent trial.

Of the letters of condolence he received none touched his heart more than the one from Edward Burne-Jones, now a baronet, who wrote to him that he knew

> no mortal sympathy can stand between you and your pain, but we must make a sign to you and you must forgive it if it is the wrong sign. Come to us in the New Year please. We go away on Thursday for a week, troubled by your trouble, and feeling how really we care for you. The swing of the mind to a friend in adversity proves this always.

Burne-Jones was to die of heart-failure the following June in his Fulham house The Grange, aged sixty-five.

2

Though Margaret had been unsuccessful in steering her husband towards a seat in parliament, she did manage to make a part-time industrialist of him, albeit a reluctant one. By reason of their substantial shareholdings he was elected to the boards of the Cannock Chase Colliery Company and (on the death of Margaret's brother-in-law George Bidder who had been the chairman) of the Danish Gas Company. At first his duties were far from onerous, except that they necessitated his staying from time to time in London which he didn't care for, always longing to be back among his beloved pinewoods at Parkhurst; but the additions to his personal income they brought were welcome. Then Sir Corbett Woodall, the new chairman of Danish Gas and a good friend, persuaded him to play a more executive part in the company's affairs and began to take him with him on his continental tours of inspection, which involved exhausting journeys visiting gasworks, meeting officials of various governments, and attending luncheons and dinners. In 1897 they crossed by boat to Flushing — Lewin, as ever, being miserably seasick — and spent the next day in a train rolling through Holland and Germany. After inspecting a gasworks at Hanover, where Lewin's mind reeled amid a confusion of purifiers, condensers, scrubbers and residual products, they went on to Berlin to attend a grand municipal dinner for gas engineers in the Great Hall. Being expected to make a speech, Lewin drank nothing but light moselle and mineral water, but managed to cry "*Hoch!*" with the best of them when toasts were proposed. He took time off for sightseeing, doing the round of Unter den Linden, University, Museum, Reichstag, Kaiser's Palace, Tiergarten and the rest, more from a sense of duty than for pleasure, before the two of them proceeded on their way, visiting Copenhagen, Odense and Flensburg before returning home.

Two years later they crossed by cattle-boat from Jutland to Copenhagen for more meetings and inspections, thence to Flensberg and Viborg, back to Copenhagen, and home again by way of Brussels, Antwerp and Harwich. They were on the circuit again in 1904, and Lewin in a letter to Margaret complained of the heat and dirt at the Odense works among coke-crushers, coal-conveyors, retorts, tar and chemicals, his discomfort the worse for his not having been able to get a bath since he left home. They had clambered up iron ladders to giddy heights, then climbed down again into cellars vibrating with the clang of mighty machinery, Lewin bemusedly following in Woodall's footsteps amid the fiery turmoil and awful heat of the furnaces, all the time wishing with all his heart he was walking peacefully round the garden at Parkhurst with Margaret.

He began to worry about the future prospects of the company, whose profits were being cut into by the spread of electric lighting: perhaps they should sell out half their holding, for everything depended on Woodall whose health was giving cause for concern. The idea that he might himself accept the chairmanship he dismissed out of hand; not having the technical ability, he would be dependent on others for financial and technical advice. In any case, as he wrote to Margaret, "I fear my soul is not keenly commercial, and I find it difficult to take an intelligent interest in the relative carbonizing capabilities of two sorts of coal". Besides, it would mean his having to travel up to town every week ... no, it was out of the question.

And he had plenty with which to occupy himself at home, for the range of his interests was unusually wide. He sat as a justice of the peace on the Dorking bench, being noted for the leniency of his sentences. He was also a commissioner for taxes, a member of the rural district council and an active supporter of Abinger parish church. He read voraciously, anything from Tolstoy and Matthew Arnold to Stanley Weyman and Rider Haggard — indeed, Meredith had poked fun at him by praising Margaret's tolerance of his devotion to *She* as a Celestial Philosophy in itself. Lewin's philosophical researches were no less eclectic as he consulted Spinoza, Descartes, Swedenborg and Richard Haldane for some convincing answer to the riddle of existence. His questing mind hovered constantly over the eternal questions and never arrived at any solution that satisfied him.

> My own problem in life has been from early days, since I began to think, how shall a man become superior to circumstance? how obtain and maintain freedom of spirit and moral independence? The old questions faced one. Whence come we? ... Whither do we go? ... Our ethics, our rules of conduct are at the mercy of every kind of accident. Pain, fear, sickness, or the contempt or anger of the world, meet us on the threshold and accompany us through life. We must then I think confess that there is some power that controls circumstance, otherwise we have no basis for determinate action. The glimpse of a purpose, the hope of betterment,

the use of effort are our sole aids in the struggle against the black despair of Pessimism.

So he wrote to a friend in 1905, propounding a treatise that is difficult to reconcile with the outline of his religious beliefs he gave to a clergyman seven years later.

> I am a Bible Christian, brought up since my earliest childhood on the Scriptures, so they are bone of my bone, flesh of my flesh; and I do not care a button about the Higher Criticism. The Word of God is good enough for me. What! you or others may say, do you believe in verbal inspiration? My answer to that is in the eloquent words of St. Augustine who, writing to St. Jerome, says: 'I have learned to ascribe such reverence to the Scriptures that I believe most firmly that there are no mistakes in them; and should I light on anything which may seem opposed to truth, I believe that either the manuscript was full of errors, or that the translator has not comprehended what was said, or that I myself had not understood it in the least degree.'
>
> I have nothing to do with answering objections or reconciling Religion and Science. I am content to take the Christian Religion as the noblest and purest ethical system that the world knows or has known, & try to reconcile my own life with it.

From time to time Lewin turned his mind from literature, philosophy and religion to such scientific matters as happened to catch his interest. He consulted an expert on the possibility of extracting malt from horse-chestnuts on a commercial scale, and about some aphid disease that had afflicted his spruce trees. ("The nests on the leafy shoots which you sent," he was told, "are the winter residence. As summer comes on, the imperfect wingless insects (the woolly lice) work over the bark. The full-winged fly you have probably not noticed ...") For a while the classification of the British fungi engaged his attention, then it was bacteriology. Inevitably he turned his mind to the question of spiritualism, in the practice of which both his sisters were regular participants. The ghost of Brockley Court in Somerset, of which he obtained what purported to be a photograph, provided a convenient case study, and after lengthy correspondence with the perpetrators he satisfied himself that the whole thing was a hoax.

3

Sometime after Lewin had settled at Parkhurst he began to make notes in a small black notebook 'On love in men and women', apparently for a magazine article, and continued to make entries on the subject over a number of years, at one time contemplating a longer work to be called *The Book of True Love*, which in the event he never wrote. The notebook jottings consist mainly of a series of aphorisms, and because some may derive from his own experience it is necessary to give an account of those which appear to have especial biographical relevance to himself or to Margaret. He began with a definition.

> There exists a certain mental and physical condition in man in which the mere thought of another being of the opposite sex causes us to forget everything else — to put

aside our ambitions, our duties, our past, our present, our future — changing both our habits & our wants. This condition I call Love.

An entry enlarging on this echoes something Margaret had written to him in the early days of their courtship.

When you truly love a woman all other women in the world seem unattractive. You see her not as she really is but through a magic medium which endows her with every perfection and makes her all that you wish her to be.

He repeated the commonplace that "Of two lovers, one always loves more than the other" and referred to the strange feeling, when one is in love, of being doubled, the interior 'me' gazing astonished at the antic doings and sensations of the other 'me'. Few men and women, he wrote, during the first two years of marriage do not earnestly wish they had never taken the plunge, for the loss of individual liberty, the dissipation of the initial stage of glamour, the prospect of his or her perpetual companionship for life, the irrevocable nature of the bond — all cause an unutterable revulsion.

He was aware that to men and women love appeared in different guises, the man saying 'Can I please her? Will she love me?', the woman reflecting 'Is he earnest? Will his love endure or is this only a fugitive attraction?' The man was more concerned with its physical aspects: the simple contact with the skin of the woman you really love, be it merely the touch of her hand, gives a sensation of such intensity that nothing else in the world is comparable with it. And yet, physically speaking, one woman is very like another, and the mystery of mysteries is why one particular woman should make all others indifferent to the man who loves. He described the stages of love from the first moment of attraction: the man's admiration for the woman; the feeling how delightful it would be to be loved by her; her presence becoming a necessity, her image following him everywhere so that he can think of nothing else; his doubts and fears; his one thought that this woman alone can give him back his peace of mind.

On the other hand, "A woman's love is like the ivy: it dies if it cannot cling and attach itself". How strange, she thinks, that a man has no sooner got possession of the woman he loves than his one desire is to render her ill and deformed by subjecting her to the pains and perils of childbirth, even endangering her life, an entry that perhaps refers obliquely to the three miscarriages Margaret had suffered during their married life. What women cannot endure is to be a mere *machine à plaisir* for the man they love; what they value is his liking, his tenderness, his attentions, not the action itself which at the beginning seems an indecency and an outrage and even when habitual has the disadvantages which are attendant on conception.

Many of the entries in the notebook are concerned with jealousy, which Lewin calls the grimmest of torments, a pain that surpasses all others, though in family life it is the deceiver who is the most unhappy because he has no security, being always afraid of being found out. Like a moral cancer jealousy works under the surface, destroying the whole character, and its only palliative is absence. (Since the subject is unlikely to have had reference to the Lewin marriage, it is probable that his thoughts on jealousy derived from Meredith's sonnet sequence *Modern Love*; he had sent Lewin a copy of the new edition in 1892.) Other entries deal at length with the Solitaries who for one reason or another are deprived of love; with the various sorts and conditions of women — the Seeker, the Actress, the Imitator, the Gynarchist-Dominatrix, the Envious Woman — all of whom love with the head, not the heart; and with the ordinary woman of society whose lot makes her a bad wife, a bad mother, and a worse friend. He distinguished between the Honest Flirt who, seeing the man becoming earnest, will hasten to terminate the incident, and the Coquette who will proceed with ingenuity to torture him.

In all this it is seldom possible to connect an entry with a particular event or relationship in Lewin's life, to which the following is clearly an exception:

> That there should be another man in the life of the woman you love, that she should have given him her virginity and borne him children is and must be always an incurable sorrow. The regret will ever be present that those children were not his own.

His comfort will have been in an earlier reflection that every woman truly loves but one man in her life.

Later he called love a sickness, a malady, a disease, of which none can cure you save the loved one only; and a terrible and insidious madness which raises man above humanity and gives him the greatest pleasures that can be known on this earth. In a uniquely lyrical passage he attempted to describe the indescribable.

> When one follows the path of love it is like the entry to a lead or salt mine — down a dark narrow & difficult descent into darkness & doubt — but when in the heart of the earth the guide lights a torch or sends up a rocket, the whole place is illuminated and one sees oneself in a fairy place hung with silver plumes & lacework & sparkling with the brightest diamonds.

4

After his children were grown up and had left home Lewin began to use the blank pages in the children's *Life History Album* to keep a record of his own health as he entered upon old age. There was nothing but minor ailments such as lumbago, toothache, piles, influenza and indigestion to record until 1897 when he became aware that he was suffering from an enlargement of the prostate, which was successfully treated and gave him little trouble until his last years. In 1890 he began to wear spectacles to read the newspapers at night, though he did not need them during daylight hours. The same year he noted that his hearing of music was not so keen as it had been. He continued to play tennis until 1898, in which year he found his interest in men and women much decreased and that he neither desired nor enjoyed anything keenly. On his birthday in 1909 he commented: "Age 70 — Things look bad & I suppose I shall not last long", but four years later he could write: "Weight gone down to 10 stone, and little appetite. Nothing else much wrong. I sleep, eat & live without pain".

He had first begun to take an interest in his ancestry in 1866 when he had been stationed at Chittagong, asking his mother to get aunt Charlotte to send him some account of the Lewin pedigree, of which he was then quite ignorant. After settling at Parkhurst he had set himself the task of gathering as much information as he could about the origin and ramifications of his family, his pursuit being simply one of curiosity and dilettantism. Since his aunts Charlotte and Harriet Grote were both dead, he tried to tap the memory of aunt Babbie in Sweden before she joined them. Writing to him in 1884 she promised him an account of his father, her beloved brother George, though one chapter of it (she said) was still a painful subject to her, and in the event she never could bring herself to undertake the task. She deplored the mislaying of her father's pedigree and personal history, which she knew had been delivered to her late brother Frederick, but thought it was likely to float up some time, unless it had been destroyed by malice prepense. Nevertheless she solemnly cautioned her nephew against letting his level of soul descend merely to ancestry. "I well know," she wrote, "that nothing human is insignificant or worthless, but still I would bid you beware of too exclusively devoting yourself to tombstones, dust and buried memories."

His inclination to research into the lives of his forbears received an unexpected impetus when out of the blue he was offered the chance of buying the family property The Hollies at Bexley, his share in which he had sold long ago because it had then seemed impossible that he should ever be able to acquire the whole estate. It had passed through many vicissitudes since his grandfather Thomas senior had died there in 1843. It had been purchased from his executors by his eldest son Thomas, Lewin's godfather, who had pulled down the old mansion and built a commodious modern house in its place, where he had lived intermittently in gloomy bachelor solitude until his death intestate eleven years later. The property thereupon becoming divisible among his heirs male, the remainders were eventually purchased by his fox-hunting uncle Frederick — according to Bob, a libertine, a cynic and a bad husband — who had squired it there until his own death in 1877, when it passed to his surviving children. After various lettings it had been decided in 1892 to sell the place, but first an approach was made to Lewin by his cousin Mortimer, to see whether he would like to buy it in order to keep it in the family. The offer had come too late, for by then he and Margaret had invested too much, both materially and spiritually, in Parkhurst for them to consider moving. Accordingly, the property was divided into lots and sold off as a housing estate, the big house being purchased by the local authority and turned into a boys' home for workhouse children, and such it remained until 1910 when it was destroyed by fire.

Meanwhile Lewin's researches into the history of his family were beginning to take the tangible form of a collection of letters and diaries written by, or relating to, the Lewin family covering the period from 1756 to 1885. Embellished with portraits, it was privately printed at Lewin's expense and issued under the title *The Lewin Letters* by William Meredith's firm Archibald Constable & Co. Ltd. in 1909 in two large handsome volumes for distribution among members of the family and Lewin's closest friends. It was a princely achievement, the fruit of much patient research, assembled and edited with considerable artistry. His preface explains what his intention had been:

> Here they are — the dear dead far-away people from whom I have my being, and whose blood flows in my veins for a brief space. How often have I longed to look back into the past, to know the lives they lived, and the loves they loved! And so at last, with some toil and much pleasure, I have gathered together such relics of the past as came to my hand, so that when I, too, travel the Dark Road, I may leave behind for the children whom I love, and for their children whom I may never know, this record of our common ancestors, their lives and deaths.

The collection comprises extracts from diaries, autobiographical sketches, and letters of all sorts, written by young and old, men and women, some grave, some gay, some dull as ditch-water. The first volume centres round Lewin's grandfather, Thomas Lewin of The Hollies, his wife Mary Hale, and their immediate family and takes the story down to 1840 when Thomas made his will, three years before his death. Already Harriet, who by reason of the early, unhappy marriage of their eldest daughter Mary and the death in infancy of their second daughter Anne had assumed her natural place as head of the younger generation, is beginning to play a leading part in the story, a section each being devoted to her relationships with Fanny Elssler and Jenny Lind. The second volume contains letters written by various members of the younger generation between 1840 and 1885, including the series Lewin wrote to his mother during the Indian Mutiny, his account of the durbar held in Cooch Behar when he was superintendent there, and a number of letters written to him on the first publication of *A Fly on the Wheel.* What gives the volume its literary richness is the correspondence that passed between Harriet Grote and her sister Babbie over a long period, which bears comparison with the classic collections of English letters. The volume ends with Lewin's tribute to his aunt Babbie who had died in 1888 at the house of her son Fabian von Koch at Falun in Sweden, which has been quoted on an earlier page.

By this time not only the nineteenth century but, with the death of the old queen in 1901, the Victorian Age had come to an end. Closely involved as he had been with tombstones, dust and buried memories, Lewin was unable to ignore completely what was going on in the world at large. Along with his fellow countrymen, he was deeply moved by the death of General Gordon at the hands of dervishes at Khartoum in 1885. The reality of the massacre of the chief commissioner of Assam with the commander of his escort and a number of Europeans during the Manipur uprising in 1891 was brought home to him, because one of the young officers who died of his wounds was the son of his neighbour and friend Colonel Brackenbury. He followed the Dreyfus case with interest. The outbreak of the Boer War in 1899 had a personal significance for him, because his son Charlie having passed out of Sandhurst was serving as a lieutenant with the 4th Hussars in India, which was awaiting orders to embark for South Africa; though in the event he did not serve in South Africa until some years after the war was over. His daughters and step-daughters had all left home by this time, and he and Margaret often had Parkhurst to themselves. It suited them well enough, for (as he wrote to one of his sons-in-law) "we are never less alone than when alone".

Chapter Nineteen
Old and New

1

In 1899 a letter arrived at Parkhurst with news of the Lushai Hills. J. Herbert Lorrain and his friend F.W. Savidge were missionaries unaffiliated to any official organization who had first tried to enter the hills from Chittagong in 1891, but owing to the disturbed conditions prevailing there had not been allowed to go beyond the confines of Kasalong and Rangamati. Nor were the Lushais, smarting from the attentions of a punitive expedition sent against them, in a mood to listen to their overtures. Two years later the missionaries tried again from Cachar and this time were permitted by the authorities to build a house a mile from Fort Aijal where they set about mastering the Lushai language with the help of Lewin's *Progressive and Colloquial Exercises.* They were supported in their efforts by the political officer Major John Shakespear, who a little later opened a school near the fort for the education of such of the chiefs as cared to come in and enrol themselves as pupils. Going about the nearby villages Lorrain and Savidge were amazed at the readiness of the people to receive the Gospel they had come to preach: "They were," wrote Lorrain in his letter to Lewin, "as prepared soil for the good seed". After a few years the missionaries had to leave, because the Welsh Presbyterian Mission was moving in, and the philanthropist who was financing Lorrain and Savidge as private missionaries would only allow them to work in places where no regular society operated. They brought away with them the manuscripts of their translations into the Lushai language of the Gospels of St. John and St. Luke and the Acts of the Apostles, which were published by the British & Foreign Bible Society, and of their *Grammar & Dictionary* which was published by the Government of Assam. Having given Lewin a brief outline of their experiences, Lorrain continued:

> But I have further news to tell which will gladden your heart even more than what I have written above. Your own influence upon the Lushais is still felt. I do not think there is a man or woman in all those hills who does not know the name of 'Thangliena' or 'Lewin Sap [Sahib]'. It is handed down from father to son, and they are never tired of singing your praises. We have sat for hours and listened to them all talking of the bygone days and the wonderful white Chief who has become to the Lushais their ideal sahib. Some few men we have met who could boast that they had actually seen the great 'Thangliena' in the flesh. One of these you will I am sure remember, the Chief Savunga. He was very old when we first knew him and died about two years ago.

Another voice from the past was that of Sir John Edgar who on the occasion of Everest's marriage in 1901 wrote to Margaret from Florence where he had settled ten years before. After Lewin and Margaret had left Darjeeling Edgar had been made chief secretary to the government of Bengal, for which he had received a knighthood, and

when he had served his time in the ICS for a full pension
had retired and settled in Italy, a Falstaffian figure with
white beard and something of a round belly, who took an
interest in art. In his fulsome way he sent felicitations to
Everest on her marriage, fervently hoping that she might
be as happy as she deserved to be: "For you will perhaps
allow me", he wrote to Margaret, "to take the liberty of
saying just this once that there is not a more charming girl
among my acquaintance and that for her own sake, apart
from any deep and affectionate regard for you and her
father, my interest in her future is keen and anxious".
Soon afterwards he suffered a stroke which partially
paralysed him and seemed to be making a good but slow
recovery when he died in Florence in February 1902.

A visitor from the past who stayed at Parkhurst in 1906
was Dr H.E. Busteed, CIE, then metallurgist to the
Birmingham mint, whom Lewin had last seen when he
was superintendent of the Calcutta mint. He had served
during the Mutiny as a young assistant surgeon with the
Horse Artillery and remembered being sent on escort
duty with the long train of women and wounded men
from Lucknow accompanied by some of Lewin's old
regiment the 34th and a detachment of irregular cavalry,
returning in time to take part in the fighting in which the
Gwalior contingent commanded by Tantia Topi had
been decisively defeated. He was now doing research for
a new edition of his book *Echoes from Old Calcutta,* in which
he gave an acknowledgement to Lewin for permitting
him to use as one of the illustrations the oil painting of

Thomas Lewin senior then hanging at Parkhurst. Busteed was seeking further information about Lewin's grandfather's liaison with Madame Grand which has been recounted in an earlier chapter, but the two friends had much to talk over of old times. An admirer of Lewin's *A Fly on the Wheel*, Busteed was particularly interested in the description he gave of the fighting at Cawnpore. He had known Munro the police officer at Akyab who had been with Lewin when, after bumping into the Lakher war-party, they had taken to the jungle; and Sir Arthur Phayre's name was familiar to him from his tombstone in a quiet churchyard near Bray in County Wicklow, for Busteed's seven-year-old son was buried nearby. He remembered, too, Lewin introducing him in Calcutta to "the old freebooter Lushai chief 'Rutton Poia' converted into a grateful and loyal friend by your kindly tact".

In 1910 came a letter from Colonel Shakespear in Imphal, the capital of Manipur:

> I send you a photograph of Nepuitangi, the widow of Vuta or Vatusa, whose name you probably heard of in the old days when you ruled the Border. The old lady was well when I left the Lushai Hills in 1905 but quite blind, and I had great difficulty in getting her to sit for her picture, only persuading her to do so by agreeing to include in the photograph two other women older than herself. I thought that this picture might be welcome, to show you that you are not yet forgotten in these parts.

Shakespear wrote again the following year, reporting on the changes that had taken place in the hills since Lewin's day. He himself had much reduced the Lushais' tendency to nomadism, which had been largely due to the fear that a neighbouring tribe would dispossess them of their *jhums*, by allotting to each chief a certain defined tract within which the villages under his jurisdiction might rotate their cultivation. In 1912 Shakespear wrote to him again from Imphal on the occasion of the publication of his book *The Lushei-Kuki Clans*, which he dedicated to Lewin with the inscription: "The fruits of whose labours I was privileged to reap, and who, after an absence of nearly forty years, is still affectionately remembered by the Lushais". He also reported: "Old Saipoiya [Seipuia] is still alive. He is about the last of the Howlongs you actually knew". Lorrain and Savidge had come back to the Lushai Hills bringing their wives with them and had settled at Lungleh on the site of Seipuia's old village which Lewin and General Brownlow had visited in 1871. Lorrain's younger brother Reginald was living with his wife Maud at Saiha further south, working among the Lakhers. "The Thengawl valley where you had your interview with the captors of Mary Winchester is now all cultivated."

Mary Winchester! She was the tea-planter's daughter whose kidnapping by the Haolongs during a Lushai raid on the Alexandrapur tea garden had been one of the main factors that prompted the Lushai Expedition. The last Lewin had heard of her came in a letter from General Brownlow written in September 1881 when he was aide-de-camp to Queen Victoria, after he had attended the christening of his infant godson, Charlie Lewin — "a sturdy little fellow with an expression about his big toes and the carriage of his legs and arms which promises or rather confirms his character as depicted in his face — a young Attila". Brownlow had taken up an Aberdeen newspaper and to his astonishment read the name of Mary Winchester in a list of examinees of the Royal Moray College. She had taken a considerable share of the marks in all manner of different subjects, and considering that when she was recovered from captivity less than ten years before she could barely speak a word of English her achievement was very creditable to the young lady. Lewin had heard no more of her until a letter arrived in October 1912 bearing a Hampstead Heath address and written in bold copybook handwriting.

Dear Colonel Lewin,
I have just finished reading "A Fly on the Wheel". In fact I knew nothing of it, until last mail brought a letter from Mr Lorraine, suggesting I should read it.
You will be more than surprised, that after 40 years I, like the leper who returned to give thanks, now write to say 'Thank you' & 'God bless you' for the many acts of courage you must have performed & the many hardships & anxieties you must have suffered to rescue poor me. God does work in a mysterious way, & to me it has always been a puzzle why God took my devoted Father & left me, but now the answer comes.
The Lushais are in possession of the Word of God, & are becoming good Christians.
Only a few weeks ago I had a letter from the grandson of the old woman who had charge of me in that Howlong village.

Your description of me amuses my husband & family! It is true the child is father to the man.

I had a very generous education, thanks to my dear old grandparents.

At fourteen I was dux of the Elgin Academy a high class public school of over 500 boys & girls. At nineteen, I was Head Mistress of a High School, having taken Higher Women's University Certificates. So 'sententious commands' learned even at the expense of my rescuers, have stood me in good stead.

I have a hazy recollection that the Lushai children used to play soldiers in order to fight the English, & I was evidently, with pipe in my mouth, Commander in Chief.

For 25 years, I have been married, & we have three children — Frank, Molly & Peggy, ages 24, 15 & 13.

If ever you can visit us we shall be delighted to see you, but if travelling is too fatiguing, I shall be only too pleased to go & see you & have a chat about the Hill people for whom you have so much love.

Pardon my letter but I felt that I must write.

There is so much one would like to know, but I must not worry you.

With every good wish, I am, yours very sincerely,

Mary Innes Howie
(*née* Mary Winchester)

For whatever reason Lewin was reluctant to meet her, but Margaret insisted, and so the visit to Parkhurst took place a month later; and from the brief account of it he wrote to Everest one can only wish it had not: "Mary Winchester was a stuck-up conceited little half-caste woman, and I am sorry I had her down here, but Mother wished it". It seems that Mrs Howie made the most of her new-found knowledge, for early in 1913 she called on

Field Marshal Lord Roberts of Kandahar, VC, who had been the principal staff officer with the Cachar Column during the expedition. It was reported to Lewin by his kinsman Major Harry Lewin, RA, ADC to Lord Roberts and engaged to his second daughter Lady Edwina, that the field marshall had been more charitable in his verdict on Mrs Howie, merely observing that he was glad to find that she was comfortably provided for.

News of Sir Charles Brownlow was given to Lewin in February 1913 by his old friend Colonel Jarrett, who had been staying with him at his house at Warfield in Berkshire. He had been promoted field marshal in 1908 and at eighty-two was in good health, though the effects of an old war wound were affecting his spine, giving it a double curvature that made walking painful. He had everything about him that material comforts could give to prolong his life and a peace of mind nothing disturbed. The only shadow on his days was the memory of his wife who had died the previous year, whose companionship he had not recognized to be so necessary to him until it was withdrawn.

And still the past refused to let Lewin alone. Two months later Lewin heard from one of his fellow cadets Colonel Vibart, urging him to attend the forthcoming Addiscombe dinner at the Café Royal in Regent Street, at which Lord Roberts was to be the guest of the evening; but such reunions were not to Lewin's taste, and he declined the invitation, as he had done in previous years.

"But now," Bob complained to Lewin, "when I send you a long letter I get in return a short scrap chiefly referring to Everest and her children 'who arrived yesterday' or that 'Nicholas and Audrey come tomorrow'. These facts may no doubt be interesting to you, but they leave me cold." They were more than interesting to Lewin, for as he grew older the doings of his children and stepchildren became his chief interest in life, their concerns of vital importance to him.

Alex Mackenzie had relinquished his governorship of Bengal in 1898 and brought Mabel and their two young children Maggie and Jock home. He was planning to stand for parliament for the Chichester division of Sussex representing the Protestant interest against the Roman Catholic candidate supported by the powerful influence of the Duke of Norfolk, but had to withdraw owing to ill-health and died in 1902 aged sixty. Early the following year William and Daisy Meredith with their two children took Mabel and her children on holiday to Hyères on the Riviera overlooking the Golfe Juan, where Lewin, Margaret and Audrey had stayed in 1893. From there William wrote to Lewin that the *enfant terrible* Maggie had made herself ill by eating over-rich food, and that Jock was a nice bright boy who should, when he mixed with other boys, develop a straightforward and open character.

> Mabel, dear simple soul, is most loveable and quite helpless by herself. Smiles, weeps, reads packets of letters, dons the crape bonnet, discards it again, and so

from hour to hour! *Mon Dieu!* what a conglomerate of contradictions constitutes a woman.

They expected 'our friend' Noel Farrer to join them next day, the inverted commas suggesting some unstated nuance that Lewin would understand, the key to which may lie in the fact that a year later Mabel and Noel were married.

Noel was the younger son of the Lewins' neighbour, by now Lord Farrer of Abinger Hall, who had spent forty years at the Board of Trade. Since Noel was a member of parliament, Mabel's life was henceforth to be involved with such political questions as the Port of London bill and votes for women. They had two children, their first-born Anthony being born in 1910, the year in which Jock, who had been born in Burma in 1894, died after a lingering illness. Although the Farrers lived for many years in Ennismore Gardens, for Mabel there was never any other "home" than Parkhurst, where she often took her children to stay.

> Visions of past holidays flitted across my mind [she wrote of one such visit], as if another existence — another being. How little that girl knew what lay in front of her! and there was 'home' just the same, everything practically the same, hay, strawberries, sunny weather, the old house, the garden, the cedars, only ourselves changed — and the three unconscious little children, Anthony, Eileen and Joan, playing in the haycocks, while Maggie is just about setting out on the same quest that we all feel so certain about, when we are young!

Anna and her husband John Young had four children, two sons and then two daughters. Whenever she came to London her mother would see her, and sometimes Anna brought her children to Parkhurst. One Saturday in the summer of 1904 she spent the day there with her two girls, little Margaret bringing with her a canary, and Lilias two boxes, one containing a dormouse, the other a caterpillar. The children spent most of the day playing in the hay, happy and thankful to be out of the dust and heat of London. John arrived later in genial and expansive mood, though his law practice had recently suffered owing to the death and failure of solicitors. Knowing him to be reliable and a specialist in company law Margaret wrote to Lewin, who was then in Denmark on Danish Gas business, asking him to suggest to Woodall that he should send him work.

The Merediths with their two children Margot and George divided their time between London and their house at Fleet, and often it was William working from home who looked after the children in the country, while Daisy stayed in London; for she had become a professional musician. She not only composed songs and choral works, but also took charge of their production, her work being performed at various times at the Albert Hall, the Court Theatre, the Chapel Royal and the Queen's Hall. In 1909 she was in Leipzig seeing to the publication of her music and in 1910 was described as wrestling with conductors, choirs, crochets and jealousies at Harrogate. Her preoccupation with musical business involved some neglect of her children and put a strain on her relationship with William, whose easygoing nature was fortunately pliable enough to put up with it. A thoughtless reference to "her extreme poverty" in a letter to her mother earned Daisy a rebuke which brought her sharply to earth. In her reply Margaret spelled out in detail the extent of the financial benefits conferred on the children since her first husband Charles Elliot's death, reminding Daisy that on her remarriage she had allowed the girls to share their father's fortune amounting to £70,000, wanting them to be independent. Moreover, on Daisy's marriage she and Lewin had put up capital to enable William to buy a partnership in his publishing firm; so if Daisy was really in poverty as she said, this could only be because she was spending more than she ought. How much Margaret had been hurt by Daisy's claim to be poverty-stricken can be inferred from her closing words:

> I hope you will find your way to light some day when you are not bewildered by vain shadows and false hopes. That I cannot follow you in them all may be because I am old and tired of life's vain show and care only for those I love and who are good enough to love me.

3

The little girl called Eileen who had been playing with Mabel's two children in the haycocks at Parkhurst was Charlie's eldest child. On his return from soldiering in South Africa he had married in 1908 Beatrice Barlow-

Webb (always called Queenie) whose family lived in some style at neighbouring Holmdale St. Mary, and because her father, who had amassed a fortune in South Africa, would not allow her to live abroad had got himself the job of adjutant of the Derbyshire Yeomanry. In 1910, a year after Eileen was born, he had been brought to the point of death by a serious illness from which he never fully recovered. He was warm-hearted, attractive to other women and like the rest of his family passionately fond of music. When off-duty he liked to organize musical evenings at home, when they would play Schumann, Dvorak, Bach, Mozart, Brahms, Mendelssohn, Chopin, Beethoven or Tchaikovsky. Following in his father's footsteps, his chosen instrument was the 'cello. If no other players were available, he would press into service instrumentalists belonging to the regimental band.

"Sergeant-Major, are you there? Yes? Well, I want four strings to be out here tomorrow morning by eleven o'clock."

"Four what, sir?"

"Four players, good ones — two violins, a viola —"

"What, sir?"

"A v-i-o-l-a and a violoncello."

"Very good, sir. They shall be there."

Queenie bore him a son in 1912 who was christened Thomas, and two more sons were born to them in later years. Charlie had still been unmarried serving in India when he received news of Everest's engagement to Tom Macdonald. "How strange it will be at home without

Effie," he wrote. "I suppose she will have to live in the Isle of Skye."

Macdonald was a member of a Scottish family with properties in the highlands and islands, which also had commercial interests in India. Soon after their wedding in July 1901 the couple sailed for India, a country Everest had last seen as a baby in 1879, where Tom Macdonald took charge of the family indigo and sugar businesses in the Saran district of Bihar. The letter she wrote from there in February 1904 will have stirred in Lewin memories of his own early days in India nearly fifty years before.

> At night when I go to bed there rises on the air the monotonous sound of the 'tom-tom', which always reminds me of Kipling's 'Little Toomai', and I see you in your big chair reading to us. The sound comes from a strange squat little village just outside our compound. The thump thump of the rhythmic beat grows louder, and then a faint faraway clamour of distant voices rises on the night air in chorus, while the drum goes on beating, and I hide my head in the bedclothes and think of the dark wild faces and what a tiny handful of intruders we English people are in this foreign land.

The indigo side of the Macdonald business had been adversely affected when a synthetic indigo manufactured in Germany came on the market, and there were indications that the industry was entering a depression from which it was unlikely to recover; so Macdonald decided to concentrate on the sugar side of the business and brought a new factory into commission. Though Everest found much to interest her in her new life, she was often homesick, missing more than anything the musical evenings at home, which for her, too, always meant Parkhurst. As the hot weather approached Tom took her and their first-born the year-old Ursula to Mussoorie in the lower Himalayas north of Dehra Dun, where their second child Neil was born. The family returned to Scotland in February 1905.

At Barquillean, their house at Taymuilt in Argyllshire, Everest did what she could to recreate the atmosphere of Parkhurst by arranging occasional musical weekends when a small circle comprising violin, flute, clarinet and piano would sit in the music-room by gaslight — for they had no electricity — playing the pieces which she had asked her father to suggest. Or she would work at his favourite Beethoven and Mozart piano quartets; for emotionally she and her father were still very close. So much so that, when that autumn he wrote reproaching her for not having written to him, she poured her distress into her reply, explaining how her love for him was so great and so vital a part of her life that she sometimes forgot that the outward and visible signs were a necessary part of it. "It is," she confessed, "so much more 'Me' than even my love for my children, I think."

There were now four of them, Diana and Thomas having been born after their return to Scotland, and when in December Tom Macdonald had to go out to India again to cope with a crisis that had arisen affecting the sugar business Everest was expected, besides looking after the children, to deputize for him as the laird, visiting the tenants' cottages when someone was ill and giving instructions to their farm manager. There was money to be raised to pay for a district nurse, and when funds were needed in aid of the cottage hospital she invited the local ladies to a sewing party, and while they sewed she read them one of Kipling's stories — perhaps it was 'Toomai of the Elephants' — and afterwards they sang songs. One evening she visited the cottage of a shepherd on the estate who was sick, and writing about it to her father described her walk back down the hill to Barquillean in the darkness:

> So still it was coming back down the hill to the house. Ben Cruachan lying like a faceless grey image of stone, against which the house glowed dimly with its lights. The broken country seemed flattened into a soft dark carpet with silver streaks of streams as pattern. No sound but the murmur of water hurrying to the sea from a hundred tiny rills which made a soft all-pervading voice, and occasionally the cry of a curlew or the sound of a flight of ducks overhead ... I lay a long time in the deep sweet-smelling heather watching the beauty of the night, and the weird cry of a small owl kept me company. Then the kitchen light at Barquillean went out, and I knew it must be late, and I ran down the hill into the deep grey velvet land, sad to leave behind me the mystery and the magic of it all.

She had come to love Barquillean, feeling it was good for the children to grow and develop in such surroundings so as to acquire an instinct for freedom, even unconsciously, before coming in contact with the machinery of life and before the complexity of convention swaddled them round. In such tentative language did she try to express what the rugged landscape round her Scottish home had come to mean to her.

Although her father only once went to stay at Barquillean, Everest enjoyed taking her children to stay at Parkhurst where they could run wild in the garden while she played billiards with him in the billiard room; and after the children had gone to bed there would be music. Lewin became fond of her children, saying they were the nicest he had ever seen, especially Ursula whom he called Starry Eyes, Wild Rose or Sweet One. Her younger brother Neil once earned the reproof "Barbarian!" when he had behaved badly at table, but so mildly delivered as not to make him quail; and when on another occasion he had been in a tantrum his howling brought no sterner rebuke from his grandfather than "You roar like a bull of Bashan". Looking back over eighty years Ursula wrote down her memories of Parkhurst seen through the eyes of a little girl which is included as an appendix.

Everest's younger sister Audrey lived in London. Both were attractive women, Everest softer featured and more motherly, Audrey finer drawn but very feminine. Both inherited their father's musical and artistic talents. Everest in addition wrote poetry, in later life having a book of her poems published which she dedicated to Sir John Squire with an acknowledgement of the encouragement he had given her. Audrey composed light music hall songs and loved clothes and décor. In her unconventionality there was much of her uncle Bob about her, and every Sunday evening she would keep "open house" for friends from all walks of life. In August 1903 she had married Nicholas Waterhouse, also from a neighbouring Surrey family and a junior partner in the firm of City accountants Messrs Price, Waterhouse & Co. Having no children meant that she had to fill up her day as best she could, and the programme she devised for herself she explained in a letter to her father: "Two days of the week I philander; the other two I philanthropate (if there be such a word); and the remaining three I vegetate". Her philanthropy took the form of visiting the indigent Jewish immigrants from south Germany who had settled in London, excursions that provided incidentally a chance to re-experience one of the childhood pleasures she used to share with her father at Parkhurst.

> Another charm of old Soho is the freshly roasted chestnuts which one can buy in the streets, straight off the fire and (chiefest of charms) eat as you walk along, which you can hardly do in Regent Street. Doing this, I often think of you and wish you could share my chestnuts with me, done to a turn just as you like them.

In 1908 Nicholas took her with him on an extended business trip to America, and they often took their summer holidays in France, touring in a chauffeur-driven car. One year it was "châteaux, parks, cathedrals, all delightful" and thence to Poitiers and Biarritz; another year Pau, Biarritz again and San Sebastian. Still finding she had time on her hands, Audrey enrolled as a student at the Royal College of Music, and although she had not had a lesson since she was at school and could not read a note of music, she could play anything by ear, astonishing her professor by an impromptu performance on the piano in which she wandered from Wagner to Brahms to Saint Saens to Dvorak without a pause between pieces.

Among the musical friends with whom she played Debussy quartets and César Franck was a young French violinist André Mangeot, who was later to form his own string quartet with the then unknown John Barbirolli as 'cellist and to employ the young Christopher Isherwood as the quartet's secretary. Mangeot helped Audrey with a piece she had composed for performance at Parkhurst, refusing payment for copying out all the parts which he offered as his Christmas present "*à cet homme charmant monsieur votre père*". Unfortunately on the occasion when the music was played Mangeot unwittingly annoyed Lewin by behaving in a way he thought lacking in respect for his daughter. Mangeot was all contrition and Audrey stoutly defended him, praising his many good qualities, and asked her father to forgive his recreant and un-conventional daughter and to put up with her shady foreign friends.

In the spring of 1913 she and Nicholas were staying at Barquillean for a musical festival — Haydn, Mozart, Glazunof, Schubert — organized by Everest, whom she still called by her childhood nickname "Peffkin". After dinner a piper was summoned and they danced reels in the kitchen with the retainers, while Mangeot who was among the party sat in a corner writing down the weird bagpipe tunes on a bit of paper with the keenest interest.

Chapter Twenty
Shadows of the Evening

1

Lewin's curiosity about the way people meet their death dated back at least as far as 1871 when he had written to his cousin Jeannie from Rangamati after learning that George Grote had died, asking her to give him some account of his illness and end. This interest developed into something of an obsession, which began to take tangible shape when he read a passage in Florio's translation of Montaigne's *First Book of Essays*, in which the essayist professed to desire nothing more than to be informed of the death of men, what words they spoke and what countenance they showed at their death. "Were I a composer of books, I would keep a register, commented of the divers deaths, which in teaching men to die, should after teach them to live." Lewin began to compile such a register himself, and the result was his last book, a large and handsome volume titled *Life and Death / being / An Authentic Account of the Deaths of one hundred celebrated men and women, with their portraits / collated and re-told by / Colonel Thomas H. Lewin / Author of 'The* [sic] *Fly on the Wheel,' 'Wild Tribes of the S.E. Frontier,' 'The Lewin Letters,' etc.* On the title page the publishers are named as Constable and Co. Ltd. of London, William Meredith's firm, but in fact the book, like *The Lewin Letters*, was privately printed at Lewin's own expense and cost him, as he wrote to Everest, a considerable sum. It was published in 1910 when he was seventy-one years old.

The celebrated men and women whose death-bed scenes he recounted ranged from figures of classical times like Socrates and Nero to his own contemporaries such as General Gordon and Robert Louis Stevenson. They included Saint Peter and Saint Paul, kings and queens, dictators, religious leaders, poets and writers, philosophers and composers; among them the Prophet Mohammed, Charlemagne, Saint Teresa, Montaigne, Donne, the Emperor Aurungzeb, Rousseau, Samuel Johnson, Marie Antoinette, Nelson, Warren Hastings, Napoleon, Mozart, Beethoven, Prince Talleyrand, Schopenhauer and Thackeray. As he wrote in his introduction, what astonished Lewin when he read through the deaths he had recorded was the fearlessness and ease with which human beings in general leave their human habitation. To die is not so terrible, for longevity is not a blessing, and only the form and manner of dying are to be dreaded. We all must die, but hardly one of us (he added) but thinks he may live another twenty years. He did not try to answer the eternal questions — Shall we meet again those who have gone before? What is life? What is death? — dismissing them as insoluble problems, for it is the quest itself that raises men from the level of the beasts, the search for truth that fills up the measure of life and gives it purpose. Death in itself is a negative and natural experience, he concluded, which should not be dreaded and, indeed, was not dreaded by the dying, as confirmed by the historical instances he had given in his book.

The introduction also contains Lewin's most considered reflections on human life as his own entered its final phase, and three quotations from it may be said to summarize his last thoughts.

> Old age is, on the whole, a much pleasanter period of life than one expects; it is less full of anxiety; the stress and strain of ambition have gone, with the attainment of an assured position; strength is less, but the spirits are more equable; and greatest boon of all, man escapes from the yoke of the passions.

> We start on our pilgrimage full of enthusiasm. Life's cup is nectar at the brink. Hope beats high as we think how much there is to be done and what we shall do. The world is full of prizes for those who dare; but as the years go by, we cannot satisfy ourselves.

> Our labour seems endless and unprofitable, and, when the time comes for us to cease work — lo! it is as a tale that is told, and all we have done and suffered seems of little worth: worldly success, rank, pleasure, love, all fail to satisfy. It is something different from all these that we seek. It is the peace that passeth understanding, only to be found in Death.

For with the march of the years had come a deeper and deeper melancholy as Lewin gloomily contemplated his relations and friends departing one by one for the Beyond. Before the turn of the century the last survivors of the older generation had gone, aunt Babbie in 1888, his mother two years later. Will had been murdered in 1897, and Edward Burne-Jones died the following year. The new century was still in its infancy when, in 1902, it was Sir John Edgar's turn and, a few months later, that of Alex Mackenzie.

Now old Bankes seemed to be heading the same way. When Lewin stayed with the Tomlins in their modern house in Earls Avenue on the sea front at Folkestone, equipped with electric light and telephones, on the occasion of Bankes's seventy-ninth birthday he seemed much older and more tottery, with a nurse permanently in attendance. Four years later he was still alive but behaving childishly, endlessly playing with the Gobang board (a Japanese game played on a chequer-board) which Margaret had given him. When in 1907 she went to stay with them their son Gore was away visiting his fiancée, but his brother Julian came in for Sunday lunch. Bankes seemed much the same, though he complained that he was fading away. Harriet was understandably in an unsettled frame of mind, not only worried about her husband's health, but also about Gore's engagement. She was under the influence of a spiritualist medium and had come away from a session convinced that the responsibility for her son's engagement lay with the spirit of Will Terriss, who had also been manifesting himself in the house by means of portentous knockings. This was not the only appearance of Will's ghost, which was frequently in evidence at night in the Adelphi Theatre after the audience had gone home, and much later was often seen by the railway staff at the Covent Garden tube station. Margaret was persuaded by Harriet to attend a *séance* but came away more sceptical than ever. Bankes eventually died in 1909.

His widow was soon to be seen consoling herself at Monte Carlo, where she was joined by her friend General G. Fitzpatrick Browne, CB, DSO; "making the most of her flying remnant", as Bob put it; "but I have passed that feverish stage and am now what is termed 'a Quietist'". Harriet moved to a cottage at St. Peter's and soon settled down to the humdrum Thanet life, where, despite her sixty-five years, she was still able to enjoy the pleasures of nature, music, change, food, society and, above all, the priceless gift of love and affection of those most dear to her, especially her loving and dutiful sons. In 1910 she spent four months with them holidaying in France, ending their tour in Venice where General Browne joined them. Shortly after their return Lewin received a letter from the general announcing that in a few days he would have the pleasure and great privilege of assuming responsibility for Harriet's future happiness, and the ceremony was duly performed in Broadstairs Church on 19 April 1911 in the presence of Gore and Julian, the bride being dressed in sombre grey.

A year later she wrote to Margaret: "I often think I should have been wiser if I had remained single, although the general is sweetness itself"; and Bob reported that when she had looked in at Cornwall Gardens where he lived she had seemed worried and restless. On holiday with her new husband at Montreux in 1913 her great daily treat was to go down to the Casino by herself and listen to the fine orchestra, the music inducing in her the fancy that the whole place was teeming with the spirits of those who had "gone over". She knew her brother Tom did not hold with such dreams, but she was still dabbling in spiritualism and by a strange coincidence asked him, if he died first, to come and tell her, and she would come to him if she went first, provided he made the way clear for her; the very request Lewin had made to his mother from Muzaffarpur fifty years before.

Lewin's increasing depression was of concern to his friends as well as his family. Lady Burne-Jones, who in her widowhood had been writing a biography of her husband, tried to talk him out of it. "I thought it was only in youth," she wrote from Rottingdean, "that one so nursed melancholy, or that the end of life seemed so terrible ... I wish you would dig your melancholy into the soil of your garden and let the green grass grow over it." She remembered Ruskin (who had died in 1900 after many years of insanity) telling her of the circle reserved by Dante in the *Inferno* for those who cherished sorrow. Comforting words were also received from Laura Forster writing from her neighbouring house West Hackhurst at Abinger: "It reinforces what I had been putting before my nephew [E.M. Forster the novelist] this Christmas, that the happiness of old age differs more in kind than in degree from that of our youth, and specially if we accept each day as it comes does the passing life bring its own sweetness and brightness". It was all to no avail.

A more effective tonic was the inveterate cheerfulness of his brother Bob, who could write that he might have to start at any moment for the Beyond as casually as he could decline Tom's invitation to meet him in London because he was engaged to go a-fishing. In an effort to cheer his elder brother up he embellished his letters with little rhymes of his own composition illustrative of the themes he introduced, as when, approaching the psalmist's span of life, he confessed that his greatest solace was playing billiards at his club:

> I have lived my life: I am nearly done
> And soon shall slip my cable,
> But I freely admit that the best of my fun
> I owe to the billiard table.

When his game began to go to pot, he had to fall back on his books and his pipe, enjoying what he called the "desolate freedom of the Wild Ass". He also brought him news of Harry Graves, who was now over seventy-five and living in a cottage in Cornwall on twenty shillings a week "because of hard times at Talbot Road", which may have meant that his children were finding it hard to support him. "A slight theological thread, never noticeable before, now runs through his letters to me", Bob wrote. "'Twas ever thus —

> For nearly everyone when age or sorrow
> strike him
> Inclines to think there is a God or something
> very like him."

He reported later in the year that, since even that meagre source of income had dried up, Harry had submitted his application for an old age pension, on hearing which Bob had sent him a fiver he could ill afford. Rather than see his old friend living on the parish Lewin arranged to finance what they called the Sustentation Fund out of which Harry was to be paid an allowance, and Bob was to let his brother know whenever the fund needed replenishing. Since no mention was made of the Sustentation Fund in Bob's last letter to Lewin in 1915, it may be assumed that by that date Harry Graves's inglorious life had come to an end.

Nothing could for long quench Bob's inexhaustible cheerfulness. Even when another of his friends died, a pal from boyhood and the only human being in whom he could confide, he managed to come up with a cheerful verse:

> They stirred him up with calomel
> And tried to move his liver;
> 'Twas all in vain, for poor old Bill
> Was wafted o'er the river —

though the cheerfulness was now becoming rather strained, for he added: "So now like a periwinkle I shrink into my shell and live from day to day. I made a break of 40 at billiards at the Club last week ...". He was now growing weak in the knee-joints and feeling distinctly aged and arthritic —

> Man's a vapour
> Full of woes,
> He cuts a caper
> And down he goes!

All in all, so many of his friends having died and his happiest memories gone with them, life was beginning to lose its savour, even for Bob, and he was quite ready, he said, to "'up anchor' for the *Ewigheit. Lusisti satis ...*".

In May 1909, a month after Lewin's seventieth birthday, his friend and neighbour George Meredith died at Flint Cottage. His death was honoured as a national event, and Lewin was particularly moved by J.M. Barrie's fanciful obituary piece that appeared in the *Times* newspaper. Next year Mabel's elder son Jock still a schoolboy at Eton had died after a long illness, and the following year Lewin's younger sister Bella became a widow on the death of her husband Nathaniel Stevenson. In 1892 he had been made a lieutenant-general, rising to full general six years later, and from 1894 to 1899 was lieutenant-governor of Guernsey and Alderney. These distant commands coupled with Bella's disinclination to write letters had resulted in her staying aloof from family affairs. At the time of his death at the age of seventy-one the general had been visiting Machrihanish in Montrose with Bella and their two daughters. After a game of golf and a swim near the links he had gone to dress for dinner in his hotel room, where he was found dead on the floor. His coffin draped with the Union Jack and many wreaths had been taken to St. Skeoch near Montrose in a gun-carriage with an escort provided by the Royal Field Artillery for burial beside his mother. Bob sympathized with his sister in her bereavement, pointing out in his robust way that she had lost not only an entirely honest husband, but £1,000 a year to boot. "Fate," he observed, "is inscrutable, and one never knows where the blow will fall next."

It fell soon enough on Lewin's medical adviser Dr Rawlings of Dorking who was stricken with cancer of the throat causing him much suffering and preventing him from speaking. On the day he died, 17 July 1914, Lewin had written to him:

> We only heard on Saturday that you were ill and by your note received this morning I judge you consider your case hopeless. My dear fellow! I am more grieved than I can say. I always looked to you to see me out of this world on which my hold is now so light, and that you in your full vigour and strength with all your powers for usefulness and mercy to your fellow men should be taken seems impossible. I have written asking your sister for news of your health, but to yourself I can only say God speed you on your way when He calls you.

Soon afterwards Lewin heard from an old comrade of Mutiny days Colonel Dudley Sampson, commiserating with him on the state of the world in which they had grown old, what with Socialism, coal strikes, cotton strikes, Home Rule, insurance bills, the shortage of Territorials and in the Navy, a shortage of horses, and a very distinct shortage of patriotism and "vim" all round, to say nothing of possible civil war in Ireland. "Well, old man," he concluded his letter:

we can only look on and wonder at this extraordinary planet, with its multi-millionaires on the one hand and its hooligan starvelings on the other, and smile at Browning's demented observation 'God's in his heaven, All's right with the world'. I am in a new doctor's hands. *Eheu.* We are both of us getting pretty waterlogged to get over 'the Bar', but I suppose there is fair anchorage on the other side.

The next one to test the anchorage on the other side was another Mutiny veteran Dr Busteed, who died in the following month; but an even heavier blow was yet to come.

"My dear old Tombo," the letter began, bringing a host of memories flooding back, for only one family had ever called him by that nickname, and turning to the end he read "Your affectionate cousin, Fanny Green". It was from Jeannie's younger sister, who thought he would be interested to receive an account of the condition of someone whose character had at one time had a great influence on his life, and who had watched over his welfare so tenderly in his young days. Earlier that winter Jeannie now aged eighty-four had been staying at Tunbridge Wells, being pushed about in a bath chair, but after a fall in November her condition grew worse and she had been confined to bed with a nurse in attendance, though she hated being fussed over. She slept much of the time, but her mind was clear and she liked to have a daily chapter of the Bible read to her, which she would then discuss. Fanny had read her the verses in 1 John dwelling on the purifying powers of the truth that by faith we are led to God, and having closed the book was sitting writing beside her when she heard Jeannie talking to herself.

"Gracious Father, purify my spirit so that I shall not mind the vexations and disturbances which are necessary." Then, after a pause: "Gracious Father, when some time soon I shall slip away, let Thy presence be very near me".

Sometimes after Jeannie had been tidied up for the night the two old ladies would read a psalm together or quaveringly sing a hymn, calmly waiting for the end which could not be far away.

Lewin's own health was now beginning to fail due to his enlarged prostate gland, a condition which in those days was inoperable, and for some time he had been undergoing treatment that caused him great discomfort. He was put on a diet which enjoined no milk, no sugar and no eggs, and since these had formed the chief part of his food, he found the change unpleasant. Going upstairs had now become more and more difficult, even leaning on Margaret's arm, until he had to accept the indignity of being carried up by one of the menservants; and he began to suffer from frequent painful heart-attacks. These days there was no more music at Parkhurst and the house became very silent, though on some evenings Margaret would put a record on the gramophone, which he seemed to enjoy.

The time came when she could not leave him for more than an hour day or night. Each day she would get up at 7.45 while Lewin read in bed before getting up himself.

After breakfast he would retire to the billiard-room which served as the living room and consider his next move in the game of chess he was playing with a friend by correspondence, and at 10.30 Margaret would read to him aloud from the *Daily Telegraph* while he practised billiards strokes. He would then look through his letters and take a little food, after which he would read or doze. Before lunch they would spend half an hour on the terrace or in the garden, depending on the weather, and afterwards play billiards together. At three she would read to him from the *Times*, which was not delivered until the afternoon, and after tea if it was fine they would walk in the garden and perhaps trim the laurels. At six he would be taken upstairs to dress for dinner, and when it was over they would talk while he smoked a cigar. At nine if he felt well enough they would play another game of billiards and at ten retire to bed.

To Everest he described her mother and himself as two old spectres, just hanging on to the fringe of life. "The oil in the lamp sinks," he wrote to her in May 1914, "and with it the flame of vitality subsides." .

2

And now the war clouds that had been massing on the horizon were moving closer, threatening to darken the world. At the beginning of August Everest was on holiday with a woman friend at Brabazon in France when the

crisis was suddenly sprung upon them. There was no
authentic news, but reports kept coming in all day long,
each one contradicting the one before, and everyone in
the hotel was tense and excited. The war had, then it had
not, been declared; there was talk of mobilization, though
nobody seemed to know what that meant; all the guests'
motor cars were commandeered, and there were no seats
to be had on the trains because they were all reserved for
the troops. At 10.30 p.m. next night they were allowed on
a train waiting at Melun station, packed and seething with
passengers, and spent the night sitting on their luggage
in the corridor as the train jolted on its way to Paris, which
they reached at one in the morning. With difficulty they
secured a cab, for the place was crowded with men,
women and children, and found their hotel at sixes and
sevens because many of the staff had gone to join their
regiments, leaving only two elderly waiters who were
worked off their feet. It was now two o'clock and they
were very hungry, but managed to get coffee and rolls at
a nearby café. All night long the searchlights crossed and
recrossed in the sky over the city, companies of soldiers
marched by, but otherwise absolute quiet reigned. It was
all very wonderful and terrible.

Colonel Davidson, a fellow director on the board of
the Danish Gas Company, reported to Lewin ten days
after war had been formally declared that Dover was a
fortress with torpedo flotillas in the harbour and cruisers
scouring the straits. Vexing to an old soldier like himself
unable to join the fighting line was the anxiety of waiting

for news of the North Sea fleet while all around there was a massing of troops, silent marching, the changing of garrison soldiers, and the constant rumbling of baggage waggons transporting camp equipage and ammunition. "What an evening to our life!" Lewin, too, chafed at his inability to be of use.

In September Mabel in Camberley wrote of a friend of her elder daughter Maggie being brought back from the front in a hospital train with a shattered shoulder and one eye shot out. At night she could hear German prisoners singing part-songs in their camp a mile away, and during the day aeroplanes swooped overhead on test flights from Farnborough. Lord Roberts who had come to make a recruiting speech had warned of the country being in great danger. Mabel had been organizing the collection of bedclothes, pyjamas and dressing-gowns for use in a convalescent home for the wounded, while Maggie was helping out at Guildford hospital. Meanwhile, a German army was marching on Paris and refugees from France and Belgium were pouring into the English ports. The wildest rumours were current. Mabel had heard on the best authority that Russian soldiers on their way to Dover, from Archangel it was said, had passed through Basingstoke in sixty trains with their blinds down. And all night there was an incessant rumbling of trains carrying troops to unknown destinations.

Barquillean was no longer the peaceful haven where only a few months before there had been a family gathering, when Nick Waterhouse and Tom Macdonald had gone fishing in the daytime, and in the evening there had been music, Everest and Audrey rejoicing in this reminder of childhood days at Parkhurst. In Argyllshire, too, rumours were the order of the day. "We heard it from a girl in the village," wrote Everest to her mother, "whose brother works as a Post Office sorter on the London & Carlisle Mail" that forty trains carrying Russian soldiers had been sent through from the far north of Scotland to some east coast port in England for transport to Ostend. News reached them of the destruction of Louvain, of a battle in the North Sea, and tales of German brutality. Everest meanwhile found herself appointed convener of the Prince of Wales's National Relief Fund and was expected to make speeches. Tom was trying to get back to India.

Nothing but war news poured into the old couple at Parkhurst, every one of whose empty rooms reminded them of their children now scattered far and wide. Colonel Davidson was, as ever, full of inside information, glad that Kitchener had gone over to Paris and had threatened to withdraw our army if they were left unsupported on the left flank. "I hear the French general who was in fault was tried by court martial and shot. Destroy my letter or I may meet with the same fate." In November 1915 he wrote in a less bellicose mood, telling Lewin that his son had been killed, leading his men in action. They heard from Harriet that Julian had gone to France and was to take charge of wireless communications in a cavalry corps then being formed, and from William Meredith that they had George at home, wounded in the hand while serving with the 8th Hussars at Ypres, when every officer had either been killed or wounded. Lewin and Margaret will have felt relief mingled with regret that Charlie's state of health rendered him unfit for active service. (He was to die in the epidemic of influenza that swept the country in the winter of 1918-19, shortly after the Armistice.) Audrey's husband Nicholas was also non-combatant, but put his accountancy skills to military use as Director of Costings, for which he received a knighthood after the war.

General Browne had been put in charge of Special Constables at St. Peters in Thanet and was sometimes hauled out of bed in the middle of the night to deal with reports of airships flying over towards Dover or London. Harriet, now past seventy, had lost all her courage and pleasure in life, bemoaning the awful war: "Everyone will die from it", she wrote. Bella had last been heard of at a spiritualist *séance* at St. Helen's on the Isle of Wight where once again brother Will had materialized, this time accompanied by Sir Henry Irving. She had now, Harriet reported, left town and would soon have to settle down somewhere, whether she liked it or not.

> Well! [she wrote] We have had a far happier life than the majority of people. God has been wonderfully good to me who deserve nothing and now when one thinks of these countless young lives, full of hope and vigour and now all gone and what for? It is too terrible.

As for Bob, even a war and the humiliations of old age

could not quite quench his indomitable spirit. "Why this sombre silence?" he wrote in his last letter to his brother. *"Où sont les neiges d'antan?"*

> A man they say is as old as his arteries and mine are rapidly hardening, my temporal arteries curling over my forehead in convoluted tubes — this is accompanied by head symptoms which are alleviated by 10 gr phenacetin, but I need hardly say that this points to probable apoplexy in the near future; but are we down-hearted? No.

3

To the end, even had he wanted to, Lewin was never allowed to forget his Indian years. In November 1915 Colonel Dudley Sampson wrote from a sick bed to send his "best wishes and remembrances on our old Baptism of Fire at Cawnpore, which will be 58 years ago tomorrow. How are you and yours? We are passing on in terrible times, but if England holds out, the future of the world will be cleaner and brighter for the dreadful struggle. God bless you dear old man". Colonel Shakespear had been brought out of retirement and was now commanding the 18th Northumberland Fusiliers soon to be subjected to a long spell at the front in France. There were plans, too, to recruit two thousand young Lushais and ship them to France to serve in one of the Indian Labour Corps then being raised.

Dr Herring the Harley Street specialist Lewin had consulted had little comfort to give him, advising him frankly that he was paying the penalty for prolonged existence. He must continue to be careful with his diet, submit to being carried upstairs and be content to go along as best he could. Then, not long after being presented with this bleak prospect, he received a long letter from Herbert Lorrain, written at Lungleh in the Lushai Hills in October. Consisting of fifteen handwritten foolscap pages, its purported occasion was the publication of a new edition of *A Fly on the Wheel*, but since that had appeared four years previously this may have been a pretext; and the timing and contents of the letter were such that it may be inferred that Margaret had written privately to Lorrain, asking if he would let her husband have news of the places where he had once lived and of people he had known in the old days.

When Lorrain had visited Sirte Tlang some years previously, the Lushais with him had pointed out to him the two small knolls separated by a slight depression with moss-grown steps leading up to them cut in the solid rock where Uncle Tom's Cabin had once stood. The place was gay with marigolds, no doubt descendants of those Lewin had planted in his garden long ago. Between Lungleh and Demagri there was a stream still known as Thangliena Bawkte Lui meaning Thangliena's Camp, on the banks of which he had once pitched his tent.

> The brook still runs on beneath its overhanging tangle of dense tropical growth as it did in those days long ago, and although the mosquitoes, sandflies and leeches which no doubt tormented you have passed away the

new generation still keeps up the prestige of its ancestors and makes camping in its midst an event not easily forgotten.

He gave Lewin news of Lushais he had known in the old days. Seipuia, who had declined to accompany the party of chiefs he had taken to Calcutta, had died a few years before and the site of his village on Zo Tlang was deserted, but his widow still lived and ruled over a new village on Khawthir Hill one day's march to the north. The three sons of Lalngurha, two of them chiefs, were all living within a few miles of Lungleh. "Rutton Poia" had left two sons. Lalchheuva, afterwards chief of Belkai, who had been a child in Lewin's day had died some seventeen years before, and Lorrain had seen in the centre of the village in front of his house his *lungdawh*, or memorial platform, decorated with animal skulls, the deceased's guns and, dangling from one of the posts, a pair of hob-nailed boots he had cherished. Thailala, a son by one of Rothangpuia's concubines, was then chief of Hruizam. He wrote, too, about Vanhnuaia, Lalchema, Lalngura, Khamliana, Lal Thangrunga and Lianchungnunga, all names that echoed in Lewin's memory. And then without preamble came one which surely set Lewin's heart knocking and brought tears to his eyes. "Amongst all my Lushai friends," he read, "the one who remembers you best is an old lady named Dari." Lorrain gave no explanation as to who she was, knowing full well that none was needed, and continued:

She lives in Lungchem [Lungsen] village on the Luangmam Range. When I was on tour out that way a few years ago I heard that her husband was very ill, & by the time I reached the village he was in a dying condition. I was very sorry that I was too late to save the poor old fellow. They had just bought a gayal [mithan] & were making arrangements for him to be brought out on the log platform in front of the house so that he might himself transfix it with a bamboo spear, in the hopes that such a sacrifice might prolong his life. He was however too weak to be moved & in the night he passed away. It was most distressing to hear poor Dari's lamentations. My heart went out to her in great sympathy. She had no children left to console her & she was practically left alone in the world.

The next day a strange ceremony took place. Dari's husband in his lifetime had killed a tiger, and although he had performed the 'ai' ceremony to get the spirit of the creature under his control after death, his friends did not seem quite easy about the matter. The gayal was sacrificed early in the morning & the flesh cut up into innumerable little pieces. The dead hunter was dressed in all his best clothes & propped up against the wall in a sitting posture. The house was full of friends drinking who had come to comfort the widow.

Dari herself sat in front of her dead husband & every time a fly settled on the corpse she would give a loud cry & drive it off. Outside the house all the boys of the village were gathered, each with a great stick of firewood in his hand. Dari's cry was the signal for them to perform their duty, & they did it with a right good will. Quickly surrounding the house many of them belaboured the bamboo walls with their sticks & shouted with all their might, while others creeped beneath the building & banged the floor in the same manner. The din & the dust raised were tremendous. When they were tired they stopped & a man came out of the house with a tray of gayal meat & divided it amongst the perspiring dust-covered youngsters who ran to their homes with it & returned quickly to the front of the house. Every time a fly settled Dari would cry out & the whole performance was repeated over & over again until there was no gayal meat left to distribute, & consequently no boys willing to beat the house.

When I asked the meaning of this strange ceremony I was told that the flies were really incarnations of the tiger which the dead man had shot when alive, and that it was necessary to drive them off in that way in order to prevent the tiger-spirit from devouring the man-spirit.

Although the majority of people in Lungchem village are Christians, Dari, during her husband's lifetime, had no inclination to learn anything about the new religion. Since that sad event, however, she has somehow been attracted to the Saviour, and not many months ago she threw in her lot with the Christians, much to their joy & her own. Her sister Chongi (whom she assures me you will remember) has also become a Christian, & as they are both widows, & neither of them has sons or daughters living, they live together for mutual company. They have adopted two young people who are orphans which makes life a little easier for them than it otherwise would be.

Dari asked me to tell you this news as she is sure you will pity her when you hear that she has been left alone in the world without husband or children to love & care for her in her old age.

At Christmas time Lewin wrote to Lorrain sending him a photograph of himself and a sum of money to be given to Dari. That Christmas Day, when Audrey and Nicholas, Charlie, Queenie and their daughter Eileen, came over to lunch, Margaret was to describe as "our last happy day", for when it was over the clouds closed in and Lewin had little peace. Far away in Lushailand Dari came in to see Lorrain at Lungleh, carrying a fine-textured Lushai cloth, which she had woven out of red, blue and yellow threads with her own hands before old age had dimmed her eyes, from cotton of her own growing and spinning. She thought of it, perhaps, as a *zawlpuan*, the special cloth kept safe by every Lushai wife in which to wrap her husband's body when he dies. Would he, she asked, pack it carefully and send it to Thangliena, as a gift from her?

When it arrived at Parkhurst Lewin was not there to receive it. On 2 February 1916 he and Margaret had gone to London and put up at the Langham Hotel so that he could be under Dr Herring's care and also visit his dentist, for his teeth had been giving him trouble. On the eleventh after seeing the dentist he had returned to the hotel and was being attended to by Dr Herring in the bedroom when at ten minutes past five he fell. The doctor came out to the sitting-room and asked Margaret for brandy, which she had ready, but by the time he got back his patient had died, without pain or suffering or knowledge that the secret of the mystery that had so long obsessed him was about to be revealed. He was seventy-six, and he and Margaret had been married for forty years.

As he had wished, his body was cremated that Sunday at the Golders Green crematorium, there being present Charlie, Nicholas Waterhouse, Noel Farrer and Tom

Macdonald (who had come down from Scotland with Everest by the night mail), Julian Tomlin and Bella. The casket containing his ashes was taken to Parkhurst and the following Wednesday in the presence of his three children lowered into the family vault in Abinger churchyard.

Appendix
A Memoir of Parkhurst
by Ursula Currie

We were four children, and every year we spent a month with our grandparents, Colonel and Mrs Lewin, at Parkhurst. 'Best behaviour' was the rule, they lived in formal Victorian style which we found cramping after the freedom of our home in Scotland, but there were many pleasures — we had 'nursery quarters' in the old wing of the house with the use of an ancient upright piano, many children's books and a cuckoo clock. There we made a lot of noise and were very happy.

The butler whose name was Bending (Dun Dun to us) was a good friend. He lived in a big pantry downstairs where he brewed lovely ginger beer in a large wooden wash-tub and showed us the big, dark safe full of shining silver. He used to ring a gong summoning everyone to meals — this gong had eight notes like a xylophone, and Gran'pa had taught him to play 'Come to the cook-house door, boys'. Dun Dun had a 'wreath of hair' and a nice sense of humour. It was at Parkhurst that I first heard a gramophone — Gran'ma had been a good pianist, and when she was smitten with arthritis collected records of all sorts, mostly classical, but Harry Lauder and the pipe band of the Argylls for our benefit — the latter most exciting — heard far away, coming nearer, very loud, and finally fading into the distance, then silence.

Gran'ma's personal maid Simmie needs a chapter all to herself. She was sweet and cheerful with a soft Surrey accent which Gran'ma used to mimic, though Gran'pa didn't like her doing so — 'unkind' he said, which was true. She was married to the under-gardener, 'moi Bill' who had a big drooping moustache and wore a bowler-hat when off duty, and she was constantly dashing 'over 'ome', as she called the little flat overlooking the back yard where they lived, to see to his comforts. The gardener was Brewer, and his round and jolly wife had command of the dairy providing butter and cream from the herd of Jersey cows at the Farm.

When we children were staying at Parkhurst the day would begin with Simmie calling ''Urry along, moi dears, yer Gran'pa and Gran'ma's on their way down to breakfast', and there would be a headlong rush of grandchildren down the back stairs so as to be in the hall outside the dining-room by the time the grandparents came slowly down the wide front staircase, always arm in arm. There were eggs and bacon and kippers on silver chafing dishes being kept hot over methylated flames presided over by Dun Dun, and Gran'ma sat at the head of the table behind a battery of silver coffee and teapots, while Gran'pa sat beside her and ate brown bread and butter with a plate of salt beef and fresh watercress — he didn't hold with luxury eating.

These were very early memories, but from about 1910 the fun of outdoors began. We had hoops and were allowed to bowl them along the main road mostly between Parkhurst and Feldemore — the road by our standards being immensely wide, and of course no traffic except the occasional horse-drawn vehicle. The hoops were large and my brother and I made vain attempts to jump through them while running. Theodore Waterhouse at Feldemore had a 'grey nannie' and wasn't allowed to run with a hoop like the rough Macdonalds! We often took letters to the post office where there was a gate across the road, usually open. We thought this strange as gates in our northern world had to be kept strictly closed because of animals — Surrey was different.

It was opposite the well that I first saw my 'dream house', through an archway in the hedge. A little paved path led up to the door between lavender hedges, and I used to linger, gazing through the gate hoping that someone might ask me to come in; nobody did, and my secret house remained my precious and private property.

I can remember the big clock over the stables at Parkhurst being built, and three splendid horses, two for the carriage (always in double harness), and the cob which was for the dog-cart used for parcels and station work. Stores had to be met at Gomshall station, and my brother and I loved to go on these errands with Retford the coachman. He told us hair-raising stories — accidents with horse vehicles — specially exciting was the one about a huge dray drawn by two great Clydesdales which stampeded and all went hurtling down the lane near the 'hatch' ending in blood and disaster. He also told us that people would probably be taking holidays in space by the end of our young lives!

There was a Brougham, a closed carriage which smelled of sour leather and had a rack on the roof for the heavy luggage. I can remember my small brother's pram being hoisted and strapped precariously with the various trunks with which my Mother always travelled. Then there was the Victoria for fine weather and visiting neighbours — Waterhouses, Lugards, Merrilees, Barlow-Webbs. We sometimes went as far as Dorking to catch the 'express' train to London. Coast Hill was considered very steep for horses and there was a notice which read 'Slacken bearing reins when going up the hill'. This all seems very rustic as I drive along busy roads in a Mini. For formal occasions Gran'pa wore a grey top hat and frock-coat, and Gran'ma a bonnet with a bunch of violets in the front. Gran'pa disliked 'formal' dress in the evenings, but wore a long black velvet jacket to the knees, lined with dark red. This last became a family heirloom and was used by my Mother for many years on cold evenings in Argyllshire.

When we were old enough my brother and I went daily to the Feldemore swimming-bath, and it was there that we learned to swim from a Mr Seer. We followed a stony little path down the hill from the main road by the Feldemore 'new drive' to Holmbury St Mary. I well remember the hot climb up after bathing. It seemed a long way, but there was always a good lunch to look forward to in the big dining-room with the grandparents and served by Dun Dun — probably strawberries with 'one spoonful only' of cream.

Before the 1914-18 war there was a sawmill on the Common under the pine trees — I recall that most of the woods on the

Common were pine, and their scent in hot sunshine is still vivid in my memory. I think that a child's sense of smell is very acute — Surrey was full of nostalgic scents for this child coming from the North. Gran'pa's study smelt of pipe-tobacco smoke and wood polish — much of the woodwork at Parkhurst was of his own carving — and Gran'ma's boudoir, of roses and lavender. It was a round room lined with bookshelves, and of course the gramophone, and looked into the branches of the biggest cedar. The gardens at Parkhurst were lovely. There were many lawns, all mowed by an old pony wearing leather shoes, and a mossy path said to be a mile long round the perimeter of the fields through a boundary of trees. This was an almost daily walk for the grandparents, Gran'pa always carrying a hatchet for casual pruning and also a 'spud' for weeds in the lawns — a good tool now obsolete. In earlier days there had been much music at Parkhurst, a family of six, and they all played stringed instruments. Every evening after dinner the little orchestra would play a large repertoire of chamber music. When asked what happened when there was a guest who didn't like music the Colonel replied 'That makes no difference, we always play'!

A few years ago I was driving past Abinger Hammer and suddenly decided to go and see Parkhurst, so I took the Holmbury St Mary road, drove up the lane to the Common, past the well, and the dream house, up the drive ... all was just as I had remembered. Preparing to ring the bell and ask who lived there I turned the corner over the right of way bridge and, to my horror, there was NO HOUSE, only rough grass showing the outlines of where it had been ... and there was the big cedar normally hidden by the high roof. I had a vivid illusion of seeing the grandparents having tea as usual under that tree on the lawn ... I turned the car and fled from something that was very like childish fear.

BIBLIOGRAPHY

BESSAIGNET, P. *Tribesmen of the Chittagong Hill Tracts.* Dacca, 1958.

BRAUNS, C.D. AND LÖFFLER, L.G. *Mru: Hill People on the Border of Bangladesh.* Basel, 1990.

BROWNLOW, C.H. *The Despatches of the Chittagong Column, Looshai Expeditionary Force.* Calcutta, 1872.

BUSTEED, H.E. *Echoes from Old Calcutta.* 4th edn. London, 1908.

CAREY, B.S. AND TUCK, H.N. *The Chin Hills.* 2 vols. Rangoon, 1896.

CARRINGTON, C.E. *The British Overseas.* Cambridge, 1950.

CECIL, D. *Visionary and Dreamer: Two Poetic Painters: Samuel Palmer & Edward Burne-Jones.* London, 1969.

DANZIGER, M.K. AND BRADY, F. (eds.). *Boswell: The Great Biographer, 1789-1795.* New York, 1989.

DONNISON, V. *Burma.* London, 1970.

EAST, C.J. *An Account of the Proceedings of the Chittagong Column of the Lushai Expeditionary Force, 1871-1872.* 1873. [Not located].

FARRINGTON, A.J. *The records of the East India College, Haileybury, and other institutions.* London, 1976.

GAIT, E. *A History of Assam.* 2nd edn. Calcutta and Simla, 1926.

GROTE, MRS [H.]. *The Personal Life of George Grote.* London, 1873.

HATHORN, J.G. *A Hand-book of Darjeeling.* [Calcutta, 1863].

HILLS, P.J. *Dane Court, St Peter's-in-Thanet: a Kentish Manor and its Families.* Gainsborough, 1972.

KYLES, D. *Lorrain of the Lushais.* London, [1944].

LEWIN, EVEREST. *Poems.* London, 1931.

LEWIN, T.H. *Chhota Haziree* by "Jeannie and Tom" [pseud. Jane Lewin and THL]. Calcutta, 1866; *The Hill Tracts of Chittagong and the Dwellers Therein; with comparative vocabularies of the hill dialects.* Calcutta, 1869; *Wild Races of South-Eastern India.* London, 1870; *Hill Proverbs of the Inhabitants of the Chittagong Hill Tracts* [Burmese text and English translation]. Calcutta, 1873; *Progressive Colloquial Exercises in the Lushai Dialect of the 'Dzo' or Kuki*

Language, with vocabularies and popular tales. Calcutta, 1874; *An Account of the Koch Bihar State.* Koch Bihar, 1876; *A Manual of Tibetan, being a guide to the colloquial speech of Tibet, in a series of progressive exercises, prepared with the assistance of Yapa Ugyen Gyatsho, a learned lama of the monastery of Pemiongehi.* Calcutta, 1879; *Dhammapadagatha. A Burmese translation from the edition prepared by THL.* 2nd ed. American Mission, Rangoon, 1882; *A Fly on the Wheel, or How I helped to govern India.* London, 1885, 2nd ed. 1912; *The Lewin Letters: a selection from the correspondence & diaries of an English family, 1756-1884[5].* 2 vols. London, 1909; *Life and Death: being an authentic account of the deaths of one hundred celebrated men and women.* London, 1910.

LORRAIN, J.H. *Dictionary of the Lushai Language.* Calcutta, 1940.

LORRAIN, R.A. *Five Years in Unknown Jungles.* London, [1912].

LOTHIAN, A.C. (ed.). *A Handbook for Travellers in India [etc.].* London, 1955.

McCALL, A.G. *Lushai Chrysalis.* London, 1949.

MACDONALD, BETSY. *India ... Sunshine and Shadows.* London, 1988.

MACKENZIE, A. *History of the Relations of the Government with the Hill Tribes of the North-East Frontier of Bengal.* Calcutta, 1884

PARRY, N.E. *Lushai Customs and Ceremonies.* Shillong, 1928; *The Lakhers.* London, 1932.

PHAYRE, A. *History of Burma.* London, 1883.

REID, A.S. *Chin-Lushai Land.* Calcutta, 1893.

REID, R. *History of the Frontier Areas Bordering on Assam, From 1883-1941.* Shillong, 1942.

ROBERTS, F-M. LORD. *Forty-One Years in India.* 2 vols. London, 1897.

ROWELL, G. *William Terriss and Richard Prince: Two Players in an Adelphi Melodrama.* London, 1987.

SASSOON, S. *Meredith.* London, 1948.

SHAKESPEAR, J. *The Lushei-Kuki Clans.* London, 1912.

SHAKESPEAR, L.W. *History of the Assam Rifles.* London, 1898.

SMYTHE, A.J. *The Life of William Terriss, Actor.* London, 1898.

TALUKDAR, S.P. *The Chakmas: Life and Struggle.* New Delhi, 1988.

TERRISS, ELLALINE. *Just a Little Bit of String.* London, 1955.

THANSIAMA, C. 'Tom Herbert Lewin — Thangliana'. *Lunglei Centenary Souvenir.* Lunglei, 1990.

WHITEHEAD, J. *Far Frontiers: People and Events in North-Eastern India, 1857-1947.* London, 1989.

WOODTHORPE, R.G. *The Lushai Expedition, 1871-1872.* London, 1873.

VUMSON. *Zo History.* Aizawl, [1987].

YULE, H. AND BURNELL, A.C. *Hobson-Jobson: A Glossary of Anglo-Indian Words and Phrases.* London, 1903.

INDEX

Cook, Mr, 203-4
Cox's Bazaar, 102, 104, 117, 123
Crimean War, 53, 60, 62
Crouch, Mr, 212, 218, 253, 262

Daletme, 140, 145
Dalhousie, Earl of, 57-8
Daly, Mr, 204
Dari, 269, 282, 416-19
Darjeeling, 311-27 *passim*
Davidson, Col., 410-11, 412, 416
Deb rajah of Sikkim, 293-4, 316-17, 319
Demagri, 252-3, 267
Dumpton Park, 273, 320
Duncan, Dr, 184

East, Capt. C.J., 240, 241-2
East India Company, 5, 6-7, 8, 11-12, 50-1, 75, 101-2
Eden, Sir Ashley, 310, 316, 319, 325
Edgar, Sir John, 198-9, 202-3, 207, 210, 216, 235-6, 256-8, 311, 313, 325, 327, 352-3, 378-9
Elgin, Lady, 351
Elgin, Lord, 351, 352-3
Elliot, Anna. *See* Young, Anna
Elliot, Sir George, 287, 315
Elliot, Mabel. *See* Mackenzie, Mabel
Elliot, Margaret. *See* Lewin, Margaret
Elliot, Margaret ("Daisy"). *See* Meredith, Margaret
Elliot, Ralph, 287
Ellis case, 99, 114, 179, 261, 280
Elphinstone, General, 57
Elssler, Fanny, 37-8

Faizullah Khan ("Fuzlah"), 138, 143, 147, 164-5, 170
Farrer, Anthony, 386.
Farrer, Joan, 386
Farrer, Mabel. *See* Mackenzie, Mabel
Farrer, Noel, 386, 419
Farrer, Sir Thomas (later Lord), 344, 386

Fayette, Marquis de la, 11
Forster, Laura, 402
Francis, Sir Philip, 9-10
Friend, Mary. *See* Lewin, Mary

Gentz, Chevalier von, 37
Gillette, William, 358
Gordon, Lieut., 252, 253, 262
Graham, Capt., 115, 134-6, 205-6
Grand, George, 9-10
Grand, Noël Catherine, 9-11, 20
Grant, General Hope, 71
Graves, Annie, 96, 97, 108, 157, 322
Graves, Harry, 47, 94-5, 97, 108, 119, 157, 201, 273, 321-2, 358-9, 360, 403-4
Green, Fanny (*née* Lewin), 50, 407-8
Grey, Sir William, 197
Grix, Mr, 47, 96
Grote, Arthur, 38-9, 61, 80, 87, 88, 100, 114, 152, 168, 335
Grote, George, 33-40 *passim*, 209-10, 272
Grote, Harriet, 14-17 *passim*, 20, 21, 25, 27, 28, 31-40 *passim*, 44, 45, 96, 110, 124, 183, 185, 200, 208, 210, 271-2, 285, 288, 294, 304, 305, 311, 318, 324-5, 345

Hale, Jane, 32
Hale, General John, 12, 16
Hale, Mary. *See* Lewin, Mary (1)
Hamirpur, 83-4
Hampden, John, 34
Hampton, Major, 81, 82, 84
Hankey, Mr, 217, 259, 271, 275
Harris, Sir Frederick, 315
Hastings, Warren, 8, 9, 10
Hatch, Miss, 285, 293, 296
Havelock, Gen. Sir Henry, 60, 63
Haydn, Joseph, 37
Hazaribagh, 91-4, 97-100
Herring, Dr, 414-15, 419
Hicks, Sir Seymour, 358, 360
Hills, Lieut.-Col. J., 227-8
Hogg, Sir James, 51